To learners everywhere,
especially those who want
to understand more of the daily news.

PEARSON   ALWAYS LEARNING

Dinner Party Economics

The Big Ideas and Intense Conversations about the Economy

Eveline J. Adomait • Richard G. Maranta

Pearson Learning Solutions, 501 Boylston Street, Suite 900, Boston, MA 02116
A Pearson Education Company
www.pearsoned.com

Printed in Canada

1 2 3 4 5 6 7 8 9 10 XXXX 18 17 16 15 14 13

000200010271823904

BK

ISBN 10: 1-269-59092-8
ISBN 13: 978-1-269-59092-1

TABLE D'HÔTE[1]

---

1. This kind of menu is fixed price and offers a limited set of choices as opposed to a menu that is à la carte. *Table d'hôte* literally means "host's table," and that is what I am going to offer you in the way of economic "courses" throughout the book.

ABOUT THE AUTHORS

Evie Adomait was born to Dutch immigrants in rural Ontario. She attended the University of Guelph, intending to become a doctor, when she realized that she couldn't use a scalpel on anything alive. This required a change in direction. Fortunately, she was taking an introductory economics course and fell in love with the ideas (*and look, Mom . . . no blood.*). She has a Master of Economics degree from the University of Guelph, and while she was a grad student she also fell in love with her future husband Martin, an engineering grad of the University of Guelph.

For the past 25 she has made her career as a teaching professor at her alma mater. (She has a gold watch to prove it.) By her calculations, she has taught the equivalent of the population of a small city various economics courses at the first-, second-, and third-year levels. Her favourite is the first year, with class sizes ranging from 300 to 600 students, because this is the year many students experience "aha moments" when it comes to economics. Their 18-year-old minds also keep her young. Speaking of young minds, Evie and Martin's oldest son, Kristian, is a graduate of Guelph and their youngest son, Jordan, has just begun his post-secondary career at the U of G. The University of Guelph has been a very important place for the Adomaits.

Richard Maranta grew up as the son of a wonderful German mother and Italian father, both of whom immigrated after the war and met in southern Ontario. With two brothers, their house in Brampton, Ontario, was loud (some might call it passionate) and the conversation usually centred on food, with his dad talking about the veal he was going to cook next week, while the chicken he cooked this week was still in his mouth.

After some wayward years, Rick (which he refers to himself as these days because his brothers started calling him Richie) eventually graduated with a Bachelor of Arts and a Master of Arts in English Literature from the University of Waterloo, focusing on critical theory and self-destructive American authors such as William Faulkner. Richard went on to obtain a Bachelor of Education degree from the University of Ottawa, with the goal of becoming a secondary school teacher and eventually teaching English in China. That never happened. Instead, after not finding a job in teaching (funny how things come around again), he ended up working for the dearly departed Nortel Networks in technical education and communications. He went on to co-found a company called Pinched Head, which develops innovative online courses for corporate clients, which was fun, except for the dealing with the clients part (if you are a former client, just kidding). Richard currently works in a communications role where he writes, works with other writers to say what needs to be said, as well as gets involved in a wide variety of projects such as developing apps, launching websites, copywriting, script writing, and providing creative direction as part of a very talented team.

Rick lives with his amazing wife of many years in the underbelly of Oakville, Ontario. For fun, he plays video games but has reluctantly come to realize that he will never be as good at them as his two sons Andrew and Ian (whom he used to let win . . . shh don't tell them!).

Introduction to Dinner Party Economics

Only dull people are brilliant at breakfast.
—from
An Ideal Husband (1895),
by Oscar Wilde (1854–1900), Irish writer

Chapter 1

Making Introductions

At a dinner party one should eat wisely but not too well, and talk well but not too wisely.
—*W. Somerset Maugham (1874–1966), British author*[1]

For those of you who read *Cocktail Party Economics: The Big Ideas and Scintillating Small Talk about Markets* welcome back! If you haven't read *Cocktail Party Economics,* no worries. It isn't a necessary prerequisite for understanding the content of *Dinner Party Economics.* What is necessary is an interest in the intersection of economics and politics in terms of the role of government. You should also like to spend long dinners either debating or listening to others debate the relative merits of various economic policies.

When I came up to Cambridge (in October 1921) to read economics, I did not have much idea of what it was about.
—*Joan Robinson*[2] *(1903–1983), British Economist*[3]

In many ways, this book covers the topics that a layperson would expect in an economics book. I know this because when I mention to people that I[4] wrote an economics book they usually respond, "Oh good, it will help me understand what is going on in some country or other that is in the current economic spotlight." I always sound a little apologetic when I have to tell them that *Cocktail Party Economics* doesn't actually help one understand how economies work as a whole. Rather my first book helps readers understand how particular markets work. Now market analysis is "nothing to sneeze at."[5] The U.S. housing and derivatives markets have affected the entire world, so the topic of markets is definitely worth a book. However, the understanding of particular markets doesn't cover such newsworthy topics as the role of governments and central banks as they cope with economies that aren't doing well—that suffer from such maladies as high unemployment, prolonged recessions, inflation or even hyperinflation, balance-of-trade issues, and government debt levels.

---

1. Taken from *A Writer's Notebook* (1949).
2. Joan Robinson was one of the circle of young economists around John Maynard Keynes, who essentially invented macroeconomics as a field of economics. Both taught at Cambridge University in England.
3. Taken from *Contributions to Modern Economics* (1978).
4. Like *Cocktail Party Economics,* this book is a joint venture between Evie and Rick but in order to keep the voice personal it feels like Evie is doing the talking. (Some things never change.)
5. This phrase was first seen in the early nineteenth century because *sneezing* and *snorting* meant essentially the same thing. You could show your distaste for something that was beneath you with a snort; thus, if something is nothing to sneeze at, it merits a closer look.

DIFFERENT STRANDS ONE CORD

A threefold cord is not easily broken.[6]
—*Ecclesiastes 4:12b*

Fundamentally, economics is divided into two strands: micro and macro. There is also a field called *econometrics,*[7] which can feel like a third strand because it is always part of an economics core curriculum. Econometrics emerged because it enables economists to test economic theories using statistics, whether they are micro or macro ideas, with real-world data. All of these fields are steeped in mathematics but, in keeping with my earlier book, this one will have next to no mathematics. I will endeavour to restrict myself to words and the occasional graph.

So what are the salient features that make macro as a field different from micro?

SIZE ISN'T THE ISSUE

Some writers maintain arithmetic to be only the only sure guide in political economy; for my part, I see so many detestable systems built upon arithmetical statements, that I am rather inclined to regard that science as the instrument of national calamity.
—*Jean-Baptiste Say (1767–1832), French Economist*[8] *and businessman famous for Say's Law*[9]

You would think that with a name like "macro" it would be about big money, and micro would be small money or at least smaller in monetary value. Not true. Rather, the distinction is about complexity. Microeconomics is usually about individual markets (less complex) whereas macroeconomics is about many different markets interacting with each other as a whole (more complex).

Essentially, *Cocktail Party Economics* is a microeconomics book because it deals with topics related to particular markets, such as cars, houses, or chocolates. However, a particular market can be very large in total value. For example, the largest market in the world, the foreign exchange market, is estimated to be worth more than 4 trillion[10] US\$ in trades per day. (Yes, that is trillions/day.) Here is an example of a micro story that explains currency values in the foreign exchange market. When Canadians want to buy anything[11] from the USA, they buy or *demand* U.S. dollars. Because of this buying behaviour, the price they pay for those U.S. dollars goes up. Moreover, in order to purchase those U.S. dollars, Canadians sell or *supply* Canadian dollars to that market, which

---

6. Taken from the Douay-Rheims 1899 American edition. This is the only version of the Bible that I could find in the public domain.
7. I have no intentions of ever writing a chatty book about econometrics (the combination of economic questions and statistics). *Naked Statistics: Stripping the Dread from the Data* by Charles Wheelan would be a good place to look if you are so inclined.
8. Taken from *A Treatise on Political Economy* (1832).
9. Say's Law has had a revival of sorts since the austerity movement following the financial crisis of 2008, having gone out of fashion with advent of Keynesian economics in the 1930s. Essentially, Say's law says that the source of wealth is production and the act of production creates demand because people don't want to hold money but would rather buy stuff instead. Thus, Say's Law can be stated as "supply creates its own demand."
10. In 2011.
11. This could include American goods and services and American financial assets such as bonds and stocks. It turns out that for Canada, financial sales and purchases are the most important reason for change in the CAD–US\$ exchange rate.

causes the Canadian dollar to lose value against the U.S. dollar. In microeconomics, the words *supply* and *demand* come up a lot in relation to markets.

COMPLEX NUMBERS

We sometimes chafe at the burden of our obligations, the complexity of our decisions, the agony of our choices.[12]

—*John F Kennedy (1917–1963), American president*

So, how is macro more complex than micro? It has to do with the numbers used and the kinds of questions those numbers answer. For microeconomics, the numbers are very straightforward. Just go to a particular market and find out the price of the product and the number of units that changed hands. For example, you can Google "U.S. exchange rate" to find the currency exchange in a matter of seconds.

The kinds of questions micro economists ask are all related to the market:

"Is the price right?"

"Why did it recently change?"

"What is going on with production levels?"

"What is the price expected to be in the future?"

"What is the source of the market failure if there is one?"

"Would regulations help correct the price?"

GO BIG OR GO HOME

And therefore someday, not only my writings but my whole life, all the intriguing mystery of the machine will be studied and studied. I never forget how God helps me and it is therefore my last wish that everything may be to his honour.

—*Søren Aabye Kierkegaard (1813–1855), Christian philosopher and theologian*

Because this is a macroeconomics book, it deals with the economy as a whole. Granted, economies such as those of the USA[13] and China[14] are quite large in their annual income, thus matching the "macro" moniker; however, some macro economies, such as that of Zimbabwe, are quite small—worth as little as 6 billion US$ per year, which is less than the annual expenditure on beer[15] in Canada.

Here are some examples of complex macroeconomic questions:

"Why is the economy in recession, and what can governments do (if anything) about it?"

"What can central banks do (if anything) about recessions?"

"What causes inflation, and when does it become a problem?"

"If China pegs its currency to the U.S. dollar, what does this do to the American balance of payments or balance of trade?"

---

12. Said at the annual message to the Congress on the State of the Union (January 11, 1962).
13. 15 trillion US$ in 2011.
14. Over 7 trillion US$ in 2011.
15. "Control and sale of alcoholic beverages, for the year ending March 31, 2012," Statistics Canada, http://www.statcan.gc.ca/daily-quotidien/130411/dq130411a-eng.htm.

"Are budget deficits and government debt a bad thing?"

"What causes economies to grow, and are there limits to their growth?"

This brings us to the issues concerning macro numbers. Specifically, how do you compare the economy of the USA with that of Zimbabwe? What numbers are appropriate? For example, we often talk about national income, but no economy gets a paycheque—so what really makes up its "income"? It turns out that measuring national income takes a team of statisticians[16] to get it right. Furthermore, it would be completely meaningless to compare income in U.S. dollars for the USA with those denominated in the South African rand or the Botswana pula,[17] which are only two of the currencies currently used in Zimbabwe. Therefore, macroeconomists have to standardize how they measure things in order to compare them across countries. In this example, we can have the national incomes (measured using similar data) for both the USA and Zimbabwe cited in terms of U.S. dollars. It takes a fair amount of work to get these numbers right, and isn't straightforward at all.

FALLACY OF COMPOSITION

Fallacies do not cease to be fallacies because they become fashions.
—*G.K. Chesterton (1874–1936), British writer*

Macroeconomics provides a ready source of conflict between the various economic camps. In some part, it has to do with asking the following question: Can we treat the macro economy as just the sum of the various parts? If so, then micro foundations are the most important aspect of all macro problems and market analysis contain the answers—if we take care of the pennies,[18] the dollars take care of themselves, so to speak. There are many who disagree with this view because of the problem of the fallacy of composition. So what is this fallacy? I think it is easier to see by using a noneconomic example. Suppose during a football game a short woman sitting in the crowd decides to stand up in order to see the game better. However, if everyone stands up around her, she may not be able to see the field at all. Thus, one person standing up will get a completely different result when compared to everyone standing up. The fallacy of composition states that what is true for the one part isn't true for the whole. In this case, is not true to say that standing up will help you see better—it really depends. In a macro context, this fallacy of composition makes us unable to say things like "If everyone saves more individually, then national savings will also go up." Fundamentally, the part (or individual) can be thought of as micro and the whole (or national) as macro.

Many of the conflicts between economists (and non-economists who hold economic opinions) have to do with how individual markets aggregate to the economy as a whole. In

16. "Canada's System of national economic accounts: An overview, Statistics Canada," http://www.statcan.gc.ca/nea-cen/about-apropos/index-eng.htm#frame.
17. Because of hyperinflation, the Zimbabwe dollar was discontinued in April of 2009. Zimbabweans use other countries' currencies as their money.
18. As of February 4, 2013, the Royal Canadian Mint ceased its distribution of the penny. If a person pays cash for anything after this date the amount is rounded to the nearest 5 cents. It is anticipated that the elimination of the penny will save Canadian taxpayers $11 million per year. Electronic and cheque payments will still have numbers to the penny. See http://www.mint.ca/store/mint/learn/phasing-out-the-penny-6900002.

other words, how significant is the fallacy-of-composition problem? In particular, the major disagreements centre primarily on how labour markets clear[19] and how financial markets change the level of business investment. The famous "fathers" of this debate are John Maynard Keynes and Friedrich von Hayek, whose ideas will permeate *Dinner Party Economics.* Keynes, the true father of macroeconomics as a field, did not believe that markets left alone would correct the economy and thus the government had an obligation to intervene with appropriate spending programs. The fallacy of composition is a big problem for Keynesians. On the other hand, Hayek,[20] the Yoda of free-market types, wanted as little government intervention and spending as possible. In other words, the fallacy of composition isn't significant enough to interfere with markets. Even today, both camps have major political clout, and I hope by the end of the book you will see why.

VOCABULARY LESSON OR STORYTELLING: GETTING A CLUE

Stay is a charming word in a friend's vocabulary. But if one does not stay while staying, better let him go where he is gone the while.
—Amos Bronson Alcott[21] *(1799–1888), American writer,[22] teacher, and reformer*

Like any discipline, macroeconomics has its own particular vocabulary. There is constant chatter in the media and on the street about the economy, and it is important to understand the lingo before you can speak with some intelligence whether—as W. Somerset Maugham pointed out in the chapter-opening quote—your comments are said "wisely" or not.

Let's say you are at a dinner party and the conversation drifts to whether or not the government should use deficit spending by borrowing from the central bank, from the public, or from foreigners to get the economy out of recession. This is actually a complicated question because you need to know precisely what is meant by *deficit,* what is meant by *recession,* and what difference it makes in whom you borrow from. You will also need to know how concepts are connected to other economic aspects such as unemployment, the debt level, interest rates, balance of payments, the trade balance, inflation, business investment, and consumer spending, all of which have precise measurements. Furthermore, in keeping with the fallacy-of-composition problem, it isn't appropriate to use the analogy of personal debt levels and scale up to the country as a whole to prove your point, unless you are convinced that there really isn't a composition problem. Just so you know, your seemingly benign conversation may have just entered what is called a "political economy" minefield, especially if the other folks at the table have different political leanings than you do. It would be helpful to know what these economic terms mean and how they are connected to each other before you enter into the fray.

---

19. Reach an equilibrium price and quantity with no excess supply or demand.
20. According to Samuel Brittain's entry on Hayek, in the Oxford DNB, titles involving "von" were eliminated in Austria in 1919. Brittain says that the only people who referred to *von Hayek* were some of Hayek's English-speaking critics.
21. Father of Louise May Alcott, the author of *Little Women* (1868–1869).
22. Taken from *Concord Days* (1872).

Once or twice she had peeped into the book her sister was reading, but it had no pictures or conversations in it, "and what is the use of a book," thought Alice, "without pictures or conversations?"[23]

—*Lewis Carroll, pen name for Charles Lutwidge Dodgeson (1832–1898), British author, mathematician, and clergyman*

This means I need to cover basic vocabulary about the economy. I don't know about you, but I have always found vocabulary lessons to be rather boring, so this posed a real problem for me in planning an approach to the text because I want this book to be fun to read, not just a glossary of terms.

After a little reflection, I came up with a structure that I thought might make this book more interesting to read. The book will centre around a dinner party scenario. Each chapter will start with a vignette that introduces the concept of the chapter, with the various chapters of the book laid out like the courses of a meal. Sounds yummy, doesn't it? (I hope you aren't saying, "Actually, sounds cheesy[24]!") The guests attending will be made up of a diverse group of students who were put into a study group by their professor (me) but have become somewhat friends over the term. I will introduce you to them in the next chapter, but I do want to let you know that each person represents a character with traits that I have noticed tend to go together—those of stereotypical types of students, so to speak. I hope the profiles I have created don't offend anyone, and if you happen to see yourself in any one character, I want you to know that I think of each character respectfully. More to the point, their ordinary conversations should demonstrate how macroeconomics affects the everyday lives of people. I also think adding a little fiction to the facts should lighten the tone and make the whole learning process more palatable.

Some of my youthful readers are developing wonderful imaginations. This pleases me.[25]

—*Lyman Frank Baum (1856–1919), American author of* The Wonderful Wizard of Oz

The progression of ideas follows a set menu. The appetizers will cover the vocabulary and basic concepts. You will notice from the menu that this is more than half of the book. The entrée consists of the economic policy options available to a country to solve its economy's problems. Finally, for dessert, we get to the disagreements. In macroeconomics, the fights seem to be more intense and political, where sharp divisions between left- and right-wing[26] individuals dominate the discussion. (Actually, the fights can also happen if people drink too much.)

---

23. Taken from *Alice's Adventures in Wonderland* (1865).
24. This term probably evolved from the Urdu word *chiz*, which means "thing." The British turned the word into slang, and it now refers to a tacky, cheap, or inferior thing.
25. Taken from *The Lost Princess of Oz*.
26. The terms *right wing* and *left wing* originated during the French Revolution and originally referred to where particular politicians sat with respect to the chair of the president. On the right sat those who generally supported the way things had been before the Revolution (1789–1799).

DÉJÀ VU

In short, the feeling of Déjà vu corresponds to the memory of an unconscious fantasy.[27]
—Sigmund Freud (1856–1939), Austrian neurologist

Please forgive me if I keep referring back to *Cocktail Party Economics,* but it was my first book and, as such, has marked me for life. There are a couple of features in it that worked well and I think are worth repeating in this book. You will notice the multitude of quotes,[28] each of which may be directly or indirectly tied to the message at hand. I have included them as a fun diversion but also a bit of a mental break—a chance to think sideways,[29] which is good practice for an economist . . . or artist or scientist, for that matter.

You will also find a gossip column in each chapter featuring the biography of an economist famous in that chapter's area. Some will be Nobel Prize winners.[30] These biographies are meant to flesh out the individuals behind the ideas, which I think is good way to remember the ideas. Many of these economists were fascinating dinner companions[31] in their own right. In this chapter I decided to reuse one from *Cocktail Party Economics* because Hayek is unavoidable[32] in a macro book of this type.

GOSSIP COLUMN: FRIEDRICH AUGUST VON HAYEK

Friedrich August von Hayek (1899–1992) was born in Vienna into a line of scholars and minor nobility. During World War I he was stationed on the Italian front, and this experience caused him to worry about the damage political organizations could do. He vowed to make the world a better place and decided to become an academic. He thought and wrote about the role that socialism played in fascism, and how collectivism (even when done in a voluntary way) usually leads to totalitarianism. (That's a lot of –isms.) During his life, he saw it all and came out in support of a laissez-faire (free and decentralized) system.

Hayek attended the University of Vienna, where he earned two doctorates, in law and political science, but he also studied philosophy, psychology, and economics. For a short time, he also studied at an institute of brain anatomy, which led him to think about economics systems in the same framework as neurological ones. He was truly a well-educated Renaissance man.

---

27. Taken from *The Psychopathology of Everyday Life* (1901).
28. For copyright purposes and in order to expedite the publishing of this book, most quotes are from people who have been dead for at least 50 years. That seems to be the dividing line. In a couple of places it is unavoidable to exclude a quote by a famous economist just because that individual didn't die conveniently. In that case the quote is carefully referenced. I hope we don't get into shades of grey over this 50!
29. Stephen A. Butler, 2010, "Solving business problems using a lateral thinking approach," *Management Decision,* vol. 48, no. 1, pp. 58–64.
30. There is technically no Nobel Prize in Economics. Rather, it is called the Sveriges Riksbank Prize in Economic Sciences in memory of Alfred Nobel, the inventor of dynamite. This prize was established in 1968 by Sweden's central bank long after the original Nobels of 1901.
31. *Companion* literally means "with bread"; thus, friendship is very connected to eating.
32. I highly recommend watching the PBS documentary *The Commanding Heights: The Battle of Ideas* if you want to get a sense about how significant Hayek and Keynes are in macroeconomics. See http://www.pbs.org/wgbh/commandingheights/hi/story/.

GOSSIP COLUMN *(CONTINUED)*

His influence on economists was extensive. He was one of the most important members of the Austrian School of Economics in the 1930s and was scooped by Lionel Robbins to join the London School of Economics (LSE). He is the second most frequently cited economist (after Kenneth Arrow) by other Nobel Prize winners in economics when they give their Nobel lectures.

Hayek's impact hit the political streets when conservative politicians took his ideas and ran with them. Margaret Thatcher is said to have slammed down on a table Hayek's book, *The Constitution of Liberty*,[33] saying, "This is what we believe," during a party meeting.[34] Students of Hayek became part of Reagan's administration. (Maybe Hayek sensed he could be hijacked, because he wrote an essay titled, "Why I Am Not a Conservative," found in the appendix of the book. Hayek identified his political stance to be basically a classical liberal or libertarian one. For subtle reasons, he disliked using either term and preferred to be called a "Burkean Whig," which definitely clears up matters.)

Hayek became good friends with Karl Popper, one of the most influential philosophers of the twentieth century, also from Vienna and who also taught at the LSE. It is unclear who influenced whom, but each dedicated books to the other in appreciation of their respective influence.

Last but not least, Jimmy Wales, the founder of Wikipedia, credits Hayek's work on prices (as signals) and his thoughts on decentralized information in "The Use of Knowledge in Society" as central to his thinking about how to manage the Wikipedia project.[35]

For a long time, Hayek had more influence among political scientists than among economists, but lately there has been a bit of a revival of the ideas of the Austrian school with which he was associated.

He shared the Nobel Prize in 1974 with the Swedish socialist Gunnar Myrdal, who said that the fact that the prize was given to Hayek and Milton Friedman showed that it should be abolished.

When one considers the impact of the man, it is worth quoting Hayek's arch intellectual rival, Lord John Maynard Keynes (1883–1946):

The ideas of economists and political philosophers, both when they are right and when they are wrong, are more powerful than is commonly understood. Indeed the world is ruled by little else. Practical men, who believe themselves to be quite exempt from any intellectual influence, are usually slaves of some defunct economist.

---

33. This book is number 9 on the list of 100 best non-fiction books of the century in the ranking found at http://www .nationalreview.com/100best/100_books.html.
34. John Ranelagh, *Thatcher's People: An Insider's Account of the Politics, the Power, and the Personalities* (1991), p. ix.
35. See the June 2007 issue of the libertarian magazine *Reason*.

POINT TAKEN

Someone else always has to carry on the story.[36]
—John Ronald Reuel Tolkien (1892–1973), English writer

Finally, because it is possible to work your way through a chapter and lose sight of the main point once you reach the end of the chapter, I will allow our tech-savvy guests to tweet[37] me a summary statement. (Personally, I don't think tweeting should be acceptable at a dinner party . . . but then again I am old-fashioned). If they get the economics right, which they will, then I guess I will be ok with it.

Here is the first tweet:

@EvelineAdomait[38]Glad there is a another econ party book #economy #dinnerandconversation

---

36. Taken from *The Fellowship of the Ring* (1954).
37. In *Cocktail Party Economics,* this was done on a cocktail napkin at the end of each chapter. At a dinner party, I don't think the host would appreciate anyone writing on cloth napkins.
38. This is my Twitter account.

CHAPTER 2

Character Assignments

Character is so largely affected by associations that we cannot afford to be indifferent as to who and what our friends are.
—M. Hulburd[1]

A small group of students are seated around a table in the study area looking like they've been there for a while. Papers are sprawled across the table along with empty coffee cups and the odd half-eaten muffin. Salim, a second-year coop student in mechanical engineering, quickly gathers his books into his backpack while the others continue to study.

Salim is medium height, with a muscular build, looking more like a kinesiology student than an engineering student. He tends to hold right-wing political views and is taking macroeconomics for his business administration minor because it compliments his engineering major well. He is really interested in patent laws because he wants to own his own business one day and is currently inventing something that he hopes will send him on his way. His parents are hardworking immigrants from Pakistan; he eats Halal[2] food and doesn't drink alcohol.

To his immediate right is Brooke. Brooke is a slight woman with light brown hair that she wears in ponytail most of the time. As a passionate first-year environmental science major, she places global warming high on her list of concerns and is solidly on the lefthand side of the equation politically. She feels strongly that globalization is a major source of the economic problems in the world and that governments have sold out to the big multinationals because of greed. She loves the Occupy Wall Street movement. Brooke has to take an economics course because of its relevance for environmental policy but is very suspicious of the discipline. She is vegan for ethical reasons, wears Birkenstocks almost exclusively, has a pet dog, and only drinks the beer found on PETA's[3] "Acceptable for Vegans" list.

On her right, Elizabeth, or Libby as she was called in the small town she was from, peers at her books through her heavy-framed glasses almost mechanically. Crisply dressed, Libby a fourth-year political science major, is a member of the student wing of the liberal-leaning political party. Her goal is to one day join the Foreign Service, and she is taking an introductory macroeconomics course because it is a prerequisite for the Master in Public Policy program she has her eye on. Libby enjoys an occasional libation from either the beer or wine category.

David, a first-year Bachelor of Commerce student, sits across from Libby and takes introductory economics because it is core to his marketing major. He seems to like making presentations for his classes but is sick of SWOT[4] analysis. David leans more to the right ideologically. David values the Jewish culture and work ethic his grandparents brought with them after leaving Europe in 1905. Although he doesn't eat Kosher, he does avoid pork out of respect for his religion. As for beverages, David likes rum and vodka but drinks beer as well occasionally.

---

1. Reported in *Dictionary of Burning Words of Brilliant Writers* (1895) by Josiah Hotchkiss Gilbert (1834–1909). I would love to be in someone's dictionary someday, especially in a book with this title!
2. Means lawful or permissible in Arabic.
3. See http://www.peta.org/about/faq/which-beers-are-suitable-for-vegans.aspx.
4. SWOT stands for Strengths, Weakness, Opportunities, and Threats.

On his right is Emma whose major is English literature. She favours writers like Jane Austen and Emily Bronte and is big into art-house movies playing at the local student-run repertory movie theatre. She's not a big "math person"; in fact, she gets down right intimidated when confronted with too many numbers that need to be crunched. Her parents made her take a business administration minor so she has something "marketable" once she graduates and so now finds herself in macroeconomics hoping that things don't get to "mathy." Politically, she is on the left side. She is a health-conscious vegetarian, although she will eat fish from time to time. She will also partake in some higher-quality wine and micro-brewed beer on occasion.

Leaning back on his chair to her right is Justin, a third-year history major and big fan of documentaries on The History Channel and Netflix. Justin wants to understand the role the economy has played in history and is taking Intro to Economics as a free elective. A political centrist, Justin is convinced that right- and left-wing governments are fundamentally dangerous to a free society. He immigrated to Canada with his parent as a small child from the United States when his dad became a professor at the University of Guelph. Justin attended Catholic schools and is a huge admirer of the Kennedy dynasty. He is the kind of guy who eats almost anything placed before him but prefers very expensive dry red wines, gourmet beers, and the occasional glass of aged Scotch—the older the better.

FELLOWSHIP SUPPER[5]

In the adversity of our best friends we always find something which is not wholly displeasing to us.[6]

—*Edmund Burke (1729–1797), Irish politician*

"I gotta go," Salim exclaims as he packs up his books and slides them into his backpack. "I have a fluid mechanics assignment due tomorrow and I have a couple of hours left on it."

Libby, the oldest of the group, takes charge and quickly asks before Salim leaves, "So how is next week looking for everyone? Want to meet same place, same time next Thursday?"

Almost simultaneously, both Emma and Justin answer, "Not for me!" Justin stops to let Emma proceed as she explains that she has three major papers due next Friday, so Thursday night is completely out for her.

Justin nods as he says, "Same for me. Between my French Revolution course and senior seminar, I'm swamped."

The first-year students, Brooke and David, indicated that they are fine with Thursday night, but by now everyone realizes that it doesn't matter that they can make it because it isn't going to happen anyway.

"How do you guys feel about coming over to my place on Saturday night?" offers Libby. "My roommates are gone for the weekend and we can have dinner and go over the course before finals. We can make it potluck."

---

5. Common phrase in Baptist circles.
6. Taken from *A Philosophical Enquiry into the Origin of Our Ideas of the Sublime and Beautiful* (1757). You have to admit that book titles had more flair in the olden days.

"That would be great," says Justin. "It would be nice to have a more relaxed study group as we close out the year."

Salim looks antsy and says, "Sounds good. Can we sort out the food by email? I have a lot of work to do."

"Make sure most of it is vegan, okay." Brooke interjects. "Also, I would prefer if there wasn't meat at the meal. I think everyone knows how I feel about eating animals, and I don't really want to watch you guys doing it."

After an uncomfortable pause, Emma pipes up with: "Fine with me, I am vegetarian anyway."

As Salim rushes out the door, he says, "Fine, fine. Let's deal with this by email. I have to go!"

The remaining students look at one another, realizing what a pain it will be to sort through 30 emails to arrange a simple dinner. "Let's figure it out now and just tell Salim what he is bringing," Emma suggests. "Given we're going meatless, I don't think we need to worry about Halal."

Libby proceeds to pull up a new Word file on her laptop. "OK, how about everyone bring an appetizer? I will do a main meal because I have the stove. Who wants to bring dessert—maybe one vegan and one not?"

"I'll bring a vegan dessert," offers Brooke.

"And I make a great chocolate caramel cheesecake," announces Justin. "A really great cheesecake!"

"Sounds good," laughs Libby before she directs her attention toward Brooke. "You OK with a Chinese stir-fry?"

Brooke nods affirmatively.

David, who had been silent for most of the exchange, chimes in, "I'll bring some bread from the organic bakery just off campus."

Libby finishes typing and attaches the file to an email for everyone. It reads:

Libby—entrée (stir-fry and noodles)

Justin—cheesecake and appetizer

Brooke—vegan dessert and appetizer

Emma—two appetizers

David—bread and an appetizer

Salim—two appetizers (We made the decision so we hope you are OK with this. Make sure the food is vegan, please.)

As Libby presses the send button, she concludes this meeting with one more directive: "Bring your own alcohol if you want to drink. I will have water, juice, coffee, and tea. Well, it looks like we are set. See you on Saturday night, six-ish."

Looking forward to a little party, Emma seemed delighted. "This is going to be fun—can't wait!" she exclaimed.

With that, everyone starts to gather their things and head to the door—a very productive end to a very productive meeting.

Key Economic Concepts and Relationships

"They are Man's," said the Spirit, looking down upon them.
"And they cling to me, appealing from their fathers.
This boy is Ignorance.
This girl is Want.
Beware them both, and all of their degree,
but most of all beware this boy,
for on his brow I see that written which is Doom,
unless the writing be erased."

—from
A Christmas Carol (1843),
by Charles Dickens (1812–1870), British novelist

CHAPTER 3

Measure for Measure

Wonder, Carlyle declared, is the beginning of philosophy. It is not wonder, but rather the social enthusiasm which revolts from the sordidness of mean streets and the joylessness of withered lives, that is the beginning of economic science.[1]

—Arthur Cecil Pigou (1877–1959), English economist

In one of those unusual coincidences, everyone arrives at the same time—promptly at 6:05 P.M. to be exact. As Libby opens the door, the fragrance of garlic, onions and bell peppers wafts into the hallway of the apartment building. "Welcome to my place, guys," Libby says. "Come on in and make yourself at home. I have to get back to the stove or we could have a bit of a disaster on our hands."

As they file into the room, they all make appreciative comments about the smell of the food.

"Just put your stuff on the table," instructs Libby. "Help yourself to a glass from the counter if you want a drink. Can someone pour me a glass of red wine?"

As they all head toward the counter, it becomes clear that everyone will not fit by the counter. Justin "wins" the race and picks up the corkscrew. He proceeds to uncork his offering of a $20 bottle of Shiraz from Australia. After pouring a glass, he hands it to Libby who thanks him. "Mmm, nice wine," she murmurs to Justin. Justin then pours himself a glass.

"Anyone else want red?" he calls out to the others, who place their appetizers on the table and proceed to inspect the choice of beverages for consumption. Most of the others decline Justin's invitation and opt for beer instead while Salim comfortably replies "No thanks" and pours himself a glass of ice water from a jug on the counter near the sink.

After surveying the table, now completely covered in food, Emma raises her beer to propose a toast: "To awesome friends, amazing food, and an A in economics!"

As the glasses clink, David adds, "Life is good isn't it?"

MEASURES OF LIFE, LIBERTY, AND THE PURSUIT OF HAPPINESS[2]

"Business!" cried the Ghost, wringing its hands again. "Mankind was my business. The common welfare was my business; charity, mercy, forbearance, and benevolence were all my business."[3]

—Charles Dickens (1812–1870), English novelist

As mentioned in the introduction, one of the first issues we have to deal with when discussing macroeconomics is the problem of measurement—and there basically are two important issues that we must contend with. First, when we want to look at a macro economy, we can find many things that *could* be measured because the data is readily available. But that doesn't mean that these things are necessarily

---

1. Taken from *The Economics of Welfare* (1928).
2. We hold these truths to be self-evident, that all men are created equal; that they are endowed by their Creator with inherent and inalienable rights; that among these, are life, liberty, and the pursuit of happiness. Taken from *The Declaration of Independence*. Thomas Jefferson (1743–1826), American president.
3. Taken from *A Christmas Carol* (1843).

important in order to get a sense of the economy as a whole. Second, we can easily measure the difficult and important things, incorrectly. As economists, we want to measure the right things, and we want to measure them accurately.

So what do we think is important to measure? Let me give you a literary example to illustrate the issues of measurement and importance. I recently saw a draft for a book that had this printed on the cover: "78,000 words." While I am sure that this is an important measurement of sweat equity for the author and also may be relevant for the readers as an indication of how long it might take to read the book (although, do we really know how many words we read in a given period of time?), it doesn't really capture what we might value in a book of 78,000 words. It captures neither the significance of the ideas nor the quality of the writing. Similarly, economists don't want to measure simple things like word counts just because they are easily measurable when what we want is something like The New York Times Best Seller List[4] ranking which would be a much more significant indicator of worth. The former, while quantifiable, isn't as important as its ranking[5] in determining whether a book is worthwhile to read or not. To be honest, it would make me really, really happy if either *Cocktail Party Economics* or *Dinner Party Economics* ever made that list!

All that Mankind has done, thought, gained or been: it is lying as in magic preservation in the pages of Books.[6]
—*Thomas Carlyle (1795–1881), Scottish writer and historian*

The measurement that macro economists most want to quantify is called *economic welfare,* which captures some aspect of the happiness[7] of people—or their well-being.[8] Well-being is what people ultimately care about and that is essentially what we want to measure if we can. You can imagine that the idea of "general well-being" is complicated to measure. Having said that, we are not totally ill-equipped to determine what makes people happy. We all know that such things as food, clothes, healthcare, books, films and leisure can improve the well-being of people.

When David says, "Life is good isn't it?" he is making a statement that the dinner party has the makings of a very happy night—fantastic food, refreshing drinks, good friends, and the promise of engaging conversation. In order to get to some composite measure of happiness for a country, we need to aggregate or add up all of the individual levels of happiness in that country. If we are feeling like we should be world citizens, we can try to find out the level of global happiness of everyone in the world. That's an idea that makes you want to hold hands and sing "We Are the World,"[9] doesn't it?

---

4. This list was first published on April 9, 1942.
5. The exact method of ranking books is a trade secret.
6. From *The Hero as Man of Letters.*
7. Economists call this *utility,* and it enters into the social welfare function. Economists say that people try to maximize their utility subject to budget constraints. In other words, they make choices that enhance their happiness given they live in a world of scarcity. See *Cocktail Party Economics* for a more comprehensive discussion.
8. Well-being is actually broader than happiness. For example, getting a root canal may be unpleasant but it enhances human well-being.
9. In 1985 this song raised money for famine relief in Africa. It was written by Michael Jackson and Lionel Ritchie and as an album sold more than 20 million copies worldwide. Less than 30 songs have made the select group of 10 million copies or more. After the earthquake in Haiti, a reprise called, "We Are the World 25 for Haiti" was produced to help survivors.

EXTREME MEASURES

From the sublime to the ridiculous is but a step.[10]

—Napoleon Bonaparte (1769–1821), first consul of the French Republic

Some years ago while in an elevator at my university, a colleague of mine from another department asked me what I was teaching. When I replied "Economics," he responded with "Well everyone knows that money can't buy happiness." I must have had my oatmeal that morning because I shot back, "Yeah, that may be true, but poverty really sucks!" My point is that I am pretty sure that if the average person were offered the choice between prosperity and poverty, he or she in most cases[11] would take prosperity over poverty any day. Now prosperity and poverty may be extremes in the standard of living continuum, but often the point is easier to see in the extremes. When stated this way, my colleague agreed with me.

Notice that my colleague also equated prosperity with money. Of course, this isn't strictly true and I will devote the next chapter to the concept of money, but suffice it to say, that although money isn't the same as the standard of living, we can use money to measure the standard of living and it proves to be quite a good way to do so. Money measures the standard of living much the way that feet and inches (or metres) measure height. For instance, if you can say that a female who is 6′8″ (2.03 metres) is tall, then you don't really need to see her to believe that she is tall. All you have to know is the measurement and compare it to your knowledge of how tall other people are in your culture. However, if you saw this person on the street and didn't know her actual height, you would still say that she was tall just by looking at her. There is something intrinsic about "tallness" in our culture that isn't dependent on the units we use to measure it. Measures just make the pronouncement of tallness quantifiable. In the same way, money is measuring something that really can make you happy and it communicates information succinctly.

It's a kind of spiritual snobbery that makes people think they can be happy without money.[12]

—Albert Camus (1913–1960), French philosopher and writer

I can already hear people object that the really important things in life like love, friendship, and good feelings can't be measured by money and that any attempt to measure of well-being without these factors becomes a futile pursuit, as if it is almost sacrilegious to try to do so. However, I am going to have to cut this conversation short and say that once we overlook the arguments about the psychological and sociological "un-measureables," which, of course contribute to our ultimate happiness, I think we can agree that there are many good things that *can* be measured that make us happy. It is a wonderful thing to have your basic needs met: food in your belly, a roof over your head, and a drink in your hand. Each of these is measurable. Thus, we have a fighting chance at getting to a reasonable number for the concept of standard of living by focusing on what we can quantify. It's definitely a number worth pursuing.

---

10. Quoted in *History of Europe from the Commencement of the French Revolution in 1789, to the Restoration of the Bourbons in 1815,* Vol. 3 (1842) by Archibald Alison.
11. Members of some religious orders take vows of poverty because their source of happiness is not found in material things. Most people do not choose—and therefore do not want—to do this.
12. From *Carnets, mai 1935—fevrier 1942,* or *Notebooks—1935–1942* (1962).

HAPPY STUDIES

What is the end of study? Let me know?
Why, that to know, which else we should not know
Things hid and barr'd, you mean common sense?
Ay, that is study's god-like recompense.[13]

—*William Shakespeare (1564–1616), English playwright and poet*

There has been quite a bit of research done in the area of human happiness, and it seems to depend on three sets of factors. (I recommend you read the article "The Economics of Happiness" by Bruno S. Frey and Alois Stutzer[14] for a more complete discussion.) They found that these factors are the following:

1. Personality and demographic traits such as age, gender, marital status, children, nationality, education, and health

2. Economic factors such as income, unemployment, and inflation

3. Political factors such as the level of democracy and government involvement as well as the functioning of a country's institutions

These factors may or may not be interconnected. For example, a higher income may lead to better healthcare and education. It becomes more complicated to distinguish between the effects of the individual factors of income, healthcare, and education. Is it the income or education or both that really increases happiness? Income can also be connected to race and nationality. Thus the finding that foreigners report lower levels of happiness than nationals may be more complicated than originally thought if those immigrants also make less income. In terms of macro economies, certain types of governments tend to have particular policies with respect to unemployment or inflation. Is it the political structure or the economic policies that really matter in terms of happiness? Because there are always multiple factors to consider, care should be taken to account for all factors before definitive statements about what is connected to happiness are made.

Have no fear, though, econometricians[15] to the rescue! Now I am sure that some might find the work that these people do boring, but we need these folks to tease apart the tangles in the data and find out what correlates with what. Econometrics helps because it provides the tools to look at one variable at a time and see its impact alone. Thus all other variables are controlled for—meaning that they are fixed at a certain level. For example, after careful analysis we can say that, generally, the more freedom citizens have in a country (econometrically controlling for income and other factors), the happier they are. It looks like freedom has its own effect over and above the impact of income. We can also say that within a country, richer people tend to be report higher levels of satisfaction once the data is controlled for such things as education, health, status, and freedom. Happiness and income are very much connected to each other, and the econometricians helped us come to this conclusion.

---

13. *Love's Labour's Lost* (1595–1596).
14. "The Economics of Happiness," http://www.bsfrey.ch/articles/365_02.pdf.
15. Recall from the introduction that econometrics combines economics and statistics to handle real-world data.

Felix qui potuit rerum cognoscere causas.
(Happy the man who has been able to learn the causes of things.)[16]
—*Virgil (70 BC–19 BC), Latin poet*

However, just because we have econometrics to statistically control for interconnected variables, that doesn't mean we can start making bold claims about causation. We should also worry about reverse causation problems. Let me illustrate with an example. Research shows that married people tend to be happier than their single cohorts. But we shouldn't jump to the conclusion that we should encourage single people to marry to improve their well-being. It may be a reverse causation that happier people find marriage easier and therefore are more likely to be married.

It turns out that it is possible to tell a reverse causation story for almost any of the factors listed in the happiness studies. (See the list of factors at the beginning of this section.) Even the idea that richer countries tend to be happier can be explained by concluding that a country of happy people will be more productive and creative, which leads to higher levels of income. The most we can say about the relationship between income and happiness is that income clearly *correlates* with happiness. We can't say that factors like income *cause* happiness because it could very well be that happiness causes people to generate more income. Whether happiness produces income or income buys happiness, there is still a correlation between the two. For the purposes of this book, a correlation between income and happiness is sufficient to proceed with measuring income at a national level and believing that it tells us something about the well-being of its citizens.

However, causation becomes important in policymaking. Identifying which is "the cart" and which is "the horse" becomes crucial in setting up the appropriate government programs aimed at improving the well-being of people. For example, if marriage really makes people happier, then a government might want to sponsor online dating services. However, if it turns out that happier people tend to get married, the government might want to reconsider this costly and futile program. Perhaps the government would be better off funding psychotherapy sessions for unhappy people and not worry about their marital status.

GOOD GOVERNMENT

The care of human life and happiness, and not their destruction, is the first and only legitimate object of good government.[17]
—*Thomas Jefferson (1743–1826), American president*

Hopefully, governments will try to maximize the total welfare or well-being of all of their citizens. This can be done by creating an environment where individuals, whenever possible, achieve a higher level of happiness for themselves. When individuals can't do this efficiently,[18] governments can take over the program. Once governments take over

---

16. *Georgics* (29 BC).
17. Letter to the Republican Citizens of Washington County, Maryland (March 31, 1809).
18. Read *Cocktail Party Economics* Chapter 11 for more on the role of government.

national programs, this means they will spend some money. This raises two questions: Where do they get the money and where should they spend it? Thus governments, like individuals, have to make hard choices about where they give and where they take when they set a budget. However, governments are not like individuals with respect to the costs and benefits of their decisions. Individuals know and bear their own personal costs and benefits when they make choices, so we assume their choices are "reasonable."[19] In a country, for redistributive programs, the costs are borne by one group of people and the benefits are enjoyed by another. Debate about what is "reasonable" is inevitable.

Comparisons do ofttime great grievance.[20]
—John Lydgate (1370–1449), English poet and translator

If governments take from one person to give to another person, they usually change the happiness of both. They do this all the time when they tax a certain segment of society to subsidize another. (Generally, the taxed person's happiness goes down and the subsidized person's goes up.) Is this the right thing to do? Now the question is a "normative" one involving equity, with rhetoric in the public sphere justifying the tax policy. Politicians may argue that the happiness lost by the rich person is less valuable than the happiness gained by the poor person[21] and that the redistribution of wealth is worth it to society overall. Of course, people who are taxed may or may not see the policy in this positive way[22] and might become quite irate, intent on voting in a new government with "friendlier" tax policies. No matter what, you can always bet on one thing: There will never be an entire electorate composed of people who are completely satisfied with the level of taxes they pay or the programs that are funded. That is just the nature of governing when you make choices for aggregate happiness. "Me to We"[23] is actually difficult.

UNITED WE STANDARDIZE

Society is one word, but many things.[24]
—John Dewey (1859–1952), American philosopher, psychologist and educational reformer

Our quest for a meaningful measurement of human welfare leads us to the United Nations Development Programme (UNDP). This organization helps governments of countries,

19. Economists distinguish between normative and positive statements. Positive statements are testable, whereas normative ones express an opinion. For example, we can test the positive statement that increased spending on mathematics education will increase international test scores. We cannot test the statement that we should increase mathematics education because it is the right thing to do. Most governments try to justify normative ideals with positive arguments. The word "reasonable" has a normative component to it.
20. Taken from *Bochas Book III.*
21. Many economists say that it is impossible to compare happiness between people (sometimes called Robbins's Critique (1932) after Lionel Robbins). What units would we use and how would we know the numbers were correct? We can only use the idea that marginal utility is diminishing and the most important dollar is the first. It seems reasonable to assume that if we took a dollar from a very wealthy person and gave it to someone who was destitute, the wealthy person wouldn't even notice it was gone. This fascinating area of economics is called Social Choice Theory.
22. If they are somewhat altruistic they may be fine with the transfer of wealth to a poorer person. It might even make them feel good (which explains why the very wealthy often become philanthropists). I happen to fall into this camp and do not begrudge the taxes that I pay on the basis of equity arguments. (Furthermore, I believe we have a dynastic endowment problem. Some people have wealth because they inherited it, and I don't really see why they shouldn't be taxed and the funds given to someone who wasn't born so lucky. I might have some efficiency concerns, however. See *Cocktail Party Economics* Chapter 6 for more on this subject.)
23. http://www.metowe.com/about-us/our-story/.
24. Taken from *Democracy and Education* (1916).

especially those which are classed as a Least Developed Country (LDC[25]), to build better lives for their citizens. Since 1990, the UNDP has annually published the Human Development Report with its now-famous Human Development Index (HDI). This measurement was created by economists Mahbub ul Haq and Amartya Sen whose lofty purpose for this index was to shift thinking from income accounting to the betterment of people. They were concerned that governments placed too much emphasis on economic progress and not enough on human well-being, and this index was created to address the disconnect. Before we look at the index in detail, let's find out more in our gossip column about one of the creators of the index, Amartya Sen, who won a Nobel Prize for his work, which included a deep concern for society's poorest members.

GOSSIP COLUMN: AMARTYA KUMAR SEN (1933–)

If one word could characterize Sen's life and work, it would be freedom. He is a man who has enjoyed many freedoms, and has researched what it means to be free. Born on a college campus in West Bengal (India) and raised by academic parents, he spent all of his working life at some of the preeminent English-speaking universities in the world (Cambridge, Harvard, Oxford, and the London School of Economics, to name a few), enjoying each institution. He never lost his connection to his roots and helped create the department of economics at the Jadavpur University at the age of 23 (while waiting to have his PhD dissertation received by Cambridge[26]), taught at the Delhi School of Economics during its glory years, and focused much of his practical research on issues facing India. Even though he was a permanent resident of the USA for 50 years, he kept his Indian citizenship because it is so important to him. It seems he is free to live in the best of all worlds.

Because he was so intellectually curious, he also had an interest in such diverse subjects as Sanskrit, mathematics, physics, and economics. He says that he succumbed to economics' charms, but I think he actually chose it because of its breadth. His economic ideas are not without some philosophy[27] thrown in because he received a degree in that subject as well. He states that his interests include reading and arguing with people, and there seems to be no shortage of books for him to read[28] and debating partners for him to engage if he wishes to do so.[29]

Academically, Sen is able to freely move between the practical and theoretical. His curiosity started with the practical—Why did so many people die in the Bengal famine of 1943 when there wasn't a reduction in food production?—and branched into the theoretical with the publication of his book *Collective Choice and Social Welfare* (1970), which led to the Nobel. He returned to the practical with the development of the HDI (1990). His most recent writings are a bit of both.

There are a couple of major conclusions he brings to the social welfare table. First, his "liberal paradox" dispels the libertarian view that free markets are both effi-

---

25. A country must meet specific criteria to be classified as an LDC. Needless to say, for most of the citizens in LDCs, things are generally very bad.
26. He finished his thesis in one year but Cambridge had a minimum three-year registration requirement before submission. Because he was so young and didn't have his PhD yet, this caused an uproar.
27. While still waiting to submit his thesis, Sen won a Prize Fellowship at Trinity College, Cambridge, which gave him four years to do anything he liked. He used it to study philosophy.
28. The range of his interests is shown by the range of his book titles: *Collective Choice and Social Welfare* (1970), *Guidelines for Project Evaluation* (1972), *On Economic Inequality* (1973), *Poverty and Famines* (1981), *Utilitarianism and Beyond* (1982), *Commodities and Capabilities* (1985), *The Quality of Life* (1993), *Development as Freedom* (1999), *Rationality and Freedom* (2002), and *The Idea of Justice* (2009), not to mention *The Argumentative Indian* (2005).
29. The economist Jagdish N Bhagwati would love to debate with him.

GOSSIP COLUMN *(CONTINUED)*

cient and respect human freedom. If people have nosey preferences—these are preferences that include other people's choices—free markets don't lead to efficient outcomes. In his illustration to show the point, he has two individuals, Lewd and Prude, in a scenario where Prude would like to censor Lewd's reading habits. As you can imagine, it proves impossible to get to a "best" solution if we value human freedom. Second, freedom to choose has to be more than in name only. He developed the idea of "effective freedom," or the "capabilities approach." For example, if a woman has the political freedom to start a business but cannot secure a business loan because she is a woman, then the freedom is not effective. She isn't really able to live up to her potential. The HDI tries to get at this by including health and education in the mix.

In his personal life, he has fought and won against cancer. He has also known the love of three intelligent women. Nabaneeta Dev, his first wife, divorced him; his second wife, Eva Colomi, died of cancer; and later he married his third wife Emma Rothschild. His four children seem to have inherited his ability to be free thinkers. Two are journalists, one a rap musician,[30] and one a Bollywood actress who experienced some notoriety because she exposed her back in public and her audience had "nosey preferences."

Sen is a first-rate academic who cares about the real world.

RELATIVELY SPEAKING

What is intelligible in history can be formulated only with reference to problems and conceptual constructions which themselves arise in the flux of historical experience.[31]
—*Karl Mannheim (1893–1947), Hungarian-born social philosopher and sociologist*

In order to understand the Human Development Index, we need to chat a little about indices in general. Index numbers are created to solve a basic problem: how do you combine factors that are not in the same units? In macroeconomics, index numbers are everywhere because of the issues in aggregating things that aren't similar. In macroeconomics, we really do need to figure out a way to compare and combine apples and oranges. For example, if you want to find out how expensive it is to live in a city or country, you want to combine different essentials such as housing, food, gasoline and entertainment prices to get to an answer. Thus, we get the consumer price index (CPI), which will be featured later in this book. If you want to know how the stock market is doing (not just the price of a single stock), you can check out such indices such as the S&P/TSX, the S&P 500, or the Dow Jones. Each of these stock market indices reduces a select group of stock prices[32]—which are given a certain amount of weight depending on their size in the market—to a single number. If the market index happens to go down, analysts will usually disaggregate the number and put the blame on a particular stock or group of stocks.

---

30. http://www.youtube.com/watch?v=2xYmhPDNx-Q.
31. Taken from *Ideology and Utopia* (1929).
32. The S&P uses the top 500 listed companies on the U.S. market. The S&P/TSX 60 looks at the top 60 companies on the Toronto Stock Exchange. On the other hand, the S&P/TSX composite has no fixed number of companies but includes about 70% of the value of the Toronto Exchange and is dependent on strict criteria; thus, the number of shares considered can go up and down depending on a particular company's fortunes. The Dow Jones only considers the top 30 companies in the U.S. market.

Thus, aggregation is useful for looking at the big picture but it hides the details. The numbers you want depend on the questions you are asking, and macroeconomics asks the big-picturetype questions. For this, index numbers are invaluable.

The actual world of what is knowable, in which we are and which is in us, remains both the material and the limit of our consideration.[33]

—*Arthur Schopenhauer (1788–1860), German philosopher*

In the case of the Human Development Index (HDI), measures of life expectancy, education, and income are combined into one number. There is no way to add years and dollars together without creating something completely different: thus, the HDI is a unit-less number with the highest value equal to 1. All countries have a number less than 1, with the highest value usually above .95. (It seems no country is perfect.) In the recent past, the country that seems to come out on top most often is Norway, but the Very High Development countries are usually all above 0.80 (the top 10 countries are usually in the 0.90 range), so it is crowded at the top. On the other hand, the bottom is equally crowded, with the poorest of the poor (or the Least Developed Counties) all in the 0.3 range.

The HDI can be tracked over time to see how every country is doing relative to each other or internally with respect to progress in life expectancy, education, and income. It should be noted that life expectancy, educational attainment, and income are all highly correlated to each other. There aren't too many countries like Cuba with high levels of health and education but low levels of income. Cuba is part of the High Human Development Index group because of the weight given to education and health. Generally, only a third of the world lives in a country with Very High or High values and slightly less than 20% are in the Low category. As a point of interest, there are some countries that are not included for various reasons. Two of the most notable are North Korea and Vatican City—quite the contrast.

OH HAPPY DAY

Any reader who finds the game tiresome is, of course, naturally not of my kind; for him the game has no significance, and it is true here as elsewhere, that like-minded children make the best play-fellows.[34]

—*Søren Kierkegaard (1813–1855), Danish Christian philosopher and theologian*

There is much more that can be said about happiness and well-being. Some might debate the premise that it can be measured at all, that the standard of living really matters, or that the measures we have are adequate. Some might think that economists actually don't care about anyone's well-being! This chapter is by no means exhaustive on the subject of *economic welfare,* although you might feel a bit exhausted by what I have said so far. All I can tell you is that economists think economic variables have an impact on human well-being. Maybe we are wrong but I doubt it. The rest of the book assumes that economics does have an impact, and together we will explore all of the various and sundry economic

---

33. Taken from *The World as Will and Representation* (1819), translated by Eric F. J. Payne (1958).
34. Taken from *Either/Or* (1843).

variables that are part of the macro canon. I hope it will add to world happiness and it doesn't decrease yours. In fact, for our study group, I trust these mini dissertations will help them get an A in the course—a single letter that combines and measures everything they have learned in macroeconomics. Hopefully an A actually measures or means something.[35]

Lindsay tweets:

> @evelineadomait Income is an important measure of well-being #dontworrybehappy #wewantanAinMacro

---

35. Bar, Kadiyali, and Zussman, 2009, "Grade information and grade inflation: The Cornell Experiment," *The Journal of Economic Perspectives,* vol. 23, no. 3 (Summer), pp. 93–108(16).

CHAPTER 4

Money Is as Money Does

For the importance of money essentially flows from its being a link between the present and the future.[1]

—*John Maynard Keynes (1883–1946), British economist*

Conversation flows freely among the students as they try to avoid any topics having to do with school, homework, or economics. This proves to be relatively easy given their mental tiredness this late in the term.

"Oh, before I forget, here is the money I owe you for the pizza we ordered last week."

"No probs, David," Justin says as he takes the bill and puts it into his wallet.

Emma notices the exchange and jokes, "Any of that for me? I'm running low on money right now. I'm going to owe a fortune in student loans once I'm done if I keep spending at this rate."

Salim nods in agreement, adding, "My parents just transferred some cash into my account yesterday, and my grandparents just wired me money as well. I should be fine to finish off the term and it feels good not to be broke anymore!"

Libby is so conspicuously silent that Emma inquires, "So what about you Libby? Is money tight?"

Libby looks a little embarrassed as she confesses, "My parents set up an educational fund when I was a baby so I don't really have to worry about money."

"Lucky you," says Brooke. "I'm fortunate that my dad's company hires students of employees every year and pays more than minimum wage. I'm good as well."

"My dad is a prof here so I get a tuition break. I also live at home, so that keeps costs down," offers Justin.

All of this seems a little too personal to David, who lightens the mood with a big grin and a flippant request. "Can I borrow some money from all of you? I take cheques, money orders, and credit cards!"

SHOW ME THE SHEKELS[2]

My own business always bores me to death. I prefer other people's.[3]

—*Oscar Wilde (1854–1900), Irish writer*

Little do our students know, but they have touched on some very important and inter-related topics in economics. These include money, savings, credit, and debt. They also touch on monetary institutions that allow them to do things like write and cash cheques, transfer funds between bank accounts, and send money orders between nations. This all may seem pretty simple on the surface—much like a duck does, as it calmly glides across the surface of the water. However, the mad paddling underneath captures the idea of a very evolved and sophisticated system that supports it all. Money isn't quite as simple as it looks at first glance.

---

1. Taken from *The General Theory of Employment, Interest and Money* (1935).
2. The first mention of the Shekel is in Mesopotamia in 3000 BC as a unit of weight of barley. The word is still in usage as the currency of modern-day Israel. Wow, more than 5,000 years of history!
3. Taken from *Lady Windermere's Fan* (1892).

For starters, money is unique among things in our society because it is defined by what it does, not what it is. Money is only money if it exhibits what economists call "the functions of money." In other words, if money doesn't act like money, it isn't money. But the opposite is also true. If something acts like money, then it is money, no matter if it is also something else, like a sheep or goat. Here is a little rhyme to help you remember the concept of money; I'm sure you will want to teach this to your children someday:

> *Money is a matter of functions four,*
> *a medium, a measure, a standard, a store.*

These functions—medium, measure, standard, and store—are what makes something—and it can be anything—money. If any of these functions are missing, the item ceases to be money. Let me give you an example of the "all or nothingness" when it comes to the functions of money.

When my oldest son was born, my sister gave him a commemorative set of coins as a gift. These were of the various denominations (*measure*) of our country's currency (*the standard*) in a sealed container so that the coins wouldn't discolour with age. In this case, these coins act as a *store* of value and my sister's hope was that this set would increase in value over time as a collector's item. Although these particular coins look like money on the outside and have three out of the four functions of money, they are, in fact, *not* money because they do not have the fourth function. Specifically, they have never been, and probably never will be, used to buy anything and thus do not act as a *medium* of exchange. For these coins to be money, they must be in circulation, which means that they are constantly changing hands with relatively short stays in various wallets, purses, and cash registers. Once the cash gets stuck in someone's jar on a dresser or in the vaults of a central bank,[4] it loses its essential "money-ness" and "disappears" from the system.

Given the right circumstances, it is also possible for things that aren't usually considered money to become money. For example, in German POW camps during the Second World War, cigarettes became money. Cigarettes (the *standard)* were worth something (*store* of value), and were used to buy or sell items (*medium* of exchange) in the camp. Other items were priced in numbers or portions of cigarettes (units of *measure*). In fact, the cigarettes for smoking were usually kept separate from this stock of money. I think the reasons are pretty obvious why people didn't want to smoke cigarettes that had been through so many fingers. It also gives meaning to the phrase "money going up in smoke."

A CONVENIENT TRUTH

A "strange coincidence," to use a phrase
By which such things are settled nowadays.[5]
—Lord George Gordon Byron (1788–1824), British poet

Most civilizations developed money because it offered convenience. Why is that? Well let's imagine a moneyless economy where all trades are based on a barter system—the exchange of real things for other real things (either an immediate transaction or on an

---

4. A central bank is in charge of a nation's money supply. In Canada, this is called the Bank of Canada and in the United States the Federal Reserve.
5. Taken from *Don Juan* (1818–1824). It was the poem that didn't end.

IOU basis). For example, I give you grain, you give me a weaving. This is fine if you want grain and I want your weaving, but if we don't have what economists call a "double coincidence of wants," the system breaks down. For example, if you want grain but I want a carving, then you will have to trade your weaving for a carving and get back to me. This is a very inconvenient process, especially if goods and services are more unique, further afield, or are wanted at different times. Money solves this problem. Here is how it works. You want my grain. I sell it to you for money. I take that money and go buy a particular carving from a particular carver whenever I want. Money, in this case, keeps the value of the grain I sold (assuming there are no inflation problems), and we make the exchange using money.

Conveniently, we have saved lots of time through this latter system. Benjamin Franklin was quite right when he said "time is money." Economists would say that we have saved on *search costs* for acceptable trades, which gives us more time to make more stuff. Therefore economies that use money prosper more than economies with just the barter system. Money economies have more time to work with. Some might argue that with the advent of the Internet there has been a revival of barter because the ability to search has become easier. However, in reality, barter has not caught on in a big way because technology in the various forms of payment systems has also helped money become more convenient to use. Thankfully, I don't have to barter for my supper. "Will teach for food" doesn't quite work for me.

FAST FORWARD

In a progressive country change is constant.[6]

—*Benjamin Disraeli (1804–1881), British Prime minister*

There are many terrific books on the history of money, banking, and the monetary system,[7] so I won't go into detail about it even though it is a fascinating subject and I encourage you to read up on it. Rather than dwell on the monetary structures of the Middle Ages or the 1900s in the USA,[8] I want to focus on the monetary system of today. Having said that, here is a very quick (and some would say dirty) summary of how we got from the early days to now in terms of the evolution of money.

In the beginning, there were commodities and commodities were money (stuff like grain, shells, and animals[9]). From there, coins took over, often with the same name as the weights of the commodities previously used as currency. For example, the shekel connects the correct weight of grain with the standardized coin (like the modern-day British pound, which connects a weight with a currency). Coins were made of various metals—most

---

6. Taken from a speech in Edinburgh (1867).
7. I suggest Niall Ferguson's book *The Ascent of Money* or the PBS movie by the same name.
8. See the *Wizard of Oz* (ounces) for the allegory representing the perceived problems of this period by L. Frank Baum—i.e. the yellow brick road is for gold standard and the silver slippers for, you guessed it, the silver standard of money. Dorothy is everywoman, the scarecrow stands for the farmers, the tin man the industrial workers, and the lion represents the politicians. The wicked witches are the banks on the East and the West Coasts of the USA. The wizard is the president of the United States.
9. The February 2013 edition of *National Geographic* featured a story on Afghanistan's Kyrgyz nomads, who use sheep as money. One lamb buys 110 pounds of flour, a sheep can buy a cell phone (with no cellular service available), and a bride is 100 sheep.

notably gold and silver. Gold and silver were inconvenient to carry around due to the danger of theft and their weight, so people stored them with the goldsmiths—who kept the coins safe and provided a note or bill as a receipt. Eventually the notes (which were backed by gold at the goldsmiths) were used for trades instead of the gold itself because it was much more convenient. I can only image how frightening it must have been for the first folks who received a piece of paper instead of a bag of gold after doing a transaction. A paper note might not have looked like much, but it caught on quickly as people discovered that the goldsmiths provided security for their gold and that the network of goldsmiths redeemed notes for gold on demand. The notes were as good as gold and a lot easier to put in their wallets. (Although I love the scene in *The Count of Monte Cristo* where Edmond Dantes pays for his estate with a wagon filled with gold. Gold definitely adds drama.)

All is not gold that glisters.[10]
—George Herbert (1593–1633), English poet and orator

Before they knew it, the goldsmiths had piles of gold in their vaults collecting dust. Ingenious people that they were, they came up with the bright idea that they could lend out the gold to others customers and charge interest[11] or a fee for their troubles. As long as the goldsmith (hereafter known as a bank[12]) had enough gold on hand to meet the anticipated requirements, the system worked well. (We will discuss bank runs later in the chapter.) They didn't actually lend out the gold itself but instead provided notes that represented gold.

With banks providing notes to those who stored the gold and notes to those who borrowed the gold, there were more notes in circulation than actual gold in the vaults. This situation was the beginning of what is known as the *fractionally backed banking system.*[13] In other words, the value of money in the system is based on the gold in the vaults but the total value of gold is a fraction of the total value of money. When it became clear that there wasn't enough gold to match all of the paper money in circulation, and that the paper that was now actually functioning as money, gold could be disconnected from money fairly easily—although it would take some time to do so.

The bills or notes became money by fiat and were called legal tender because governments endorsed the paper. (Check the signatures on your bills.) Remember that money is what money does, and these bills were doing the job. If people wanted to pay for things, they could take cash (bills, not gold) out of their bank accounts or write a cheque (draft) to request a transfer of money from one person's account to another. The gold standard was dead.

With the advent of the Internet, things became even easier because money now became just a bunch of digits in people's bank accounts and could be transferred without ever needing things like cash or cheques. Today, you can directly deposit money with a click of a button—hopefully on a secure site. In a developed country, if you say, "Show me your money!" all someone needs to do is turn on his or her smartphone, tablet, or

---

10. *Jacula Prudentum; Or Outlandish Proverbs, Sentences, &c* (1651). *Glister* is the verb for *glistens.*
11. Usury, which came to mean exorbitant interest, was forbidden by Church law.
12. Banks have existed since ancient Rome. Once goldsmiths gave out loans they acted as banks.
13. If banks kept all of your savings on hand, then it would essentially be a safety deposit box for which they would charge a fee. The fractionally backed system means that your savings become loans, helping the economy to prosper. As long as the bank keeps enough on hand should you need your money, this system works well.

computer and access his or her bank accounts to show you numbers on a screen. Technically, although we are not actually cashless in North America, cash as money is really small potatoes when compared to bank deposits.

There you have it—the evolution of money from barley sacks to bank accounts: drachmas[14] to digits.

CREDIT WHERE CREDIT IS DUE

All the perplexities, confusions, and distresses in America arise, not from defects in their constitution or confederation, not from a want of honor or virtue, so much as from downright ignorance of the nature of coin, credit, and circulation.[15]
—*John Adams (1735–1826), American president*

Identifying who has or who does not have money in the age of bank accounts is relatively easy because of the accounting system consisting of debits and credits. If the bank credits your account, you possess money and it is part of the national *money supply*. If you transfer money online from your chequing account to your friend's chequing account, your account is debited and you no longer own that money. Now your friend owns the money once it gets credited to his or her account. If you add up all of the deposits (credits) in the banks along with all of the cash in circulation, then you have the value the money supply. A transfer between chequing accounts doesn't cause a change in the total money supply. It simply changes the names of the owners on the accounts.

This should be fairly straightforward for most of us to grasp so far. However, what might not be so easy to understand is how a central bank of a country can increase the actual money supply in an economy, which implies the central bank has credited people's bank accounts. We will answer the question of why a central bank may want to do so, as well as look at the unintended consequences of money supply changes, later in the book. Here I want to look at how they do it. I know you're thinking, "They can increase my bank account any time they want and be done with it!" It isn't quite as easy as magically adding a few zeros to your account.

I am sorry to tell you that I am getting very extravagant, and spending all my money, and, what is worse for you, I have been spending yours too.[16]
—*Jane Austen (1775–1817), English novelist*

In the old days, if a country discovered gold, the money supply automatically increased as the gold entered the country. But we aren't backed by gold anymore, so how does our modern system work to create money that increases the money supply? To see how this works, we need to understand the role of a central bank. It should be noted that a central bank is not the government per se. It is supposed to be an independent agency within a country. Furthermore, central banks are not your ordinary bank. They are the banker's bank. Any deposits on their books are not in circulation and are therefore not part

---

14. Drachma literally means a handful, a grasp, or a fistful. It was a measure of volume.
15. Taken from a letter to Thomas Jefferson, August 25, 1787, in *The Works of John Adams,* ed. Charles Francis Adams, vol. 8 (1853).
16. Letter to Cassandra (1811–04–18), in *Letters of Jane Austen,* Brabourne Edition (1884).

of the money supply. Modern central banks work closely with their governments with the goal of creating a safe and stable financial environment for the country. They also have the ability to intentionally change the money supply, which is known as *monetary policy.*

To explain how a modern central bank increases the money supply takes some work and becomes quite technical. I think it best to illustrate the process with a story instead using equations and T-accounts.[17] Suppose I look at my bank accounts online and I see $1500 in my chequing account. Chequing accounts[18] are always part of the measure of money in the economy, so the national money supply includes my $1500. Now suppose I decide to buy a cottage. It turns out I don't have the cash to buy it outright because $1500 isn't enough to make the purchase and I will need to get a mortgage. So I head over to my local bank to get approved for a loan. The bank representatives ask me lots of questions about my financial health in order to determine if I can repay the loan. They check my credit rating, they ask for my paystubs, they send someone to check if there really is a cottage, and finally they say yes—phew!

The bank's legal department then draws up the mortgage papers for me to sign and I get closer to relaxing on that sunny deck overlooking the lake. These papers represent an agreement between the bank and myself that says that I promise to pay back the loan in regular fixed installments over a number of years if the bank agrees to lend the money upfront to pay for the cottage. This seems like a good deal to me. The fixed amount I agree to pay depends on the interest rate at the time of signing and the spacing of the installments. Higher interest rates will mean that I will pay more. The more frequent the payment plan, for example, weekly as opposed to monthly, the lower the payment size.

Now for the magic: I sign the papers and the loans officer goes to the computer on his or her desk, opens up the file to my bank account, and credits my account with the funds. In effect the bank official has . . . wait for it . . . just created money! How can this be, you might ask? The bank has created money because at one moment there was only $1500 in my account and the next there is a whole lot more. Essentially, banks create money when they extend loans to people because those loans go into somebody's bank account and accounts are money. In my case, the funds might only stay in my account until I transfer the payment to the people selling the cottage. My account gets debited and their account gets credited, but as a whole there is new money in the system. The fact remains that my mortgage created new money.

The process by which banks create money is so simple that the mind is repelled.[19]
—*John Kenneth Galbraith (1908–2006), Canadian-born,*[20] *American economist*

For some of you this might be somewhat frightening news. Banks can create money at will by simply extending loans?! I suggest you hold the panic. Banks don't normally go around lending money to everyone and their brother (although it did looked that way dur-

---

17. Accountants use T-accounts to record debits and credits with a ledger that looks like a capital T.
18. There are many definitions of *money supply* depending on which accounts at a bank are counted. They all start with M. Cash and chequing accounts are in all of the definitions of *money supply,* but U.S. accounts are in M3 but not M1 and M2 definitions of *money supply.* If there is a + along with the designation—for example, M2+, then accounts at credit unions, trust companies, and so forth are also included. There is no standardized set of accounts that equal the money supply. It depends on how broad or narrow you want to be about which accounts function as money in the economy.
19. *Money: Whence it came, Where it went.*
20. He went to the University of Guelph for his undergraduate degree, which is where I teach.

ing the financial crisis of 2008–2009 in the USA). Also, they can only lend out the funds available to them and these funds are costly to maintain. For example, banks give some interest to depositors, especially on longer-term savings accounts. As well, they provide services such as record keeping, ATMs, and security measures on accounts, which are costly for them to provide. Furthermore, depositors often come back to withdraw funds and therefore banks have to keep some of the deposits on reserve, which does not earn them any interest because the banks don't lend out their reserves. Thus, if banks want to extend more loans in order to make interest, they need to get more deposits or other sources of funds to work with. There is only so much money a single bank can create.

MY NAME IS BOND

The whole universe is carried on the credit system, and if the mutual confidence on which it is based were to collapse, it must itself collapse immediately. Just or unjust, it lives by faith.[21]
—Samuel Butler (1835–1902), British writer

This is where a central bank comes in. A central bank is a major player in the bond market of government securities. Bonds are debt contracts of various lengths of time that can be issued by different levels of government and by corporations. The shortest-term government bonds are less than a year and are called Treasury Bills[22] because they are printed by the treasury or finance department as part of a government's debt financing of its expenditures. Once printed, these bonds are bought and sold every day by the public[23] through bond dealers. If the central bank enters this market to buy or sell T-Bills, it changes the money supply. Here's how. When the central bank buys T-Bills from the public, the central bank receives the bonds and will transfer funds into the bank account of the seller. This seller's bank account gets credited and, voila, new money. Note that the T-Bills are not money because no one goes to the store and buys things with T-Bills. It's the new deposit that is money. This act of buying these short-term bonds is called *open market operations,* and it is the way that central banks increase the amount of money or liquidity in the financial system. If they want to destroy money, they tell their bond dealers to sell T-Bills and put bonds into the public's hands. The buyers of the bonds transfer funds out of their accounts to the central bank, and once the funds hit the central bank, they leave circulation and cease to be money. Remember that money is as money does. The credits on a central bank's books are not money. No one gets to spend these digits.

Money is like muck, not good except it be spread.[24]
—Francis Bacon (1561–1626), English philosopher, statesman, and essayist

At its most basic level, all modern money is a form of debt. Even the cash in your pocket is a liability, or a debt, of the central Bank because it is legal tender. Furthermore,

---

21. *Ramblings in Cheapside* (1890).
22. T-Bills are bonds that mature in under a year and are sold at a discount. See *Cocktail Party Economics* Chapter 12 for more.
23. These are big players like banks and mutual fund companies because T-Bills are sold in lots of $1,000,000, which isn't the standard fare of the ordinary person. The little people like us save through our banks in accounts that are attached to the T-Bills that the banks own.
24. Taken from *Essays* (1625).

your bank account is the base upon which your bank has extended loans to other people, which created other bank accounts somewhere out there over the rainbow. In fact, a new deposit is just the start of a domino effect. Once my seller gets paid for the cottage that I talked about earlier, he or she deposits the money in his or her bank. That bank will use the cottage funds to make another loan. Thus deposits (money) become loans, which become deposits (money), which create more loans, and so on. What keeps this circle from exploding is the fact that the bank never lends out the entire account but always keeps a bit as a reserve. The lower the reserve amount that banks hold, the more money that gets created in the system after one open market purchase of T-Bills by a central bank.

Between the idea
And the reality
Between the motion
And the act
Falls the Shadow[25]
—Thomas Stearns Eliot (1888–1965), American-born English writer

Central banks hope the banking system is fairly predictable and that they can precisely increase or decrease the money supply by changing bond activity. It would be lovely if the central bank could pull a lever and know exactly what was going to happen to the nation's supply of money. However, the recent financial crisis taught us that commercial banks are not automatons. They, in fact, are publically held, profit-minded companies that don't want to go bankrupt.[26] Central banks can't really make commercial banks extend loans if they don't want to just because the central bank bought some bonds from the public. Commercial banks can decide to increase the amount they keep on reserve instead. The money supply expansion hoped for by central banks during the 2008–2009 crisis was impaired because commercial banks didn't keep the ball going by lending the funds. This is called a credit crunch and required even more central bank interventions. For better or worse, the money supply in the market relies on a delicate partnership between central and commercial banks that isn't always predictable.

GOSSIP COLUMN

John Law (1671–1729) tends to be overlooked in histories of economics.[27] I guess that being responsible for the first great financial bubble and bust, and bankrupting a country in the process, will tend to overshadow one's accomplishments in theoretical economics.

John Law's early history didn't seem to mark him for a career in monetary economics. After the death of his goldsmith father in 1688, Law took his inheritance and left Edinburgh and moved to London, intending to make his name as a gambler and society dandy. He had mixed success, losing most of his inheritance at the tables (his

---

25. Taken from *The Hollow Men* (1925).
26. Italian for "Broken Bench." Money changers "broke the bench" when they became insolvent.
27. John Law is not listed in *The Economics Book: Big Ideas Simply Explained,* which covers the entire history of thought for economics. This must have been an oversight—he most definitely belongs in the canon.

mother had to bail him out—I hope he was grateful to her!) and killing another society "beau" in a duel. There are differing stories about the cause of the duel—apparently it was over a woman, with some stories claiming that she was a royal mistress and others claiming that Law's victim was the homosexual lover of a high member of the royal court. Both versions of the story suggest that Law had a royal license to kill. I can't imagine his mother was happy about all of this.

Consequently, Law was arrested and condemned to death, but escaped, probably with help from higher ups, and made his way to the Continent. There he resumed his life at the high-stakes gaming tables, but with a difference. Law, who had always had a talent for math, started thinking seriously about probability and the odds of various games, something that virtually nobody else was doing. As a result, he made a fortune, mainly by offering to place bets at odds that looked absurd but that actually favoured him.

He returned to Edinburgh and took another unexpected path. He started writing about the theory of money and banking. (Now there's a contrast in things to do with your time.) He was the first economist to use the terms *demand* and *supply* correctly (he predates Adam Smith) and to talk about the demand for money. He developed a macroeconomic model in which money was an essential component of exchange, so changes in the money supply were driving forces behind economic cycles. He concluded that for a country like Scotland, whose only source of gold or silver was her trade surplus,[28] a precious-metal currency made no sense, because the money supply would fluctuate with the state of Scottish trade. He proposed instead a paper currency, on the grounds that this would let the authorities stabilize the money supply and eliminate cycles. He believed using a deposit banking system to expand the money supply would stimulate economic activity, but he also recognized that pumping up the money supply too quickly would lead to inflation.[29]

In 1705, before Law's theories could be put to the practical test, the Act of Union between England and Scotland was passed, and a death sentence passed in London became enforceable in Scotland. Law fled for the Continent again, and resumed his life as a gambler. About a decade later he made his way to France. The French secret police took the view that the flamboyant gambler with a Scottish burr and a reputation as a killer was probably an English spy and wanted to expel him. Law was spared deportation by the death of Louis XIV, which resulted in Law's friend, the duc d'Orleans, becoming Regent.[30]

Under the Regent, Law was permitted to set up a bank with the authority to issue its own paper money, backed by gold. It quickly became very successful. Law didn't stop there, though. Louis XIV had left France's finances in a mess, and Law took it upon himself to clean them up—by buying the national debt. He took over a company that had the monopoly over all French trade and colonization in the Louisiana territory. He offered to swap shares in what became known popularly as the Mississippi Company for government debt at a much better rate than the debt was trading for publicly. Debt holders grabbed at the opportunity. Law went on to take over the other French trading companies, with monopolies over French trade in Africa, the Middle East, and basically the rest of the world. He then took over the French tax collection system and

---

28. Scotland unfortunately doesn't have any gold or silver to mine. All the metal has to come in by trade, specifically by a trade surplus (exports exceed imports). Thus the Scottish would receive gold for their goods and this new gold became part of their money supply. In essence, when things were good on the trade front, it was also good on the monetary front. The reverse can be said if things were bad. This meant trade cycles were magnified.
29. See *The Genesis of Macroeconomics: New Ideas from Sir William Petty to Henry Thorton* for a more complete discussion.
30. The new Louis was only five and way too young to rule.

GOSSIP COLUMN *(CONTINUED)*

bought the Mint. At this point he essentially owned France. He converted to Catholicism in order to become controller general, in effect the prime minister of France. Shares in the Mississippi Company soared, and vast paper fortunes were made—the term "millionaire" was coined to refer to Law and his shareholders. Law closed his bank and opened a new one, the Banque Royale, to serve as the government bank. He made his banknotes legal tender and moved to demonetize gold altogether. But you know what they say about something that is too good to be true.[31]

At that point, late in 1719, things started to go wrong. Some people questioned whether the price of Mississippi Company shares made sense in view of the fact that no profits were actually coming in from the Mississippi territory, and started to sell their shares. As the price of shares fell, Law panicked. (He should have remembered to stay calm and think of England.) Then he did something that shows why central banks should always be independent of finance ministries. He printed money in order to buy up company shares, to support the price of the shares. It worked for a while, but as Law, the monetary theorist, had once predicted, the massive increase in the money supply led to a hyperinflation. To add insult to injury, in 1720 share prices crashed anyway. The millionaires, who included much of France's upper crust, were suddenly penniless and very angry. Law fled France, leaving his wife and children[32] behind, and returned to England (he had been pardoned for the murder the previous year), where the man who had bankrupted France was received as a popular hero. Nevertheless he wanted to go back to France.

Alas, fate conspired against him and it was not to be. He died of pneumonia in Venice in 1729, again a gambler, but believing to the last that given a chance he could have fixed things. This may be true, but sometimes theorists[33] should not let practical expediency corrupt good theories. When you know better, you should know better.

THE REAL ISSUES

Money is a good servant, a dangerous master.[34]

—*Francis Bacon (1561–1626), English philosopher, statesman, and writer*

You now know that the money supply in a country is predominately the sum of the deposit accounts sitting in all of the banks.[35] Money and banks go together like a horse and carriage. But who cares if there is more money or less money sitting in bank accounts? Well, we should care—and here's why.

Think of the money supply as the grease that lubricates the gears of a very big machine we call the economy. Without grease, the gears wouldn't turn the machine so that things can be produced and consumed. Even if the gears could still turn without

---

31. For an entertaining short documentary on this part of Law's career, see http://www.nfb.ca/film/john_law_and_the_mississippi_bubble/.
32. His wife may not have been a legal one, as his children were not allowed to inherit his estate because of the "vice of their birth." See the *Oxford Dictionary of National Biography.* You have to be British and dead to make it into this collection.
33. I wish to thank my colleague and friend Brian Ferguson for his version of this gossip column. I shamelessly plagiarized his work because I couldn't have said it better myself. Any errors I added by tweaking are solely my fault and shouldn't reflect on him.
34. Taken from *De Dignitate et Augmentis Scientiarum* (1623).
35. If we want to extend things we can also include accounts in credit unions and other financial institutions that offer chequing privileges.

grease it could be very painful to watch. On the other hand, too much grease means that the gears are so sloppy that the teeth may not catch each other either correctly or efficiently. In other words, just as there is an optimal grease level that promotes proper functioning of a machine, there is an optimal money supply that promotes the proper functioning of the economy as a whole. The economy with buyers and sellers needs money to facilitate all of the trades. The actual goods and services produced and purchased are real but they use money (which isn't real in and of itself) to make the buying and selling happen. If there isn't enough money to support business, then we have a credit crunch and the economy can grind to a halt. If the central bank floods the system with too much money, then we have inflation,[36] with prices skyrocketing because we are spreading too much money around over too few goods. Like Goldilocks and the Three Bears, central banks have to get monetary policy just right. The real economy of goods and services depends on it.

THROWING GOOD REGULATIONS AFTER BAD

"I don't understand you," said Alice. "It's dreadfully confusing!" "That's the effect of living backwards," the Queen said kindly: "it always makes one a little giddy at first."[37]
—*Lewis Carroll, pen name for Charles Lutwidge Dodgeson (1832–1898), British author, mathematician, and clergyman*

Because money is so integral to the proper functioning of the economy, commercial banks are highly regulated.[38] Governments want to make sure that banks don't fail, or even get into any trouble for that matter, because the entire banking system relies on public trust. Most of modern-day regulations are a result of some past crisis, while every new crisis raises concerns about the appropriateness of the current regulations or the level of monitoring by the monetary authorities.

I would like to outline just a few problems that arose due to our fractional banking system—the fact that banks loan out most of the deposits they receive and only keep a fraction on reserve at any one time—and what has been done to address the issues.

First, what happens when we start to hear whispers that a particular bank is in trouble? Immediately, everyone comes out of the woodwork to withdraw their money from the bank because they are worried that they will lose everything. We have a bank panic on our hands. Because the bank doesn't have the cash on hand, we now have what is called a "bank run." If you've seen the classic Christmas movie *It's a Wonderful Life*, you will get the idea.

Once doubt begins it spreads rapidly.[39]
—*John Maynard Keynes (1883–1946), British economist*

The problem is that once the cash on hand is drained from the bank, the bank goes bankrupt and the remaining depositors are out of luck. What's more, what if the neighbours start to worry and think that this could also happen at their bank as well? They will

---

36. We will devote an entire chapter to the topic of inflation.
37. Taken from *Through the Looking Glass and What Alice Found There* (1871).
38. The Basel Accords make recommendations to countries on how to best supervise their banks.
39. *The General Theory of Employment, Interest and Money* (1935).

probably go and withdraw their money from their own bank. The second bank could go bankrupt even though it wasn't in trouble to begin with. Remember that each bank only holds a fraction of the deposits on hand. Bank runs and bank panics are very contagious and can lead to a system failure if left unchecked. A system failure of this magnitude is a very bad situation. Thankfully, after it happened a few times around the world, governments instituted mandatory deposit insurance that commercial banks must purchase to protect their depositors. Thus if a bank has a run, these insured accounts are safe up to some predetermined amount (which is usually quite high). It is amazing how this insurance can have calming effect on people, who don't really want to stand in long lines anyway.

Second, banks can take some very big risks with other people's money. In order to make sure that bank shareholders aren't too tempted to instruct their management team to do so for profits, governments regulate commercial banks to have a certain amount of the shareholders' capital in the game. If the bank is going down, then the government wants to make sure the shareholders feel the pain as well.

All human things hang on a slender thread; the strongest fall with a sudden crash.[40]
—*Publius Ovidius Naso, known as Ovid (43 BC–17 AD), Roman poet*

Third, if banks make bad loans, they can end up in financial trouble. This was the root cause of the financial crisis that began in 2008. In order to prevent this, banks must regularly file reports with their regulators and open their books to scrutiny. In particular, they now have to show how risky their loans are. Furthermore, banks are not allowed to invest in risky assets like stocks with the deposits they receive. Most of their assets are in loans (of which the majority are mortgages) and safe T-Bills.

Last, in the USA and in China, banks are required to keep a minimum amount of reserves on hand, although countries like Canada do not have minimum reserve requirements anymore. It isn't clear that this practice really protects depositors. It should be noted that during the most recent financial crisis, U.S. banks held more than the minimum requirements, which means that this regulation wasn't really binding. Also, Canada's financial system was deemed the safest in the world without this requirement, so the jury is still out on this one.

BIG BROTHER

Freedom is the freedom to say that two plus two make four. If that is granted, all else follows.[41]
—*Eric Arthur Blair, pen name George Orwell (1903–1950), English writer*

Another thing central banks and government regulators do is monitor the transfer systems[42] where financial institutions interact with each other. With all the money transfers that happen between banks in a normal day, there has to be a place where everyone meets to make the exchange. Today it happens online with strict rules and computer algorithms somewhere behind it all to make things work smoothly. In essence, the government wants to make sure that parties in the system can trust each other and that no one bank defaults on another bank

---

40. *Epistolæ Ex Ponto IV* (AD 12–16).
41. Taken from *Nineteen Eighty-Four* (1948).
42. In Canada, this is called the Large Value Transfer System or LVTS.

at the end of the day. If one party were to default on a money transfer, the entire banking system could crash. If any bank is short the amount it needs to clear its books, then central banks act as "lenders of last resort" to the party that can't pay, in order to keep the books balanced—but regulators keep an eye on things, hoping it doesn't come to that.

Regulators attempt to curb bad behaviour and promote good behaviour of the commercial and investment banks in order to maintain a safe and sound financial system. The ultimate goal is to have the banks so much in the background that producers and consumers will use money without being aware of the banks as all. Therefore, if a problem does occur, governments, along with their central banks, need to be quick to come in and rescue the system from failure. The impact of a banking failure on Main Street would be catastrophic. It's a big job.

WHERE YOUR TREASURE IS

Instead of honoring this sacred obligation, America has given the Negro people a bad check, a check which has come back marked "insufficient funds." But we refuse to believe that the bank of justice is bankrupt. We refuse to believe that there are insufficient funds in the great vaults of opportunity of this nation. And so, we've come to cash this check, a check that will give us upon demand the riches of freedom and the security of justice.[43]
—Dr. Martin Luther King Jr. (1929–1968), Baptist minister and civil rights activist

Money is as money does—and money can do a lot. It can grease the wheels of the real economy and make everything much easier. Financial institutions such as commercial banks give great service to society because they act as middlemen or "financial intermediaries" that connect depositors with wannbe cottage owners. Savings and loans: you can't have one without the other. Commercial banks also conveniently keep our money safe—read heavily regulated by the government—as they account for all the debits and credits of our financial lives. In the end, mostly money works.

Tweet from David:

@evelineadomait Money is made by bank loans which make deposits. #greaseforthewheels

---

43. Taken from the 1963 "I Have a Dream" speech.

CHAPTER 5

An Assortment of Gross Products

The most effectual encouragement to population is the activity of industry, and the consequent multiplication of the national products.[1]

—*Jean-Baptiste Say (1767–1832), French economist and businessman*

As the students congregate at the table laden with appetizers, you get a palpable sense that they all expect a stimulating evening of great conversation and even better food. Everyone's hunger is at its peak after the preparation that has gone into the meal.

"Hey Libby, do you mind if I heat up these samosas in the oven?" asks Brooke.

Libby's reply is swift and enthusiastic, "Go ahead . . . mmm the mango chutney looks great! Did you make the samosas?"

"No, I picked them up at that vegetarian Indian store downtown. They're better than anything that I could make at home and they are really cheap."

David opens the bag of fresh, multigrain, organic dinner rolls that he picked up on his way over and places them in the basket conveniently located in the centre of the table. "Same for me. I can't imagine making bread. Besides, who has the time?" Then David pulls out humus and some butter from the insulated pouch in his backpack. "Sorry Brooke, I can't eat bread without butter, but I brought the hummus for you. I know you said "no meat" and this isn't meat. I did buy organic butter. It is a bit more expensive but at least the cows were treated OK in the making of the butter. It's the best I could do."

Before Brooke can respond, Salim removes the lid from his container to reveal an array of home-made Pakistani appetizers. "Wow, do those look good! Did you make them?" inquires Libby.

"No, I was home last weekend and I told my mom about this dinner. She made them for me."

David pipes up with, "Salim, you're such a weasel!"

Salim feigns offense. "It's not like I got them for free. I had to vacuum the house for my mom."

Emma lifts a series of freezer bags filled with cut veggies from the table and jokes, "I peeled and cut these with my bare hands." She motions to the glass jar of vegan bean dip, "But I bought that," she says with a wide grin. "Libby, can I borrow something to put this stuff on?"

As Libby moves to the kitchen to retrieve a large oval platter, Justin says, "Well, I'll have you know that I made the cheesecake completely from scratch. Although I probably spent as much as you guys on the ingredients."

The oven buzzer rings and Libby pulls the cookie sheet from the oven. She turns to everyone. "Hey guys, the samosas are hot. Let's eat because the stir-fry will be ready soon and I don't want my *homemade* [said with emphasis] food to get ruined."

---

1. *A Treatise on Political Economy,* 4th edition (1832).

EATING RIGHT

We have no more right to consume happiness without producing it than to consume wealth without producing it.[2]

—*George Bernard Shaw (1856–1950), Irish writer*

I am getting hungry just writing this, but I want us to think of the students' dinner party in our ongoing scenario as a very small and very simple economy where the only thing we are concerned about measuring is the well-being of our students. So if we were to analyse this situation, what are the major things that would enhance their lives in this particular evening that we can measure? I am going to assume that it is the food and beverages—the cheesecake, samosas, Pakistani appetizers, veggies, bread, wine, and, last but not least, the beer. The consumption (which implies the production) of this meal is going to make these students very happy. How should we get an aggregate number for the meal as a whole? How do we add carrots + chutney + chardonnay?

Recall from our chapter on money that money can act as a unit of account and a medium of exchange. Because these students went to the store to buy the ingredients for this meal, let's make sure they keep their receipts, shall we? When we ask them to hand those over, we can add up everyone's purchases—calculator please—this will give us the total market value of the food and beverages for the dinner. We now have a single number that gives us the value of the meal to the group. Consider this number to be the gross domestic product for the evening meal.

There are exceptions to the rule, but it is a rule.[3]

—*Theodore Roosevelt, Jr. (1858–1919), American president*

There are a few exceptions we need to factor in, however. How do we treat the non-market contributions? Because Justin made his cheesecake instead of buying one, the final number is not as high as it could and should be if we are trying to capture the happiness the cheesecake brought to everyone. Because the dessert is homemade, there is no market valuation for his baking efforts, which certainly increased the value of the food. A store-bought cheesecake would have included the bakery's contributions, and if he had bought the cheesecake he would have brought a receipt with more expenses on it. Not only that, Salim paid for his food by vacuuming his parent's house. Again, no market value exists in the form of a receipt because Salim bartered for his supper. We could ask his mother for her receipts, but again we don't know the market value of her labour.

In addition, many of these students went out of their way to procure vegan-acceptable food despite any additional costs this food might have. Does that mean that if Brooke wasn't vegan, then everyone would be less happy because the meal cost less? And what if Libby's food is ruined? Do we still count her receipts?

This little example shows that even measuring a simple meal can get complicated. The unaccounted labour of Salim's mom, of Justin, and of Emma will undervalue the cost of the production of the food. On the other hand, the more expensive food, as a result of a single person's preferences for vegan food as well as potential spoilage, might cause us to

---

2. *Candida* (1898).
3. *The Strenuous Life: Essays and Addresses* (1910).

overestimate the value of the evening. Hopefully, these don't end up being significant factors and in some ways cancel each other out. Also, over time it might not matter. Think of it this way—if these students were to get together for a semester of dinners, then we should be able to say that a more expensive meal indicates a better one.

GOOD ENOUGH

The cause which is blocking all progress today is the subtle scepticism which whispers in a million ears that things are not good enough to be worth improving.[4]
—*Gilbert Keith Chesterton (1874–1936), British writer*

Our little dinner party demonstrates many of the issues in measuring national well-being. But issues aside, the basic idea goes like this. We can (mostly) measure the costs of production. That production of goods and services leads to consumption, and consumption gives people a sense of well-being. Now it is time to really party and try to measure the well-being of an entire country. Let me outline the major questions we are going to look at.

1. How do we account for the production levels?
2. How does production connect with income?
3. What are the complications in getting the numbers correct?
4. How do we deal with equity issues?
5. How do we handle inflation over time?

BUT THIS IS BORING

Boredom is not an end product, is comparatively rather an early stage in life and art. You've got to go by or past or through boredom, as through a filter, before the clear product emerges.[5]
—*F. Scott Fitzgerald (1896–1940), Irish-American writer*

Before pressing on with this chapter, I have to tell you that when I told my colleagues I was writing an accessible macroeconomics book they all thought it was a great idea. (I have very supportive colleagues.) However, after a couple of minutes, it soon dawned on them that I would have to try to explain the idea of national accounting. The thought of the utter boredom of that topic caused each of them to sympathetically wish me luck as they drifted back to their offices. Optimist that I am, I am going to give it a go because I think it is very important[6] to a solid understanding of macroeconomics, and so I will attempt to make this as painless as possible. But first, let's take a quick minute to read a gossip column about a man who worked out how to think about the important inputs, outputs, and money flows in the economy.

---

4. *The Defendant* (1901).
5. *The Crack-Up* (1945).
6. In 2000, as part of a retrospective, the U.S. Department of Commerce listed gross domestic product (GDP) as one of the great inventions and the country's greatest accomplishment of the twentieth century. http://www.bea.gov/scb/account_articles/general/0100od/maintext.htm.

GOSSIP COLUMN: FRANCOIS QUESNAY

Dr. Francois Quesnay (1694–1774) had a life that seemed like an ever ascending rise to the top. Born 8th in a family of 13 children (of which only 6 survived childhood), his father was a small farmer and merchant. His father died when he was 13 years old, so from then on he answered to his mother. Because of his interest in bloodletting (this does give one pause), he convinced her to let him study surgery in Paris. Just so you know how things have changed, at that point in time becoming a surgeon was considered on par with becoming a barber.[7] Naturally, his concerned mother wanted a back-up plan, so he finished an apprenticeship for engraving first. He went on to become an excellent surgeon and worked hard to raise the status of surgeons; however, his rheumatism caused him give up his surgical practice and he took the exams to become a physician. Up to this point, his career path seems quite ordinary in a progressive sort of way.

But life can have some lucky surprises and sometimes it matters whom you know as well as what you know. One of Quesnay's friends in Paris was the First Surgeon to the king (hmm, I wonder if he cut the king's hair). It was probably because of this friendship that Quesnay became connected to the aristocracy and, in his 50s, he became the personal physician to Madame de Pompadour—the mistress of Louis XV.[8] He was also in contact with the king, who called him his "thinker." In fact, when the king made Quesnay nobility at the age of 58, part of his coat of arms was the pansy (*pensee* is French for "thought"). I guess it pays to think in front of the right people. It also helped that he saved the king's son from smallpox.

Up to this point Quesnay had written in the area of medicine, but that was soon to change. During his time in the royal palace, Quesnay was clever enough to stay out of palace politics and instead read the works of economists. He was a smart man and what he read got him thinking. As a result, he put together what is known as the *Tableau Economique,* which is essentially a flow of income and expenditures between the three groups he saw as integral to the economic system: landowners, farmers, and artisans.

In his model, only farmers (and only those with capital like horses and ploughs) produce a surplus. This surplus would work its way through each of the players to produce national income.[9] This led to the policy implication that farming should be supported through-low cost loans to entrepreneurial farmers that would enable them to buy the capital they needed. He also promoted trade to give farmers greater export capabilities, thus creating even greater national wealth. As a result of his thinking, a new school of economic thought called the *Physiocrats* was born. They opposed the ideas of the mercantilists' establishment who thought wealth came from treasure and that countries should operate like a business—protecting themselves with import restrictions, by creating monopolies, and, last but not least, acquiring gold. Because of mercantilists' policies, France's growth was choked when compared to that of England.

Quesnay was 62 when he wrote his first economic piece and he continued to work on economic ideas along with other Physiocrats. (I told you—ever onward and upward.) This brings us back to the Tableau Economique, which looks like a page of zigzag lines connecting all the players and showing the flow of goods and money between them. It is the "circular flow" that I will explain in the next section. However, in Quesnay's picture the flows aren't arranged in a circle. Rather, the diagram looks more like the laces on the back of a corset or a pair of lace-up shoes. It does, however, detail the incomes and expenditures of the various players and thus we have the theoretical basis on which to account for a nation's output. He died in 1774 on December 16, which is my birthday. Enough said.[10]

---

7. In fact, barbers and surgeons were in the same guild, and the red stripes on the barber shops represent used bandages. It doesn't look like Quesnay practiced barbering.
8. This is the Louis who was five in the gossip column on John Law. They do grow up fast, don't they?
9. We have the beginnings of a multiplier effect, which is critical to Keynesian economics.
10. See the *Genesis of Macroeconomics* by Antoin E. Murphy if you want more. You can also go to http://www.taieb .net/auteurs/Quesnay/albon.html if you happen to read French.

1. More Than One Way to Skin a Cat

"Would you tell me, please, which way I ought to go from here?"
"That depends a good deal on where you want to get to," said the Cat.
"I don't much care where—" said Alice.
"Then it doesn't matter which way you go," said the Cat.
"—so long as I get somewhere," Alice added as an explanation.
"Oh, you're sure to do that," said the Cat, "if you only walk long enough."[11]

—Charles Lutwidge Dodgson, pen name Lewis Carroll (1832–1898), British author, mathematician, and clergyman

When measuring the level of income or expenditure in a nation, we talk about production or product rather than gross consumption (and not only that, there is no such word as "consumpt"). Thus, we have names like gross domestic product (GDP) and gross national product (GNP). (We will look at the difference between these two measures a little later in the chapter.) We do know, however, that well-being has to do with standard of living—and the good life always has consumption as a part of it. So, what is the connection between production and consumption when we look at the economy as a whole? The best way to see the link is through what economists call the circular flow.

WHAT GOES AROUND COMES AROUND

For also when we were with you, this we declared to you: that, if any man will not work, neither let him eat.
—2 Thessalonians 3:10[12]

I think a story is the more interesting way to illustrate the concept of the circular flow, but this is what you should appreciate as the underlying concept: we will start with someone and follow his or her economic activity, only to find out that we are back to that person in the end. It is a circle.

Here we go. Suppose I am a farmer (I actually grew up on a farm but I don't really know how to farm) and I plant an acre of grain (Dad, I need some help!). When the season is over, I harvest 100 bushels of grain per acre. (For inquiring minds, this means my average productivity is 100 bushels per farmer and/or 100 bushels per acre, depending on what we use as the input to measure productivity.) If all we had was grain, then we could measure national output in bushels. Alas, the world is a bit more complicated than that and we don't just have a single product. Suppose the world includes my neighbour who grows apples. His crop for his acre of land is 500 bushels of apples. What is the domestic product of my grain and his apples? It isn't appropriate to say 600 bushels because grain and apples are different commodities. Neither is it correct to say that my neighbour's output is worth five times mine. The world still needs grain to make bread so it is quite possible that, in a barter economy, my neighbour would trade 5 bushels of apples for 1 bushel of grain depending on how much he values grain and on how badly I wanted

---

11. *Alice's Adventures in Wonderland* (1865).
12. Taken from the Douay-Rheims 1899 American edition.

apples. If we agree that this is a fair trade, then our crops have the same value even though they are not the same volume.

TO MARKET TO MARKET TO BUY A PENNY BUN[13]

Consumption is the sole end and purpose of all production; and the interest of the producer ought to be attended to, only so far as it may be necessary for promoting that of the consumer.[14]

—*Adam Smith (1723–1790), Scottish economist and philosopher*

Now we go to the market. However, instead of bartering grain for apples, we use money. If we feel that our respective crops are worth the same, then, at the end of the day, we will have the same amount of money in our pockets. In terms of flows, I sold my grain and bought apples. I also paid and made money equivalent to the values of those transactions. My neighbour did the same, only he sold apples and bought grain. Now, with my revenues I pay myself an income[15] and then use it to buy apples that I will turn into applesauce. My neighbour does the same, only he uses the money to buy grain and makes bread instead. If we add my purchases of apples with his purchases of grain, we are well on our way to recording our economic output[16] using money as the standard unit of accounting. How do you like them apples?

Or we could take a different tack. If we add up my income and my neighbour's income, we should be adding the same dollars together as before. After all, we paid out all of our revenues as income. (For the theory of well-being's sake, we hopefully used our incomes to buy things that made us happy. By the way, I really do like apples.)

The two approaches to account for these numbers are connected because they are part of the same circle. The income generated by the seller equals the expenditure of the buyer. Now we can ask either of the business owners for their personal income statements (*income approach*) or for the sales receipts of their companies (*expenditure approach*) to get at the value for GDP (or GNP). The dollars should match.

This is a very simple circular flow—I work for myself and get paid, then I use the income to buy apples from my neighbour, who also works for himself and uses his income to buy grain from me. The circle is complete.

MAKE THE WORLD A BIGGER PLACE

For everything that is really great and inspiring is created by the individual who can labor in freedom.[17]

—*Albert Einstein (1879–1955), Theoretical physicist*

But who really bakes their own bread and makes their own applesauce nowadays? Sure, some people might, but in the real world, I would normally sell my grain to a miller, who would sell

13. *Songs for the Nursery* (1805). Sorry Mother Goose, but no fat pigs were harmed in the making of this nursery rhyme.
14. *The Wealth of Nations* (1767).
15. A mix of wages for my labour, rent for my land, interest if I lent my company money, and profits for my entrepreneurial spirit. The mix will probably depend on what my accountant thought would minimize my taxes.
16. This number won't include my efforts to make applesauce or my neighbour's to make bread, so it is incomplete.
17. Quoted in *Educational Trends: Journal of Research and Interpretation* (June 1936).

flour to a baker, who would sell bread to a grocery store. My neighbour would probably buy bread from the grocery store instead of grain from me. Have no fear. We can use the same types of numbers as before but we are going to need a few more income statements and receipts to get the accounting correct. Thankfully, there are people who like accounting and are willing to do this kind of work. I can emphatically say that I am not one of them!

This job is not for the faint of heart, though. Lurking in the background is the problem of double counting. Let me explain. If we record the sale of the grain + the sale of the flour + the sale of bread + the sale of conveniently located bread in a grocery store together we get a much bigger number. Partly this is fine because each middle person actually works to create value, which we would want to include. Mostly this is wrong because my grain revenue is part of the price of the grocery store bread as well as in my sales. We shouldn't count it twice.

There are two ways to handle this. One is called the *value-added approach*. When the miller buys my grain, we count the grain sale. Then when the miller sells the flour, we record the sale of the flour minus the cost of the grain because grain was an expense to the miller. (Thankfully, we have bookkeepers who will keep track of this.) If we keep this approach throughout the system, we will only record the additional value that each party contributes. (This also means we can't increase the national product of a country by just having more merchants in the middle.) The second approach is to only record the purchases of the final person, which in our story would be the price my neighbour paid to purchase the bread from the grocery store. (Hopefully he had the right kind of dough!) The price of the loaf of bread will include all of the values of each player added together. This approach is a final-expenditure approach. In a perfect world, both the final-good and the value-added approaches will get to the same number. When the final buyer of bread is a consumer, we also call this consumption (C).[18]

2. Errors of Omission and Commission

There have been errors in the administration of the most enlightened men.[19]
—*Edward Law, 1st Baron Ellenborough (1750–1818), English judge*

Ok, there are a few more hiccups in all this that make the story less tidy. The expenditure approach (whether final sale or value added) only works if I and my neighbour sell everything we made that year to each other. What if we both keep some grain and apples for ourselves? What if the government regulates how I produce and also buys what I make? What if the economy goes global?

THE DEVIL IS IN THE DETAILS

Hell is paved with good intentions.[20]
—*Dr. Samuel Johnson (1709–1784), British author, linguist, and lexicographer*

In this simple economy there are a number of reasons the value of the national output will be incorrect if it only includes me and my neighbour.

---

18. As we go through this section we will derive the accounting identity that GDP = C + I + G + X − M. For our purposes this will be the approach we use in the rest of the book because it neatly matches Keynes's approach to modelling the economy.
19. Quotes reported in James William Norton-Kyshe, *The Dictionary of Legal Quotations* (1904). This case was *Rex v. Lambert and Perry* (1810).
20. *The Life of Samuel Johnson* by James Boswell (1791).

First, I might actually want to make my own bread and therefore keep some grain for myself. (I baked bread once, and the loaves turned out hard as rocks. Never again.) This is called home production, and at this point, we have no good way to verify the value of production that happens at home. Thus, a nation's GDP or GNP doesn't include the value of the output of stay-at-home moms or dads when they cook, clean, garden, provide childcare, or homeschool their children. We have no credible way to ascertain the value of their work and thus it is excluded from GDP and GNP. (I know this doesn't seem fair, but on the bright side, their work isn't taxed the way workers in a market economy are taxed.) Therefore, GDP and GNP underestimate the true value of production (and consumption) of the nation.

On the flip side, what if the government bans genetically modified grain, causing me to use more fertilizer and pesticides to get the same yield? Unfortunately, I will have to charge more for my grain due to higher costs. Technically, this increases national production when measured in money. The GDP and GNP now have higher numbers that aren't actually reflecting higher production levels of grain, just more expensive grain. Furthermore, if I cause pesticide and fertilizer runoff into the watershed, then cleanup costs actually increase national production figures. You can see that higher GDP or GNP doesn't mean we are better off in this case. Go figure.

Second, I might keep some of the grain back to seed next year's crop. In essence, this seed is an investment into next year's income and I will keep it in inventory over the winter. We count this seed as part of GDP by costing it at the market price. If any of you have ever done inventory for a company, you now know why this painful process is necessary. The inventory is counted as part of this year's production even though no one actually bought it. It was produced but not consumed. The national accountants record this grain as investment (I).

Investment also includes any purchases of equipment and facilities that I may have made from other players in my now-larger economy. GDP and GNP treat production of equipment and buildings as a final purchase even though they are inputs into making consumer products and logically seem like something earlier in the supply chain. This is partly due to the special role physical capital plays in economic growth, and we want to keep track of these numbers for their own sake.

Never, never rest contented with any circle of ideas, but always be certain that a wider one is still possible.[21]

—*John Richard Jefferies (1848–1887), English writer*

Third, what if the government comes to the bakery and buys bread as part of a school breakfast program? The cost of the bakery bread is included in national income accounts. What is not included in GDP or GNP is the value of the extra service the government provides in feeding children. No one is paying a market price for these services, so we don't know what they are worth. (And yes, no matter what your political leanings, these services are worth something.) We only know the cost of the bread. If you look at the national accounts you will see that government goods and services (G) are always recorded at factor (or input) costs because they don't sell their services for a fee.

Fourth, we add an international component. Suppose I sell some grain to another person who lives across a national border. I produced the grain and it is recorded at the

---

21. *Story of My Heart: My Autobiography* (1883).

border as exports (X). This is pure production without consumption. On the other hand, what if a grocery store bought and imported bread from a bakery across the border and sells that bread to my apple-producing neighbour? His consumption (C) is up but production in our country is not. To deal with this, GDP and GNP include our exports (X) but subtract the value of the imports (M). Again, we see the production perspective of national accounts.[22]

There are a good many real miseries in life that we cannot help smiling at, but they are the smiles that make wrinkles and not dimples.[23]

Oliver Wendell Holmes, Sr. (1809–1894), American physician and writer

The final complexity in our accounting saga is found in the distinction between GDP and GNP, which I have littered throughout the text but I haven't defined yet. This is a good spot to finally put you out of your misery and distinguish between GDP and GNP because it has to do with a global economy, which we just mentioned. The easiest way to understand the differences is in the names:

The D in GDP stands for *domestic* soil and the producer can be a citizen or a foreigner.

The N in GNP stands for a *national*, where the producer is a national and the place can be at home or abroad.

If citizens (or nationals) of, let's say, Canada have any investments of any type abroad in, for example Barbados,[24] then the GNP[25] will be larger than the GDP because Canada will have production happening in Barbados, which counts as national product but not as domestic product because the production wasn't "made in Canada." If Canada has lots of foreign investment or ownership by Americans, then GDP is greater than GNP because all of the production counts as domestic product within Canada's borders but some of the fruits of domestic production must leave the country to reward these Americans for their investment. Domestic is about production within a country (or place), and national is about ownership of the production (or people). People and places don't always match, although most of the time citizens do produce in their own country.

Here is a quick recap of the expenditure approach to measure the value of the nation's production. We ask our accountants to find the value of the purchases of the following groups and sum them in the following way:

Output = C + I + G + X − M

where C is consumer spending, I is business investment, G is government purchases, X is exports, and M is imports.

---

22. We will find out later in the book that this might not be a bad thing. It turns out that chronic net importing can lead to other problems that will reduce the well-being of future generations, so we might not want to change how we do these measurements.

23. *The Poet at the Breakfast Table* (1872).

24. http://www.international.gc.ca/economist-economiste/assets/pdfs/Data/investments-investissements/FDI_by_Country/CDIA_stocks_by_Country-ENG.pdf.

25. The USA used GNP from the time of Kuznets until 1990. The switch in 1991 to GDP occurred because most other countries had adopted GDP as their measure.

INCOME STATEMENTS

Explanations are clear but since no one to whom a thing is explained can connect the explanations with what is really clear, therefore clear explanations are not clear.[26]
—Gertrude Stein (1874–1946), American writer who lived most of her life in Europe

We have seen the value and complexities of recording the spending on goods and services by the major economic buyers. Matching the expenditure flows should be the income flows to the corresponding sellers. This gives us the income approach[27] in measuring national output. We will need to ask the farmer (in our story that would be me), the miller, the baker, and the grocer to cough up their personal income statements so we can add them together. If the miller has employees, we will need their wages as well. Don't worry about double counting because any income an employee earns doesn't go to the owner. If the baker pays rent for the bakery to a landlord, then we will need the landlord's rental income in our accounting for national income. We can only hope the baker isn't paying the rent in bread. If the grocer borrowed any funds, we will need the lender's interest income for the year. Finally, if the government made some income through net[28] taxes, then those funds will need to be accounted for as well. The theory is that the value of GDP (or GNP) has to be distributed into somebody's pocket in some form of income and we just have to find it to add together. Under-the-table or undeclared cash-only transactions make it difficult to accurately measure GDP (or GNP) because people don't declare this income and we therefore can't account for it (not without involving government officials to audit people's books).

If the circle is unbroken then both the income and expenditure approaches should get to the same final value, but in reality they aren't exactly the same due to the complexities mentioned earlier. Having said this, the gap between the two approaches is really quite small. For example, there is less than 0.06% (really, really small percentage) of a gap between the final values of the two approaches as measured by Statistics Canada, although this does amount to more than a billion-dollar difference.

A BRIEF HISTORY OF INCOME STATISTICS

As a side note, in 1932 the U.S. Congress commissioned Simon Kuznets[29] to measure the nation's economic activity in order to help in fighting the Great Depression. Obviously, the Great Depression wasn't helping increase people's sense of well-being in the USA, and Congress thought better information might lead to better policies. Kuznets came up with National Income Statistics,[30] which listed incomes by industry and type (income approach). With his continued involvement, in 1942 annual GNP (expenditure approach)

---

26. *Everybody's Autobiography* (1937).
27. The handy mnemonic "ripsaw" helps in remembering the components of total income: GDP = Rental income + Interest income + Profits + Statistical adjustments (corporate income taxes, dividends, and undistributed corporate profits) + Wages.
28. Net taxes = Taxes – Subsidies. Generally governments tax more than they subsidize, so this number is positive.
29. Kuznets (1901–1985), a Jewish immigrant from modern-day Belarus, began working in 1927 with the National Bureau of Economic Research (NBER). His first faculty appointment was in 1930 at the University of Pennsylvania. Later he would work at Johns Hopkins University and end his career at Harvard in 1971—the year he won the Nobel Memorial Prize in Economic Science.
30. The original set of accounts was presented in a report to Congress in 1937 and in a research report, "National Income, 1929–35." Kuznets's first presentation to the Senate was in January 1934.

numbers were launched and reported, only this time the reason was to help with the war effort. Governments wanted to know how much they were spending. By the mid-1940s, the income and expenditure approaches were integrated into a consolidated set of accounts.[31]

Kuznets must have been psychic (economists would say a great forecaster) because he explicitly warned[32] that we need to be very careful if we use national income as a complete measure of well-being. His work was never intended for this purpose. Rather, it was meant to assist policymakers in doing a better job in running the country by helping them understand the magnitude of the economic flows. His warnings were mostly ignored, as economists and politicians have long used both GNP and GDP to assess how citizens of a country are doing.

3. Issuing Equity

Poor nations are hungry, and rich Nations are proud, and Pride and Hunger will ever be at Variance.[33]

—*Jonathan Swift (1667–1745), Irish writer*

There's another complication that is worth mentioning. What if, in our opening story, no one had brought vegan food except Brooke? Can we say the total value of the meal captures the true well-being for everyone? Obviously Brooke would have a more limited experience because of a poor food selection while everyone else would have more food to choose from and therefore a better experience. Come to think of it, Salim doesn't drink alcohol. How does a big bar bill contribute to his well-being?

It is time to talk about fairness. So far we have dealt with totals—all the GDP or GNP for a country. The hope is that this product/income makes its way into the hands of citizens. But what if the majority of the income/product goes to very few individuals? The Occupy Wall Street movement famously captured this idea with the catch phrase "The top 1%." If these wealthy[34] folks get most of the income, then they are the only ones able to buy "the product" and thus experience the well-being. This section will look at how to measure the size of the inequality. In a later chapter we will look at the role of government taxes and subsidies to redistribute income between the haves and the have nots.

Economist Rev. (Thomas) Robert Malthus[35] made a good point when he argued that growth in income needs to be considered in tandem with the growth in population. For

---

31. http://www.bea.gov/scb/pdf/2007/02%20February/0207_history_article.pdf.
32. "The valuable capacity of the human mind to simplify a complex situation in a compact characterization becomes dangerous when not controlled in terms of definitely stated criteria. With quantitative measurements especially, the definiteness of the result suggests, often misleadingly, a precision and simplicity in the outlines of the object measured. Measurements of national income are subject to this type of illusion and resulting abuse, especially since they deal with matters that are the center of conflict of opposing social groups where the effectiveness of an argument is often contingent upon oversimplification" (1934).
33. *Gulliver's Travels* (1726).
34. The top 1% is very dependent on the pool of comparison. Obviously the income it takes to get the top 1% in Canada (income of more than $200,000 in 2010) or the United States (income of more than 350,000 in 2010) is a very different number from the income needed to make the top 1% in the world (little more than $34,000 after tax). Sometimes it is good to talk percentage of the pie. For example, the top 1% in Canada took home 10% of the nation's income, whereas in the USA this group took home 24% of the national income in 2010. It should give us pause to realize that less than 10% of the world earns more than half the world's income.
35. He wrote the classic *An Essay on the Principle of Population* (1798) and belonged to the Political Economy Club. Founded by James Mill, the purpose of this group was to act as an intellectual society to debate, provide peer reviews, and hopefully come to a consensus on the fundamental principles of political economy. This group included David Ricardo, a good friend of Malthus and a gossip column recipient in *Cocktail Party Economics*.

example, if GDP is $100 million and there are a million people, then the per capita GDP is $100. If GDP rises to $110 million but the population doubles, then things are much worse for the average person. Now per capita income is only $55. Malthus was convinced that prosperity led to the birth of more babies (who actually survived childhood) and that this increase in mouths to feed will ultimately decrease the standard of living to the point of misery for those families. This theory was convincing enough for China to legislate the one-child policy[36] as a way to reduce poverty. Although history proved Malthus wrong on his limits-to-growth model, he was nevertheless correct in thinking that prosperity should be thought of at the individual not just the aggregate level. Thus, we will use per capita (or per person) national income as the standard measure of well-being.

After all, facts are facts, and although we may quote one to another with a chuckle the words of the Wise Statesman, "Lies—damned lies—and statistics," still there are some easy figures the simplest must understand, and the astutest cannot wriggle out of.[37]
—*Leonard Henry Courtney (1832–1918), British politician*

However, there is more than one way to calculate per capita GDP (or GNP). The most common way is the one we used earlier. Divide income by number of people and, voila, we have income per person. This will give some idea about how well the hypothetical average person is living. What it doesn't address is the issue of inequality. In other words, how wide is the income gap from the person at the top to the person at the bottom? Suppose GDP went up from $100 million to $110 million and the population went from 1 million to 1.1 million (100,000 more people). It looks like per capita income has stayed the same at $100, which it did if we take the average. But what if I told you that the extra $10 million went to one individual? This would mean that most people's standard of living must have actually fallen. There are 99,999 more people sharing in the original $100 million, but the average won't tell us that.

To address this problem, we can use another measure of individual standard of living called the *median GDP per capita*. This is the income of the middle person in the economy if we line everyone up in order of income. If the mean (the average) and the median (middle) values are the same, then the middle person is actually the average. But often the average person and the middle person aren't the same. If income only goes to the top 1%, then the average income increases but the median (or middle person's income) stays the same. The bigger the gap between the median and mean implies greater income inequality in that particular country. Unfortunately, finding the median[38] is much harder than finding the mean. You actually have to line everyone up from one end of the income spectrum to the other and find a single middle person. On the other hand, you only need total numbers to find the hypothetical average person. Sometimes you can only use the data you have.

---

36. This policy was first applied in 1979 and restricts urban couples to one child. A little over a third of the population is subject to this restriction.
37. *To My Fellow-Disciples at Saratoga Springs* (1895).
38. There are other ways to measure income inequality. A famous one is called the Gini coefficient, which usually has a value between zero and one. The more equal the society, the lower the coefficient. The most equal society would have a coefficient of zero, which means that for every percentage of the population listed, that percentage has the same percentage of income (or wealth). In other words, everyone has the same income.

It is said that the children of the very poor are not brought up, but dragged up.[39]
—*Charles Dickens (1812–1870), English writer*

Finally, for this section anyway, if we want to make international comparisons we need to have income in a common currency. Because of the place the USA has had in the post-WWII period of the 1900s, the U.S. dollar is the standard unit of account. Therefore a country's income needs to be converted into U.S. dollars in order to make global comparisons. This isn't quite fair because a low income level in U.S. dollars might not be as bad as it looks on paper once you actually live in that country. What if food prices are correspondingly low? For example, if my income is $100,000 and bread costs $10, while your income is $10, 000 and bread cost is only $1, we could actually buy the same number of loaves. Internationally we need to consider what that per capita income can really buy. The technique used is called purchasing power parity, or PPP, U.S. dollars. We take the prices in the USA and the country in question and find a ratio. This ratio is used to estimate the equivalent income in U.S. dollars in terms of domestic spending power. If you search Wikipedia for statistics on any country, you will find that "real per capita GDP in PPP US$" is the standard measure of income shown. The only remaining word we need to discuss from this measure is "real." So what's real?

4. Over Time It Should Be Real

A typical vice of American politics—the avoidance of saying anything real on real issues, and the announcement of radical policies with much sound and fury, and at the same time with a cautious accompaniment of weasel phrases each of which sucks the meat out of the preceding statement.[40]
—*Theodore Roosevelt, Jr. (1858–1919), American president*

Let's start with the problem and then talk solutions. Essentially, once we want to compare income per person over time, we run into the following problem: What if the quantity of products such as bread doesn't change but the price rises? It would not be true that the citizens of that country are better off just because per capita income is up. (More income but the same amount of stuff isn't an improvement.) This calculation is known as *nominal output per person*. If you use nominal GDP (or GNP), then a rise in value can occur for two reasons: output is really up or prices are inflated. In this example, the bread is real and we want our standard-of-living numbers to reflect the fact that if bread quantities have stayed the same, then real GDP (or GNP) has also stayed the same. So how do we guarantee that?

Let's recall how GDP (or GNP) is calculated using the expenditure approach. We take the total expenditure by all the players and add them together. This is the sum of price (P) per unit paid times the number (Q) of units bought. In notation we can write the following: Total spending = P × Q. It is possible for P or Q to rise to increase the amount spent. But only the quantity or Q is real. We need a way to neutralize the impact of price (P) changes.

---

39. *Bleak House* (1852–1853).
40. "Platform Insincerity," *The Outlook*, vol. 101, no. 13 (27 July 1912).

The easiest way to disentangle quantity increases from price increases is to artificially hold prices constant. So we take a year, any year, and call it the base year. We use base-year prices as the norm and multiply those prices against the quantities of things. (You will be happy to know that the next chapter will go into this process in excruciating detail.) Thus, if *real* income per person increases, then we know it wasn't due to inflation and these folks are really better off because they have more stuff. Really!

Obviously, the task of fixing prices to a particular base year and then using them to find the dollar amounts for output takes a bit of skill, especially for a large economy with millions of products. Most government organizations[41] that calculate these statistics have hired some very qualified people to create these databases. Just so you know, there is no particular reason to pick one year over another as the base year but if you see a figure called real GDP per capita, usually the base year will be in brackets after the number.[42] Every few years, the base year is moved up and all the real numbers are recalculated to reflect different (usually higher) prices. This is done so the real income levels don't seem completely unrealistic to the general public. What really matters in calculating real growth is the change in values from one year to the next. Those changes aren't dependant on the base year used to fix prices.

GETTING TO THE BIG (BLURRY) PICTURE

That country is the richest which nourishes the greatest numbers of noble and happy human beings.[43]

—*John Ruskin (1819–1900), English writer and artist*

We have done a lot of work to get to a measure of national income—Real GDP (or GNP) per capita in PPP US$. There you have it—warts and all. These universal measures of output/income per capita are, for better or worse, the most common measures of standard of living. They are not perfect, but in year-over-year international comparisons, they do a pretty good job of making gross (although not necessary fine) distinctions. Once we are in a particular country, we can drop the PPP part and look at real GDP or real GNP per person per year. Again, if these numbers are going up consistently, this is a good sign for that country's citizenry.

Salim tweets:

@EvelineAdomait Glad to know how to put numbers on std of living #accountingrules

---

41. In Canada this is done by Statistics Canada and in the USA it is done by the Bureau of Economic Analysis.
42. For example, Stats Canada could report in 2014 that real GDP per capita is $37,000 [2007], which means that the base year price is 2007. Nominal GDP is approximately $52,000 for the same year. The further we get from 2007, the bigger the gap between real and nominal numbers if we have inflation—even low inflation, which Canada has. It might be time for a new base year.
43. *Unto This Last* (1860).

CHAPTER 6

Name Your Price

In short, I conceive that a great part of the miseries of mankind are brought upon them by the false estimates they have made of the value of things, and by their giving too much for their whistles.[1]

—Benjamin Franklin (1706–1790), Founding Father of the United States and first ambassador to France[2]

The group reclined comfortably in the living room. "Living room" is a good term for it because it functions as part study area, part dining room (because the table had to extend into the area to fit everyone around it), and spare bedroom whenever any of Libby's or her roommates' friends stay the night. It consists of various odds and ends of mostly brown beefy furniture cobbled together from family castoffs.

At first everyone ate the hors d'oeuvres quickly and in relative silence, but once the initial pangs of hunger passed, the pace relaxed and the conversation started to flow.

"I didn't realize I was so hungry," Emma declares, leaning over to pick up another carrot stick from the veggie tray.

Libby laughs as she reaches for another samosa. "These are great! By the way, I was talking to my dad about food last weekend and he says that they never ate samosas when he was a kid. He can't believe the variety of veggies and prepared foods in the grocery store these days."

"Not only the variety has increased," says Brooke, "but so has the price of things. My mom got one of those birthday cards that gives you information about the year you were born. Did you know that in 1963, the average income was, like, $5,800 per year? My grandparents only paid $13,000 for their house and $3,000 for their new car, so I guess it isn't so bad. All I know is that it costs me more to go to school than what they paid for a house!"

"1963 was also the year that JFK was assassinated," Justin adds as an aside, "Tragic."

Before things can get to maudlin, David gets back to the talk of prices with, "It turns out that my dad's family had one of the first colour TV's on their street and it cost about $500—so no deals there."

Everyone turns to Salim, who munches on the food his mom had made. "Don't look at me," he says, "my parents were in Pakistan so the prices in rupees wouldn't mean anything to you. I guess I could ask them how much of their income they spent on food but I haven't thought to ask. Mostly when my parents talk about 1963 it is about the boundary disagreement with China and the change in the geopolitics of the region because of it."

From there, the conversation follows rabbit trails from a discussion on the quality and merits of various documentaries about the Kashmir region, to the political economy of Europe between the world wars, and ending with the life of Anne Frank.

---

1. Letter to Madame Brillon (1779).
2. He was ambassador during the reign of Louis the XVI, whose grandfather was Louis the XV from the previous chapter. It was Louis the XVI who was beheaded during the French Revolution.

THE TIME HAS COME TO TALK
OF MANY THINGS—OF PRICES

Are we up to the task—are we equal to the challenge?[3]
—John F. Kennedy (1917–1963), American President

In the last chapter, we found a way to measure output. It's called real GDP or real GNP. It's real and therefore captures the idea of quantity even though it is measured in a country's currency—in our case, dollars. We can do this because we manipulated the numbers to hold prices constant so it is now really about quantity, albeit on a national, aggregated level. (You can't just go to a store and say please give me five units of GDP [in 2007 US$] please. GDP as a single product doesn't exist.)

In this chapter, we want to direct our attention to finding a national price level. Again, aggregation is going to be an issue because we need one number that combines the prices of *"shoes, and ships and sealing wax, of cabbages"* and crowns (instead of kings because we really can't buy those[4]), and this number has to be logical. This brings us to the subject of price indexes or indices, whichever spelling you prefer.

INDEX NUMBERS

How index-learning turns no student pale,
Yet holds the eel of science by the tail.[5]
—Alexander Pope (1688–1744), English poet

We have already touched on how to get an index number for well-being in Chapter 3, Measure for Measure. I have already explained why the Human Development Index (HDI) is helpful. Just to make things easier (so you don't need to flip back to find out the details), I will reiterate the main point. Index numbers help us add things together that aren't easy or possible to add together. For example, the HDI combines things like:

> Literacy rates + Life expectancy + Real gross national income at purchasing power parity per capita

Hopefully, you get why adding dollars and years isn't possible and why an index number is absolutely necessary. But here we are talking about a price index that is combining prices. I can imagine some of you might be thinking "But a price index is about prices, which are all in the same units (dollars). Why can't we just add them together and find an average price? What is the problem that we need an index number to solve?"

---

3. Presidential Nomination Acceptance Speech (July 15, 1960). JFK also said, "The New Frontier of which I speak is not a set of promises—it is a set of challenges. It sums up not what I intend to offer the American people, but what I intend to ask of them."
4. This particular part of Lewis Carroll's children's book *Through the Looking-Glass, and What Alice Found There* (1871) has many images that have made their way into our culture:
"The time has come," the Walrus said,
"To talk of many things:
Of shoes—and ships—and sealing wax—
Of cabbages—and Kings—
And why the Sea is boiling hot—
And whether pigs have wings."
5. *The Dunciad* (1728).

The problem, in this case, is the weighting. (I could tell you were waiting for that.) Not everything that has a price is of equal importance. Therefore, averaging the price of bread with that of toothpicks isn't very helpful if you buy bread every week and toothpicks only once a year. We can't treat unequal things as if they were equal and hope to find some meaningful number for average prices across a country. If bread prices rise, it should have more weight than if toothpicks become more expensive in the grand scheme of things. Therefore, even though everything has a price, we really can't just add them together to get a sense of how we are doing in terms of aggregate prices—we need to weight things by importance in an index.

As there are so many who talk prose without knowing it, or, again, who syllogize without having the least idea what a syllogism is, so economists have long been mathematicians without being aware of the fact.

—*(William) Stanley Jevons (1835–1882), English economist*[6]

Again, I will create a very simple example, this time out of children's literature, to illustrate how to construct a price index rather than just give a definition (I seem to be doing this a lot). Let's make a "Through the Looking Glass Price Index," or TLGPI for short (or maybe not so short). This bundle or basket of goods is quite unique. I will assume that in Wonderland, Alice and her friend the Walrus eat 2 cabbages, take the ferry 10 times, and buy a new pair of shoes and hair wax every fortnight (which literally means 14 days[7]). Let the construction of the TLGPI begin.

We start by multiplying the price and quantity of each item together. For example, let's say a cabbage costs $1, a ferry ticket $20, a pair of shoes $80, and hair wax $8. Thus their fortnight purchases include cabbages for $2 (2 × $1), ferry tickets for $200 (10 × $20), shoes for $80, and hair wax for $8. (I feel like I am watching Jeopardy.) They spend a grand total of $290. We need to keep track of this number.

If we want to see what happened to prices in the next fortnight, we can't just find out what happened to individual prices and average the percent changes. This doesn't solve the issue of relative importance. To see why this is so, let's assume the price of cabbage doubles to $2 (wow a 100 % increase), a ferry ticket rises to $21 (a 5% increase), a pair of shoes went on sale for $70 (prices actually fell 12.5%) and the hair wax gets topped up to $10 (up 25%). If we just average the percentages, we would report close to a 30% increase in prices. But this can't be right. Most of the 30% increase in prices comes from the 100% increase in cabbage prices. However, Alice and Walrus only spend $4 on cabbages even at the higher price because they only buy 2 cabbages and the price is relatively low.

Explanations exist; they have existed for all time; there is always a well-known solution to every human problem—neat, plausible, and wrong.[8]

—*Henry Louis Mencken (1880–1956), American writer*

One solution to the problem of accurately capturing the relative importance of a price is to "weight" each item by how many units Alice and Walrus purchase rather than treating each price as if they only bought one. Essentially a store receipt would give us this

---

6. *The Theory of Political Economy* (1871).
7. This term is so British.
8. "The Divine Afflatus" in *New York Evening Mail* (16 November 1917); later published in *Prejudices: Second Series* (1920) and *A Mencken Chrestomathy* (1949).

information because it itemizes how many units were purchased at the going price to total up the expenditure on that item. If we take this approach, then ferry tickets will now have more weight because Alice and Walrus buy so many of them.

We need to remember that in the real world, the dollar amount on the receipts can rise over time and can do so for a couple of reasons. First, prices could be higher, and this is what we want to determine in any discussion about inflation. Second, those doing the purchasing could decide to buy more cabbages and shoes for some reason, and this is a real change—not an issue of inflation. We need to be able to distinguish between these two very different reasons for why spending is up.

No problem of human destiny is beyond human beings. Man's reason and spirit have often solved the seemingly unsolvable—and we believe they can do it again.[9]
—John F. Kennedy (1917–1963), American president

The solution for measuring price changes that captures the idea of relative importance is to hold the quantities constant across time—in effect, create a fixed basket of goods and services to multiply prices against. In the case of TLGPI, the number of cabbages and shoes has to stay the same in our calculations every fortnight even if Alice and Walrus don't actually buy the same basket of goods every fortnight. This will give us a clearer picture of what happened to prices from one fortnight to the other. (I wish *fortnight* was more popular in North America. It is such a great word and we need something between week and month.) We also need the statisticians from the last chapter to help us fix or massage the numbers again. This time they will hold quantities fixed and not prices.

Let's redo the calculations using this fixed-basket method. The expenditure on cabbages is now $4, ferry tickets $210, shoes $70, and hair wax $10. In order to find out how they did overall, we calculate the grand total, which equals $304. We can now say that they are certainly spending more on aggregate because prices went up. The percentage change from $290 to $305 is just under 5%. This shows us that our initial calculation of 30% inflation was wildly off the mark.

We still do not have price index but we are getting closer. Let's take the next step. An index is a ratio. This means that in mathematical terms (sorry about this . . .) we need a denominator and a numerator to create a fraction. Let's make the first fortnight (which we will call our base fortnight) our denominator. In order to find an index number for any period, we would take the value of the particular fortnight in question and divide it by our base fortnight. For our base fortnight this means we are taking 290 (particular) and dividing it by 290 (our base). Drum roll please—290/290 = 1. Now, just to add a flourish and allow us to get rid of decimals, let's multiply this number by 100 so that we now have the number 100 as the value of the price index in the base fortnight. So far this might seem like a lot of effort for very little benefit but please be patient, there is a payoff coming.

How my achievements mock me! I will go meet them.[10]
—William Shakespeare (1564–1616), English writer

It is in the next fortnight that we see the benefits of this approach. In this case, we have a ratio of 304/290 where the new particular value of 304 when divided by the base

9. Commencement Address at American University on June 10, 1963.
10. Troilus and Cressida (1602).

of 290 equals approximately 1.05. If we multiply by 100 we get 105. Thus the value of the index in the next period is 105, and hopefully you can see the payoff for creating the index with values relative to 100. The index number 105 means that for the TLGPI basket of goods, the cost has risen 5% in the second period when compared with the base period. Another way to look at is to say that if Alice and Walrus had spent $100 in the first period, it now costs slightly under $105 to buy the same basket of goods and services in the second fortnight. The index number makes the percent change in overall prices of a fixed basket of goods easier to see.

If we do this for a year of fortnights, or 26 times, we can track price changes from the base period and see what general prices (rather than specific prices) are doing over time. Indexes are good for getting at the general gist of things.

All price indices need a base period—most often a base year. There isn't any magic in picking this point in time. The developers of the price index can keep the original base for all time (and some do), but most change the base year every couple of years. The choice of the base year is neither here nor there. Just know that whatever year becomes the base, that year's index value will equal 100 or some multiple of 100.[11] The number we finally arrive at is disassociated from any numbers related to prices such as dollars and cents. Instead, when you divide dollars by dollars and multiply by 100 ($/$ × 100), you get a proportional or relative number. In the base year that relative number is 100 but all other years are usually higher or lower depending on their relative prices to the base year.

NAME YOUR TYPE

Variety's the very spice of life,
That gives it all its flavour.[12]

—William Cowper (1731–1800), English poet, and hymnodist

There are a few ways to calculate a price index. The two most common are the Laspeyres price index and the Paasche price index. They are virtually identical except for one point—they use different baskets of goods in their calculations. Recall that if you want to see if prices are really changing you need to keep quantity constant. Thus the numerator and the denominator always have the same numbers of items (for example 2 cabbages, 10 ferry tickets, etc.). The only thing that is different is the prices we use to multiply against those quantities. The resulting ratio tells us how a particular year's prices relate to those in the base.[13] The fundamental difference between the Laspeyres and Paasche indices has to do with which period we pick our quantities from. The Laspeyres index uses quantities from a past period and the Paasche uses quantities from the present period. So, for instance, with the Laspeyres method you pick the quantities from the first period, which included 2 cabbages and 10 ferry rides, a pair of shoes, and one container of hair wax. However, with the Paasche method, we must find out what they bought in the second period and it is possible that the mix has changed. For example, in the most recent fortnight, they purchased 3 cabbages, 8 ferry rides, 2 pairs of shoes, and no hair wax. The

11. For example the S&P/TSX is a price index for a fixed group of stocks traded on the Toronto Stock Exchange and had a base value of 1000 in 1975. The base doesn't change.
12. *The Task* (1785).
13. Mathematically it reads $\sum(P2 \times Q)/\sum(P1 \times Q)$.

Paasche index would use this basket to weight the relative importance of each item when it measures price changes over time. For the same price changes from one period to the next, the Paasche index and the Laspeyres index show a similar although not identical percent change in prices because the basket of goods and services is slightly different.

Technically, the *Through the Looking Glass Price Index* is a Laspeyres type of price index because we use the basket of goods and services from the first fortnight period. Most of the price indexes that you hear about in the news are of the Laspeyres type. The most famous of them is the consumer price index (CPI), which uses a fixed basket of some 600 consumer goods and services that our country's statisticians multiply prices against on a monthly basis. The fixed basket is updated every couple of years using the information provided from surveys,[14] which can consist of phone interviews or diary keeping. This means that over time cell phone plans and Internet fees made their way into the CPI as a consumer service along with Blue Ray players, plasma TVs and international foods. Lesser known cousins to the CPI include such indices as the industrial price index, commodity price index, construction price index, wholesale price index, and so forth. Basically, you can create a price index for any basket of products.[15]

If you want to inspire confidence, give plenty of statistics—it does not matter that they should be accurate, or even intelligible, so long as there is enough of them.[16]

—*Lewis Carroll, pen name for Charles Lutwidge Dodgson (1832–1898), British author, mathematician, and clergyman*

It might be tempting to ignore the Paasche method altogether except that one very important index uses this method. It is called the GDP deflator and its basket includes all of the goods and services for the entire economy. Not one you can easily ignore. We calculate the deflator using the GDP accounts we discussed in the previous chapter.[17] Because the GDP deflator uses current quantities, it takes a bit of time to gather all of the data together after year end. Laspeyres-type indices have the advantage because they are easier to use and can generate faster results.

RELATIVELY SPEAKING

Tomorrow would be Christmas Day, and she had only $1.87 with which to buy Jim a present. She had been saving every penny she could for months, with this result. Twenty dollars a week doesn't go far. Expenses had been greater than she had calculated. They always are.[18]

—*William Sydney Porter, pen name O Henry (1862–1910), American writer*

Now that we know how to measure aggregate prices with a price index, let's look how the index is used. There are basically three uses for price indexes. Before we start, I just want to reiterate one point just to make sure it is crystal clear. Whenever we look at

---

14. In Canada this is called the Survey of Household Spending. In the USA it is called the Consumer Expenditure Survey.
15. In 2013 the University of Guelph launched a Food Price Index.
16. *Three Months in a Curatorship* (1886).
17. If you divide nominal GDP by real GDP you get the deflator.
18. *The Gift of the Magi.*

inflation issues, all numbers are either nominal or real. Nominal numbers are just the prices of the current year with no adjustment for inflation. On the other hand, real numbers have had some work done to them to remove the inflation issue in order to make real comparisons. This section looks at the work economists do to the numbers in order to make legitimate comparisons between years.

1. Price indexes deflate a number to make it real. This is done by dividing a price in any given year by the index number of that year. This allows you to compare what has happened to the real price over time. If you use 2002 as the base year, then the index number in 2002 is 100. Going back in the past, the 1963 index number is 16 and if we go forward to 2013, it equals 123. (Notice these numbers are relative to 100.) This means prices are 7.7 times higher[19] over this half century (16 to 123). A TV that sold for $500 in 1963 should be selling for $3,850 if the TV had kept up with inflation. But the TV is actually selling for $500 in 2013. We can say that the real cost of a TV has actually fallen even though the nominal price has remained the same.

    Another way to look at it is to say that a TV that costs $500 in 2013 should have only cost $65 in 1963. A TV for $500 back then was a relatively expensive item out of the household budget. (In addition to the real drop in prices, this doesn't take into account the quality improvements in TVs over this period, so if you watch TV, things are better on all fronts.)

    . . . but I will first give you an Account of the Price of Things, which I received from a private, but very credible hand, of the year 1444.[20]
    —*William Fleetwood (1656–1723), English bishop*

    But in terms of prices not all things get relatively cheaper. For instance, at the University of Guelph, tuition fees in 1996 for a BA were $1,225 per semester but grew to $2,928 per semester in 2013. If the real cost had stayed the same from 1996 to 2013, then tuition should have been $1,693 per semester in 2013. In this case both the nominal and real cost of a BA degree have risen, which means that newer students (or most likely their parents) bear more of the educational costs than earlier generations did.

    The only way to look at prices in different years and make any sense of the values is to make sure they are real. Therefore, economists talk about real incomes, real wages, and real prices. For every one of these values, a nominal number is divided by a deflator to make it real.

2. Price indexes are also used to inflate a number in order to keep real purchasing power up. In other words, indexes are used to make sure that people's ability to buy things, when prices rise, stays the same. For instance, governments often index pensions, welfare payments, and tax brackets on income tax forms using the CPI. Inflating a

---

19. http://www.bankofcanada.ca/rates/related/inflation-calculator/.
20. Page 106 in *Chronicon Preciosum* (1707). Fleetwood is credited with creating the first price index, which he used to justify why a student should be allowed to earn more outside income and still maintain his college fellowship. The statute, which limited outside income to 5£, was developed two centuries earlier in 1444. Fleetwood showed that prices for the same goods had risen close to 6 times over this time period. Thus the statute needed updating.

number is done by multiplying it by the index number in that period. Sometimes this in known as indexing because saying you are "inflating" a number doesn't quite have the right ring to it, but that is basically what's being done.

For example, a union may negotiate a cost-of-living allowance (COLA) clause in its contract, which means that all wages and/or salaries automatically increase when the consumer price index (CPI) increases to compensate workers for the higher consumer prices in the economy. In theory, the purchasing power of the compensation package should[21] remain constant for the worker, who is also a consumer in his or her non-work life and should be protected from inflation over time.

O constancy, be strong upon my side.[22]
—*William Shakespeare (1564–1616), English writer*

Sometimes pension plans will exempt the first 2% of inflation from indexing, which makes them partial indexing schemes. Over time, this can make a big difference. There is a handy rule of thumb called the rule of 72 that will help us understand what a couple of percentage points can do over time. Here is the rule: take 72 and divide it by the interest rate in percent. This tells you approximately how long it takes to double your money. In the case of a partially indexed pension, it tells us that in 36 years your pension's purchasing power will essentially be cut in half if the first 2% of inflation isn't indexed. Needless to say, the importance of this feature depends on how long a person lives after retirement.

"If I wasn't real," Alice said—half-laughing through her tears, it all seemed so ridiculous—"I shouldn't be able to cry."

"I hope you don't suppose those are real tears?" Tweedledum interrupted in a tone of great contempt.[23]

3. Price indexes are used to calculate inflation rates.[24] (I have already alluded to this idea in the previous paragraph.) In fact, an inflation rate is the preferred way of giving price level information. Normally, news outlets don't report the value of the index because it is so completely dependent on the base year. Instead, these index numbers are converted into percent changes from one period to the next. For example, the difference between index numbers of 100 to 105 from one year to the next is the same as 200 to 210 if another base year had been used. Both are 5% increases.[25] The value of the index number isn't as important as the difference between successive numbers. Consequently, when you check the CPI on any government website, they don't

---

21. In a book like this I can't prove to you the following, so you will have to accept my word for it. The Laspeyres index will overestimate and the Paasche will underestimate the cost of inflation. An average of the two should make it close to correct. Historically, pension plans that use the CPI method deduct a couple of percentage points due to this overestimation of inflation costs. With improvements in CPI calculations, this problem of overestimation isn't as big; thus, partial indexing really does cost the pensioner.
22. Julius Caesar (1599).
23. *Through the Looking Glass and What Alice Found There.*
24. Or deflation rates, which occur when the price level falls.
25. If the index went from 100 to 95 then prices deflated by 5%.

usually report the value of the index[26] number itself but instead they provide the rate of change from the previous period in percent, saving you the calculation.

This way of reporting price level information is particularly handy when calculating real interest rates because both interest and inflation are in percentages. The real interest rate is equal to the nominal rate as reported by financial institutions less the expected rate of inflation.[27] For example, if nominal rates are currently 6% and expected inflation is 2%, then the borrowers and the lenders are really paying and earning approximately 4%. As inflation increases, so do the interest rates posted at the bank. Most of this is driven by the savers, who see no reason to lend money if the amount they get back in the future doesn't compensate them for the opportunity cost of saving it—which is spending it now. No one wants to deny themselves today only to have less purchasing power in the future—at least not on purpose. Savers need a real reward to incentivize them to lend, which is some amount of interest over and above the amount of interest they need to keep purchasing power constant over time. Thus you put the expected inflation rate on the table before any negotiations about real interest rates between borrowers and lenders can begin.

INFLATION COSTS

Money often costs too much.[28]

—*Ralph Waldo Emerson (1803–1882), American philosopher and writer*

The real enemy of money is inflation, especially the deadly hyperinflation[29] strain. Inflation can take a perfectly reasonable bank note or bill and make it virtually worthless, as evidenced in pre-Nazi Germany around 1923 when, at one point, prices doubled every two days. People carried money around in wheelbarrows because each piece of paper was worth so little. When currency cannot keep its value, people either revert to the barter system or they start to use another country's currency instead. Zimbabwe no longer has a currency of its own for this very reason. Remember that "money is as money does" and hyperinflated money doesn't do much. People in pre-Nazi Germany ended up using its bank notes as wallpaper and to keep fires going because it was worth more as a product than as a medium of exchange. The previously civilized economic system fell into chaos. There are stories of elderly people gassing themselves in their apartments to avoid the economic fallout.

---

26. The only indexes that report as a level are stock indices. I find this somewhat annoying. What does a 420 point increase in S&P/TSX mean? I would prefer they said the market was up or down by a certain %. However, daily changes are often so small this might seem ridiculous. Therefore they normally say that the market is up a certain number of points to equal the new total. Thus you are left to figure the relative importance of the market movement yourself.
27. This is known as the Fisher equation after the American economist Irving Fisher (1867–1947). The equation is Nominal interest rates ≈ Real interest rates + Expected inflation over the period.
28. *The Conduct of Life* (1860).
29. American economist Phillip Cagan (1927–2012) defined hyperinflation as a monthly inflation rate that exceeds 50% in *The Monetary Dynamics of Hyperinflation* (1956). This is very high, but I guess you have to make a line in the sand somewhere.

The inflation of the currency systems of Europe has proceeded to extraordinary lengths. The various belligerent Governments, unable, or too timid or too short-sighted to secure from loans or taxes the resources they required, have printed notes for the balance.[30]
—*John Maynard Keynes (1883–1946), British economist*

The consequences of hyperinflation go far beyond the economy, as we can see from the rise of the Nazis. The German people started looking for something or someone to blame for the devastation of hyperinflation and its long-term impact. Even though identifying the root cause for something on this scale is complicated by multiple factors, human nature, being what it is, likes to find simplistic answers. As a result, people started floating a conspiracy theory that the Jews were using inflation to ruin Germany. The inflated bank notes in circulation became known as Judefetzen, or Jew-confetti,[31] on the street. Members of the German government also blamed the consequences of their inflationary monetary policy on the Treaty of Versailles and its punishing war reparations, which they felt drove their country into ruin. With this backdrop, it isn't hard to see why the German citizenry began to look for a saviour who confirmed their suspicions. Although Keynes entitled his book *The Economic Consequences of the Peace*, I think we would do well to never underestimate the peace consequences of the economics.

I don't believe that the big men, the politicians and the capitalists alone are guilty of the war. Oh, no, the little man is just as keen, otherwise the people of the world would have risen in revolt long ago! There is an urge and rage in people to destroy, to kill, to murder, and until all mankind, without exception, undergoes a great change, wars will be waged, everything that has been built up, cultivated and grown, will be destroyed and disfigured, after which mankind will have to begin all over again.[32]
—*Annelies Marie Frank (1929–1945), Jewish diarist*

GOSSIP COLUMN: ÉTIENNE LASPEYRES (1834–1913) AND HERMANN PAASCHE (1851–1925)

Both of these men were German born, although Laspeyres's name looks French. In fact, his ancestors left southern France and settled in Berlin, part of the Huguenot exodus from the Occitan region. They kept their Huguenot identity along with the non-Germanic pronunciation of their name. Étienne's father was a law professor, and Étienne studied law and public finance but went on to earn a PhD in political science and public finance from Heidelberg University. He taught in various political science departments before he settled and remained in Giessen[33] for 26 years. He is most famous for developing the Laspeyres price index, which he published in 1871. Not to

---

30. *The Economic Consequences of the Peace* (1919) was written because Keynes was appalled at the harshness of the war reparations imposed on Germany in the Treaty of Versailles. He predicted another war because of it. "If we aim deliberately at the impoverishment of Central Europe, vengeance, I dare predict, will not limp. Nothing can then delay for very long that final war between the forces of Reaction and the despairing convulsions of Revolution, before which the horrors of the late German war will fade into nothing."
31. http://www.telegraph.co.uk/finance/comment/ambroseevans_pritchard/7909432/The-Death-of-Paper-Money.html.
32. Entry on May 3, 1944.
33. A town that was heavily bombed during WWII, leaving many of its historical buildings destroyed. It also served the Nazis as a sub-camp of the Buchenwald concentration camp.

GOSSIP COLUMN *(CONTINUED)*

be a one-hit-wonder, he is also credited with establishing business administration as an academic/professional discipline in Germany as well as combining economics and statistics in his work. This combination is the norm for most economists today. It should certainly be part of any MBA degree as well.

Hermann Paasche was born in the medieval town of Burg bei Magdeburg in northeastern Germany. He initially studied agriculture but received his PhD under the supervision of Johannes Conrad (a famous political economy professor) at the University of Halle[34] in 1875. He also became a political science professor and taught at various German universities. While at his last university, he developed the Paasche price index (1874) to analyze the German sugar industry. It was this work on sugar that got him connected to the Reichstag (or German parliament). In 1906, he gave up his position as a professor to enter politics and rose to the top as the vice president of the Reichstag.

Both of these men knew each other academically and discussed the relative merits of their indices with each other. However, because they published in German, the English-speaking world didn't really know about them for some time. Moreover, Stanley Jevons had already published (in 1865) his version of a price index in England. However, these two indices, once known to the English-speaking world, would dominate in the accounting for national prices.

Laspeyres died before WWI began (1914), but Paasche lived through it. The war would prove devastating to both Germany and to Paasche's family. His oldest son Hans was charged with high treason (1917) because of his pacifist politics, but he was never sentenced, probably because of who his father was. Instead, he was admitted to a mental institution but was released to care for his children when his wife died. Tragically, only a couple of years later, Hans was assassinated on May 21, 1920, by the newly minted soldiers of the German Republic.[35] Somehow Hermann Paasche managed to carry on and was a member of the Reichstag for the German Peoples Party (DVP) during the hyperinflation years (1921–1924), where it was possible for him to see his index at work. In 1925, Paasche died of pneumonia in Detroit, a week after he arrived in the USA for a lecture tour. He was to speak on the conditions in the French-occupied German territories.[36]

WINNERS AND LOSERS

What therefore God hath joined together, let not man put asunder.

—Mark 10:9[37]

Everyone can understand the horrors of hyperinflation, but even moderate unpredictable levels of inflation have issues. One of the most significant problems is the unfair and arbitrary redistribution of wealth or income between people. For an economy to run smoothly, people need to trust each other and they need to make plans, so there has to be a level of certainty. This leads to people entering into various kinds of contracts where both parties agree to the conditions of the contracts that can bind them together for many

---

34. Now called the Martin Luther University of Halle–Wittenberg.
35. http://hanspaascheen.wordpress.com/chronology-by-werner-lange/.
36. Obituary in the *New York Evening Post*, April 11, 1925.
37. Douay–Rheims Bible.

years. Unbeknownst to the parties, unexpected inflation will change the agreed-upon costs and benefits such that one party unexpectedly wins and the other party unexpectedly loses. Inflation can make the losing party unwilling to tie itself to any more long-term agreements, and fair long-term agreements facilitate long-term investments, which are good for a thriving economy.

Here are some common contracts that are affected by unexpected inflation:

1. Loan agreements between borrowers and lenders are especially vulnerable because contracts can span many years. For example, some 25-year mortgages can fix an interest rate for 5 years at a time. If inflation unexpectedly occurs during the loan period, which it did in North America during the 1970s, the borrower wins and the lender loses. The lender can even make negative real interest rates if the inflation rate is higher than the nominal agreed-upon rate. Lenders hate to lose unexpectedly, so they stop offering long-term loans.[38] As a result, a borrower can only get a very short-term loan and hope that the lender will renew the contract once it becomes due. This doesn't lead to good planning because the basic rule of business finance is that you should match the length of time of your assets with those of your liabilities.[39] Inflation means that long-term multimillion-dollar assets such as buildings are financed with short and hopefully sequential loans.

2. Businesses sign employment contracts with their employees. For unions in particular, contracts can last two to five years. If inflation during the contract turns out to be more than the negotiators expected, then the nominal wages are worth less in real terms. The employee loses purchasing power and the employer wins in terms of lower labour costs relative to the price of the inflating product. This is precisely why union contracts often negotiate cost-of-living allowance (COLA) clauses into their contracts in order to prevent this kind of damage to their workers.

3. Contracts between businesses and their customers can have problems when inflation occurs because, depending on the nature of the service, payment can often be delayed for a significant period of time. It is not uncommon for consulting companies to wait until the end of the job to bill the client, and then the client take 90 days to pay. During this period, if inflation occurs, the business loses and the customer wins.

It seems to me that whenever circumstances arise in the ordinary business of life in which, if two persons were ordinarily honest and careful, the one of them would make a promise to the other, it may properly be inferred that both of them understood that such a promise was given and accepted.[40]

—*Lord Esher,* Ex parte Ford *(1885)*

These contracts can be entered into implicitly. For example, a company printing catalogues can list prices in them or restaurants can print menus with prices on them. (You know you are in a very expensive restaurant when the menu doesn't have prices

---

38. During the double-digit inflation years of the 1980s, banks were only willing to lock in terms for one year. Now it is possible to get 10-year terms at fairly low interest rates.

39. This is also true for homeowners who borrow at low rates at the maximum amount they can afford. If you have enough capacity to take a rate hike, then short-term variable rates will usually guarantee that you pay less interest on the same principal.

40. *The Dictionary of Legal Quotations* (1904).

on it!) These are a kind of contract between the sellers and their customers. Economists call these the "menu costs" of inflation because it costs money to print menus. During the moderate-inflation years of the 1970s and 1980s, many restaurants stopped using expensive, hard-to-change-without-looking-tacky menus and used chalkboards and simple paper menus instead. Many businesses with catalogues stopped their catalogue sales[41] altogether during this time.

4. Pension contracts with fixed benefits lead to losses for the pensioner and gains for the pension plan when inflation occurs. In democratic countries with state-run pension plans, angry seniors mobilized their votes and lobbied their governments for indexation. Now government (and non-government) pension funds are at least partially indexed. Go Grey Power!

5. Tax forms are a contract between the government and taxpayers. When inflation occurs, people tend to negotiate for higher incomes with their employers, which can push them into a higher tax bracket if the tax brackets aren't indexed. This is known as *bracket creep* and is effectively a tax increase. In this case, the taxpayer loses and the government wins, which really doesn't seem fair, as governments have some control over the inflation in the economy in the first place.

6. Money as cash is a contract between the central banks and the holders of cash. Inflation causes the holders of cash to lose and the central bank to win during inflationary periods, especially if the central bank creates more money[42] for the finance department or treasury to spend.

    Money as a deposit is also a contract between the commercial banks (borrower) and the depositors (lenders), which brings us to our first point about the unfair redistribution of income between borrowers and lenders during unexpected inflation. When unexpected inflation occurs, investors also try to convert more of their money into other assets as a hedge against inflation—assets like gold, land, equity, and foreign currency[43] that do not have the problems that debt does during an inflationary period for the lender. These assets hopefully increase in value to keep pace with the inflation.

There is more owing her than is paid; and more shall be paid her than she'll demand.[44]
—William Shakespeare (1584–1616), English writer

Notice that for each of these instances, the losing players found ways to mitigate their losses. Not many people will continue to lose wealth without some form of protest. They lobby or negotiate for automatic indexation of pensions, wages, and tax brackets. Lenders decrease the length of time they will lend for and add risk premiums to the interest rate

---

41. Eaton's was the first Canadian retailer to distribute a mail-order catalogue (1884–1976). The company especially targeted rural areas, and I remember getting the Christmas catalogue as a child and circling what I wanted for Christmas. As a preteen, I also used it to dream of how I would decorate my home one day by flipping through the furniture pages. Back then, I favoured colonial mainly because that was the style they showed. I favour Scandinavian modern and French provincial now.
42. This is called *seigniorage*, but economists often call it an *inflation tax*.
43. During hyperinflation, people don't want cash at all. They will stand in long lines as soon as they get their paycheques to get the cash to go shop and turn the money into real things or to exchange that cash for another, more stable currency, such as the U.S. dollar.
44. *All's Well That Ends Well* (1600s).

just in case it turns out they have guessed wrong again. Those who hold money get out of money and into something safer. Each of these strategies is reasonable and helps get the system running more smoothly again. Essentially, these responses take the unexpected inflation surprise out of the equation for everyone, and that is a good thing—a much better solution than revolution, war, and ethnic genocide.

DEFLATING NEWS

Es ist nichts schrecklicher als eine tätige Unwissenheit.
(Nothing is more terrible than ignorance in action.)[45]
—*Johann Wolfgang von Goethe (1749–1832), German writer, artist, and politician*

It turns out that deflation is also bad. The winners and losers discussed in the previous section simply trade places. However, the point about inflation's effect on money is critical and worth an explanation. Now people hoard money instead of spending it on real things because they anticipate that prices will continue to fall. Remember that "money is as money does." This means that the hoarded money sits idle. This is particularly bad if businesses hold on to their cash instead of investing in the physical capital that creates jobs, which benefits the economy.

Deflation also punishes businesses that previously made investments at a higher cost only to watch the prices of their products fall once they go to market. Profits are the lifeblood of industry, and deflation wipes out profits—particularly if the business[46] has debt (now the borrowers are the losers). It is easy for the economy to slow down, and deflation is usually associated with recessions and depressions (although it may be the effect rather than the cause). Whatever way you look at it, deflation isn't correlated with good news, and business needs good news to keep going.

PRACTICE TARGET

Reason, or the ratio of all we have already known, is not the same that it shall be when we know more.[47]
—*William Blake (1757–1827), English poet and visual artist*

Is there an optimal inflation rate? The consensus of central banks around the world seems to be that 2% is ideal. However, this consensus is not without its detractors. Some economists think inflation should be zero, whereas others think 2% is too low and that it should be slightly higher at 3% or 4%. Because nobody thinks optimal inflation sits in the double digits, the debate is over a fairly narrow range of rates. Let's take a moment to look at the rationale of the various camps.

Two Percent Is Too High: Those who think that inflation should be closer to zero believe this because they have a particular view of the role of prices in the economy. As a key proponent of this argument, Hayek argued that prices are supposed to give accurate

---

45. *Sprüche in Prosa* ("*Proverbs in Prose*") (1819).
46. This is Irving Fisher's debt deflation explanation for depressions.
47. *There Is No Natural Religion* (1788).

information about what is really up and what is really down in the marketplace. Prices act as signals or signs. The change in price information should help buyers and sellers make intelligent decisions. But inflation changes all prices together, which makes it hard to tell what the price signal means. Economic players (or agents, as economists like to call them) get confused about what is going on, inhibiting their ability to make good decisions. Bad decisions can have negative long-term economic consequences.

Two Percent Is Too Low: Those in this camp[48] believe that 2% inflation takes away too many options for governments to use in order to solve recessionary problems with economic policy. For instance, lowering interest rates is an important tool in solving high unemployment rates because it stimulates business investment. If the economic agents in the economy generally want a 4% real interest rate, then an inflation rate of 1% maxes out the nominal rate at 5%. However, an inflation rate of 3% could accommodate bank interest rates of 7%. If the central bank wanted to lower interest rates in bad times, the latter gives central bankers more percentage points to work with.

For example, if the central bank wanted to drop interest rates 6% (which would be massive, by the way), then, in the first case, interest rates would need to be −1%, which really isn't possible—although in the most recent financial crisis, short-term interest rates in Europe did go slightly negative. In this case, the lender is actually paying people to borrow their money. (The only argument for why the Europeans would accept negative interest rates is that they couldn't realistically take all that money out of the bank and put it under a mattress and still remain in Europe. The bank was physically keeping their money safe, and they were willing to pay a premium for that service.) However, the higher inflation rate of 3% can allow the economy to stay in the positive-interest-rate zone because 7% less 6% is a positive 1%. This argument for higher inflation targets is known as the *zero-bound-* or *zero-floor-on-nominal-interest-rates* argument.

Alice laughed. "There's no use trying," she said: "one can't believe impossible things."

"I daresay you haven't had much practice," said the Queen. "When I was your age, I always did it for half-an-hour a day. Why, sometimes I've believed as many as six impossible things before breakfast."

Furthermore, some economists[49] argue that the economy as a whole needs more wiggle room during times of economic downturns in order to be able to recover by allowing real wages to change when nominal ones can't. Let me give you an example. Suppose one country has a target inflation rate of 2% and another country 4%. Now suppose both countries have employees who resist taking a pay cut in bad times and nominal wages stay constant. Recall that real wages equal nominal wages deflated by a price index. Because of inflation, the second country's real wages will drop twice as fast as those of the first country, which means employers in the second country are more willing to hire people sooner due to the lower real costs of a worker. More employment means a quicker recovery. This is the downward-wage-rigidity argument, which we will see again when we cover Keynesian economics.

---

48. "IMF Staff Position Note: Rethinking Macroeconomic Policy," by Olivier Blanchard, Giovanni Dell'Ariccia, and Paolo Mauro, http://www.imf.org/external/pubs/ft/spn/2010/spn1003.pdf.
49. http://www.collectionscanada.gc.ca/eppp.archive/100/201/301/bank_can_review/2006/spring/cover/en/press/annexe1.pdf.

Essentially this group thinks that it isn't the exact inflation rate that is the problem per se (within reason of course); rather, it is the unexpected and random nature of inflation that creates winners and losers. If people knew the expected inflation rate, they could make their plans and negotiate it into their contracts. Prices can still act as signals if everyone knows and believes that inflation is targeted at some low stable number because the math isn't too difficult.

FIRM ON THE PRICE

"It seems very pretty," she said when she had finished it, "but it's rather hard to understand!" (You see she didn't like to confess, even to herself, that she couldn't make it out at all.) "Somehow it seems to fill my head with ideas—only I don't exactly know what they are!"[50]

Charles Lutwidge Dodgson, pen name Lewis Carroll (1832–1898), British author and clergyman

In this chapter we developed measures of aggregate prices and used them to calculate inflation and deflation. Economists have learned a lot about inflation, and this is due, in no small part, to the work Laspeyres and Paasche, who helped quantify it, and to governments, which keep track of price levels in massive databases. We also saw the damage hyperinflation and unexpected inflation can do. Last, if expected inflation is low and predictable, then the economy can merrily go on its way in making contracts. There is some disagreement about how low is the "correct low," but the spread isn't that big anyway. There are also some differences between how price indices are computed, but nothing major, really. Later in the book we will look at solving inflation problems. Just a forewarning: Excessive inflation is like cancer and, depending on how bad things are, the cure can be pretty devastating.

Brooke tweets:

@EvelineAdomait Its easy to calculate inflation. #priceindexesarefun #unexpectedisbad #dontbehyper #Iwanttogotowonderland

---

50. *Through the Looking-Glass, and What Alice Found There* (1871).

CHAPTER 7

In Labour

Measure not the work
Until the day's out and the labour done,
Then bring your gauges.[1]
—*Elizabeth Barrett Browning (1806–1861), English poet*

Libby goes to check on the main course in the kitchen and Justin follows her. Justin refills Libby's glass as they stand on either side of the counter separating the kitchen from the dining area.

"You look cute in that apron," teases Justin. "You a fan of Martha Stewart?"

Libby laughs, "Aprons are a great invention if you don't want to get your clothes ruined, but I'm not really the Suzy homemaker[2] type."

"How are your grad applications going? Have you decided where you want to go next year?" Justin asks.

Libby replies, "I applied to a couple of places. I'm just waiting on one of my references to submit her letter and my applications will be complete. The prof said she would do it over the break."

Both Libby and Justin turn in response to the joint laughter of Emma and David, who are sitting on the couch.

"What's so funny?" asks Salim.

"David was just telling me about a job interview he had last week and his description of the interviewer was hilarious. You should consider stand-up comedy!"

David replies, "Maybe I'll open a club and combine business with comedy. That would be my dream job."

"I wish I knew what I wanted to be when I grow up. All I know is that I want a job that is ecologically sustainable but makes enough money to live on. It seems all the ethical jobs are part-time or short contracts," notes Brooke. "I think I might need to go to law school."

"You know the best thing about my coop program?" Salim asks, joining in the conversation, "I can find out what I really want to do and make enough money to go to school at the same time. I really like my engineering courses, but I'll have to see what happens on the job. I don't think I could stand hating my job for 30 years. That would be awful!"

LABOUR AND DELIVERY

Jean Valjean had this peculiarity, that he might be said to carry two knapsacks; in one he had the thoughts of a saint, in the other the formidable talents of a convict. He helped himself from one or the other as occasion required.[3]

Victor Marie Hugo (1802–1885), French writer

People are more than just the consumers of products—whether we measure those products in real or nominal terms. People also provide the inputs that allow firms to actually make the goods and services

---

1. *Aurora Leigh* (1857).
2. Topper Toys launched the Suzy Homemaker line of toys in 1966. The Suzy Homemaker doll was right behind Barbie in popularity. Quite the contrast in stereotypes.
3. *Les Misérables* (1862).

that they sell to households. The most important input people bring to the business community is labour. We can look at this topic from two different perspectives depending on whether we are telling a micro- or macroeconomics story. Even though this book is essentially a macroeconomics book, I find myself reluctant to give up the microeconomics side of things totally. Therefore, I will look at the macro implications of employment but whenever possible I will give the micro foundations for why workers and businesses behave as they do. I'm going to ask a basic question because I think it's a good place to start our conversation about labour: Why do people work?

Work spares us from three evils: boredom, vice and need.[4]

—*Francois-Marie Arouet, pen name Voltaire (1694–1778), French writer and philosopher*

The most obvious reason people work can be found in microeconomic theory: that it pays to work—the paycheque people receive is used to buy the goods and services that increase an individual's utility or happiness. Unfortunately, when we aggregate that reason up to the larger economy, this reason bumps up against our chronic measurement problems. The paycheque theory assumes that all work can be counted. Recall that we found out in our chapter on national accounting that stuff like home production, such as people making their own bread or canning their own fruit or taking care of kids, doesn't get counted. These folks are getting paid in a non-monetary way, which in terms of micro analysis isn't really a problem because pay doesn't necessarily have to be monetary. Rewards can be either psychological in terms of such individuals feeling good about their decision or can also be in terms of the opportunity cost of not paying someone else to do the home production to enable these people to enter the paid labour market for themselves. Those who stay home invariably ask the micro question "Is it worth it for me to stay at home or go out to work?" However, from a macro perspective, we can't really capture the magnitude of these choices because no money changes hands. We can't count the work[5] that was performed by these people and we have no accounting for the pay. Be sure, however, that these choices influence the labour market statistics that we can measure.

In addition, just because some money changes hands doesn't mean it tells the whole story about why people work. There are many wealthy people who continue to work even though they don't need the money to buy any more happiness. For some über-wealthy people, it isn't even possible for them to spend their wealth in their lifetime, but they continue to work. Some people will run their successful family business and others will retire only to become very busy working through their foundations. Not everyone is looking for the fastest way out of paid employment into a life of leisure. For some people, because of their personal preferences, work and happiness go together and it isn't about the money . . . it is about the satisfaction of the work itself.

The ugliest of trades have their moments of pleasure. Now, if I were a grave-digger, or even a hangman, there are some people I could work for with a great deal of enjoyment.[6]

—*Douglas William Jerrold (1803–1857), English writer*

---

4. *Candide, ou l'Optimisme* (1759).
5. If you want to offend a homemaker, just ask if he or she works.
6. "Ugly Trades," reported in *Bartlett's Familiar Quotations*, 10th ed. (1919).

Let me give you a personal example. When I wrote *Cocktail Party Economics*, it took most of my free time for about two years. You might argue that I did it for the money—for the potential royalty cheques. However, when I cash my cheques once or twice a year, it doesn't even come close in compensating me monetarily for the time and effort it took to write the book. As I joke with my friends, "I'm not giving up my day job!" Yet here I am again—writing another book. I know the costs and I have made some guesses about the benefits. Again micro analysis assumes that this choice is easy to make and easy to explain with cost-benefit analysis. From a macro perspective, only paid employment counts as work and it is assumed that we only work because we get paid for it. The national employment statistics aren't going to include the writing of this book in their figures.

For of fortunes sharp adversitee
The worst kynde of infortune is this,
A man to han ben in prosperitee,
And it remembren, whan it passed is.[7]
—*Geoffrey Chaucer (1343–1400), English writer, philosopher, courtier, and diplomat*

The idea that work itself can make you happy is easier to see on the downside. In the happiness studies we talked about earlier in the book, researchers[8] found that when individuals become unemployed after being employed, they not only lose income, which correlates with lower levels of well-being, but also experience negative psychological effects associated with the job loss itself. There are also spillover effects. Even if you don't lose your job, just knowing that others have lost theirs can make you unhappy. It might be due to fears that crime will increase or that more taxation is just around the corner, or it could just be sympathy for the other person who lost the job. Therefore, high unemployment actually affects the happiness of those who are still employed. Ironically, the more global the unemployment, the less bad an individual feels about his or her own unemployment status. It must be true in this case that "misery loves company."

All of this discussion just to communicate this fact: national well-being and paid employment are connected. We won't be able to capture all of the nuances because of measurement issues, but we can establish that work is important. Garden-variety paid employment increases the welfare of a nation for whatever reason—and, yes, my day job does and should count. It behooves a government to develop employment policies that contribute to and don't detract from national welfare, and for that we need statistics. Let's look at the life of Richard Layard, a famous labour economist who specializes in happiness studies and is quite good at statistics.

7. *Troilus and Criseyde* (1380s).
8. http://www.bsfrey.ch/articles/365_02.pdf.

GOSSIP COLUMN: RICHARD LAYARD (1934-)

In order to understand Richard's work as an economist, I think you need to meet his immediate family. His father was John Willoughby Layard, a British anthropologist and psychologist from a long line of anthropologists and minor nobility. His mother was Doris Dingwell, the wife of anthropologist Eric Dingwell[9] at the time of his birth. Doris and Eric had an open marriage, and even though John and Doris were living together, Eric refused to divorce her until Richard was nine years old. Doris and John's relationship was an emotional rollercoaster. During the bitter times, John had long-term relationships with two other women, specifically Baroness Vera von der Heydt (a psychotherapist) and Lola Paulson (a psychologist). Doris and John divorced but later reconciled to end their lives as a couple. Both Vera and Lola attended John's funeral as friends.

Richard's father's interest in psychotherapy grew out his depression and attempted suicides. For example, before meeting Doris he had tried to kill himself by shooting himself in the mouth. He survived because he took a taxi to the home of W. H. Auden—a man he professed to love and whom he mentored—and asked him to finish the job. Fortunately, Auden called an ambulance instead and John would live to father Richard.

Richard, a terrific student, attended Eton, Cambridge, and finally the London School of Economics (LSE) to become a labour economics professor. He would later found and become the director for Centre for Economic Performance at the London School of Economics.

In 1991, Richard married Molly Christine Meacher, the ex-wife of Michael Meacher (a labour MP in the British Parliament and the father of her four children). She graduated with a BA in economics and a certificate in social work, and went on to work in the areas of mental health, policing, and drug reform. Because of her work, she was given a life peerage[10] to become Baroness Meacher.

Now to Richard's academic life. His early work focused on unemployment, inequity, and educational reform. Specifically, he was a senior researcher on the committee that generated the famous Robbins Report.[11] Here we see the LSE connection between Robbins and Layard. This report fundamentally changed and expanded the post-secondary education system in Britain during the 1960s and 1970s.

Later, as a labour economist, he wrote about labour market policies, which became part of the Labour Party's "New Deal." Layard proposed that policies such as training, subsidized employment, and volunteer work would reduce unemployment. Because of his efforts, he was made a life peer by the Labour government to become Baron Layard. (Note that Layard and his wife are one of the few couples to have earned these titles in their own right.)

In recent years, Layard's research efforts shifted in the direction of happiness studies, where he specifically looks at the role that mental health and psychotherapy play in well-being. He produced *The Depression Report,* which resulted in initiatives to improve access to psychological therapies in the United Kingdom. He also coauthored (along with economists Jeffrey Sacks and John Helliwell) *The World Happiness Report* (2012),[12] which questions the singular focus on the level of national income for predicting well-being.

---

9. http://libraries.ucsd.edu/speccoll/testing/html/mss0084.html.
10. In the United Kingdom, life peers (as opposed to inherited peers) are created members of the Peerage whose titles may not be inherited by their children. Life peerages are created under the Life Peerages Act of 1958, always at the rank of baron, and entitle the holders to seats in the House of Lords if they meet certain qualifications, such as age and citizenship.
11. See the Gossip Column in Chapter 1 of *Cocktail Party Economics* for more on Robbins.
12. http://www.earth.columbia.edu/sitefiles/file/Sacks%20Writing/2012/World%20Happiness%20Report.pdf.

Richard Layard is an excellent academic—the best kind, really. Just check out his homepage[13] at the LSE. Like Lord Robbins, his work became practical, as he pushed his government to make real changes in policy in order to better the lives of British citizens. Perhaps the report commissioned by the Children's Society and coauthored with children's author Judy Dunn expresses his perspective best: *A Good Childhood: Searching for Values in a Competitive Age* (2009).

CALCULATING PEOPLE

The worker therefore only feels himself outside his work, and in his work feels outside himself.[14]

—Karl Marx (1818–1883), German philosopher, economist, historian, sociologist, journalist, and socialist

Of all the inputs available to business, labour is the most personal. This may be why human resources (HR) are sometimes called *personnel*. It is important to remember this when you hear what can feel like impersonal statistics about the labour market.

There are some common ways to measure labour market activity. These include:

1. Labour force participation rates
2. Unemployment rates
3. Employment-to-population ratios
4. Duration of unemployment (which isn't a rate but is measured in weeks.)

Notice that the first three are rates (or ratios), so let's start by looking at the pros and cons of using percentages. The major pro is that a rate is easy to understand. For example, if I say that 60% of the students in my university classes are female, you can immediately picture who is in the audience. The con is that you have no idea if my class has 40 or 400 students. Rates give a sense of proportion but not scale.

In order to calculate each of these indicators of the labour market, we need data. There are at least two approaches to getting data. One is to regularly ask everyone in the country their employment status. The problem with this approach is that it is expensive and time consuming to administer. We therefore use the statistical method of random sampling, which basically asks a much smaller group of people who have been carefully selected to be representative of the whole population. When done right, this is much cheaper and quicker and is still accurate. Statistics Canada surveys 54,000 Canadian households every month, asking them questions on the age and the work status of anyone living in the home. This is known as the Labour Force Survey[15] and is the primary source for labour force statistics in Canada.

---

13. http://cep.lse.ac.uk/_new/staff/person.asp?id=970.
14. *Paris Manuscripts* (1844).
15. In the USA, this is done by the Bureau of Labor Statistics.

So what information does this survey collect? How is it related to the labour market statistics just listed? What do these statistics mean, and what issues do they raise?

1. Working-Age Population

Any population can be divided into two groups—those who are able to work and those who technically are not. The person who is not able to work may be different in various countries depending on labour laws, retirement laws, and levels of institutionalization in such places as prison or school. (My younger son is pretty sure school is a type of incarceration.) For international comparison purposes, the working-age population[16] is anyone in the age group of 15 to 64 years of age. This number gives us interesting observations about the demographics of various countries. For example, in 2011, among the G8 countries, Russia's working-age population was 72% and had risen since 2006, whereas Japan's was only 63.5% and had fallen in the same time period. If this number goes down over time, it indicates that the general population is aging, which is exactly what has been happening in all G8 countries except Russia. Obviously, this will have implications for governments as they use income tax revenues from workers to provide services—including healthcare—to an ever-aging population. It can also be the driver of immigration policy, educational policy, and child benefits.

It is not enough for a great nation merely to have added new years to life—our objective must also be to add new life to those years.[17]
—John F. Kennedy (1917–1963), American president

When Statistics Canada calculates workforce participation rates, it counts as the working-age population all people 15 years and older, including retired people. This cut-off age has changed over time. From 1891 to 1931 the age started at 10 years, after which it was raised to 14 years and older. Finally, in 1951 it became 15 years and older and has remained at this cut-off age ever since.[18] The USA uses a cut-off of 16 years and older.[19] Supposedly, this is the age at which someone can realistically be called a worker. Thankfully it isn't 10 anymore.

2. Labour Force

Just because a person is in the pool of the working-age population doesn't mean he or she wants to be working in the labour market. For example, high school students and homemakers don't necessarily have paid part-time jobs. Once we know the size of the labour force, we can calculate the participation rate for any demographic. We simply divide the labour force by the working-age population. Since the early 1960s, the participation of women in the paid workforce has almost doubled, whereas the participation rate of men has actually fallen. These trends in participation rates tell the story of women's emancipation as well as the trend for men to obtain more schooling and thus delay their entry into the workforce.

---

16. "Proportion (in percentage) of the working-age population (aged 15 to 64), G8 countries, 2006 and 2011," Statistics Canada, http://www12.statcan.gc.ca/census-recensement/2011/as-sa/98-311-x/2011001/fig/fig4-eng.cfm.
17. Special message to the Congress on the needs of the nation's senior citizens (February 21, 1963).
18. http://www.statcan.gc.ca/pub/11-516-x/sectiond/4057750-eng.htm.
19. Bureau of Labor Statistics, http://data.bls.gov/timeseries/.

3. Employment and Unemployment Numbers

Once we know the labour force, we need to separate out those who are working from those who are unemployed. Seems straightforward, don't you think? Well it is. If individuals say they have a job—whether full-time or part-time—they are considered employed.

On n'est pas inoccupé parce qu'on est absorbé. Il y a le labeur visible et le labeur invisible.
A man is not idle, because he is absorbed in thought. There is a visible labour and there is an invisible labour.[20]
—*Victor Marie Hugo (1802–1885), French writer*

Individuals are considered unemployed and still in the labour force if they indicate that they are in any of the following situations: (a) they are without a job but have actively looked for work in the past four weeks, (b) they are laid off but expect to be called back, or (c) they are in transition to a new job that will begin in the next four weeks. The unemployment rate is calculated by taking the number of unemployed people and dividing it by the size of the labour force.

Once you know how to calculate the unemployment rate, getting the employment rate is easy. The employment rate is just the number of employed people divided by the labour force. Or, we can just go with the fact that the employment rate and the unemployment rate should total 100% of the labour force. If you know the unemployment or employment rate, just subtract that number from 100 to find the other number. In notation it looks like this:

$LF = U + E$ (where LF is the labour force, E is the employed, and U is the unemployed)

Therefore, we can say

$(LF/LF) \times 100 = (U/LF) \times 100 + (E/LF) \times 100$

Or

$100\% = U\% + E\%$

This categorization of who is in the labour force and who is unemployed can do interesting things to the unemployment rate. To see what I mean, let's follow a hypothetical person through the numbers, shall we? For the purposes of illustration, assume that there are 100 people in the labour force and 9 are unemployed workers. That means the unemployment rate is 9%. Suppose an individual is laid off from a factory job but she expects to be called back to work soon. That means that there are actually 10 unemployed workers and the unemployment rate increases to 10%. Sadly, the factory actually shuts down and this worker isn't called back. If she can give specifics about her job search, she continues to be counted as unemployed and the rate doesn't change. However, things become grimmer and this person experiences depression about her joblessness. The individual can't motivate herself to leave her home and she stops searching for about a month. (This is known as a *marginally attached worker*, who can quickly become a discouraged worker over time.) Technically, this person has left the labour force, which now drops to

---

20. *Les Misérables* (1862).

99 workers. and the number of unemployed drops to 9 again. The unemployment rate is 9/99 rather than 10/100 as a percent. Because that individual is a bigger proportion of the unemployed pool (in the numerator) than the labour force pool (in the denominator), the unemployment rate actually falls from 10% to 9.1%. I hope you see that, in this situation, a drop in the unemployment rate isn't actually good news.

Fractions were a subject of very great difficulty with the ancients. Simultaneous changes in both numerator and denominator were usually avoided.[21]

—*Florian Cajori (1859–1930), American professor of mathematics and physics*

The national employment and unemployment rates are pretty black and white. Either the person is working or not. There is a third rate that tries to capture the idea of under-employment. This would be the person who works at a part-time job but really wants a full-time job. Technically such individuals are classified as employed for the purposes of the unemployment rate, but this positive characterization misses something pretty important about this person's work status—that he or she isn't working enough.

Therefore, Statistics Canada takes the number of people who report that they are in this situation and divides that number by the labour force to get the involuntary part-time rate. If the unemployment and employment rates stay constant, but the involuntary part-time rate falls, it means that workers have moved from part-time to full-time employment status and things are getting better for workers. In recessions, the number tends to go in the opposite way, so things are actually worse than the straight-up unemployment rate indicates.

In terms of employment, there is one other ratio we need to consider—the employment-to-population ratio. From the name, you should guess that this is the number of employed people divided by some measure of population. For this calculation we use the working-age population rather than the entire population. Essentially, this ratio captures the idea of who is working compared to who could work. If we track this number over time, we can get an indication of how the population is aging. For example, a population whose average age is rising will have an employment-to-population ratio that is dropping. (i.e., lots of population with fewer workers.) We can also get some indication about how the economy is cycling. This ratio will go down in recessions as people lose their jobs but will go up in good times. As you can see, policymakers can use this information to help determine how the economy is performing as well as the age demographics of the citizenry.

4. Duration

The Labour Force Survey also collects information from unemployed workers about how long they have been out of work and provides a statistic known as the duration.[22] Short durations can be actually good for the economy. Hopefully, it means that people are leaving jobs for better ones, with short periods of transition. For instance, in Canada, about 60% of the unemployment resolves itself within 13 weeks of a job loss. If you look at all of the Canadian workers who lost their jobs, the average length of time of

---

21. *A History of Mathematics* (1893).
22. "Labour force survey estimates (LFS), duration of unemployment by sex and age group, unadjusted for seasonality," Statistics Canada, http://www5.statcan.gc.ca/cansim/pick-choisir?lang=eng&p2=33&id=2820047.

unemployment in the winter of 2013 was between 21 and 22 weeks (or less than half a year). If we compare the median and mean duration for Canada, this means that the average unemployed worker is out of work for half a year but the median (or middle) unemployed worker is unemployed for less than three months. The 40% who are unemployed for more than three months are pulling the average duration up because they have a much longer unemployment problem. In many ways, the duration numbers are actually more important than the unemployment rate. If this number increases, as it does in recessions, it indicates more hardship for individuals and their families because of how long it takes to find work again. Durations also change with the generosity of unemployment benefits because many of the 40% tend to find a job once their benefits are close to running out.

NOT ALL UNEMPLOYMENT IS CREATED EQUAL

If the concept of probability and the formulae of the theory of probability are used without a clear understanding of the collectives involved, one may arrive at entirely misleading results.[23]
—*Richard von Mises (1883–1953), American scientist and mathematician*[24]

We have ways of measuring unemployment, but the number we come up with is not necessarily indicative of the underlying problem creating that unemployment. Unemployment is much like bacteria. It sounds bad but there are different types—some are deadly but others are actually helpful for a healthy body.

Unemployment can be categorized as frictional (healthy), structural (semi-healthy), seasonal (healthy), and, finally, cyclical (unhealthy) unemployment.

Frictional unemployment occurs when jobs exist and there are workers who could fill the position but they haven't found each other yet. This type of unemployment isn't a problem as long as it isn't too large or the duration too long. For a country to have a dynamic labour force, it must have churning (or turnover) in the labour market. If people are in jobs they hate, it isn't necessarily a bad thing when they quit. Governments can help reduce frictional unemployment duration by sponsoring job banks or employment centres to aid in the matching of workers with employers.

But job search is never costless to either the worker or the business. Search theory[25] explains why people can end up with different wages for the same job. People with different search costs will accept different wages, and this has implications for government-sponsored programs. On one hand, if unemployment benefits are easy to get and have very few conditions, this raises the opportunity costs of job search and lowers the person's willingness to accept a job offer. As a result, frictional unemployment goes up. On the other hand, the government might give tax credits for coop programs because cooperative education provides valuable information to students during their schooling— information that should reduce the mismatching of workers and jobs once the students enter the permanent labour market upon graduation. This should cause frictional unemployment to fall.

---

23. Taken from *Probability, Statistics and Truth*, Second Revised English Edition (1957).
24. The younger brother of the economist Ludwig von Mises of the Austrian School of Economics.
25. George Stigler (1911–1991), a Nobel Prize laureate in economics, developed the theory of search unemployment and published "Information in the Labor Market" in 1962.

What you call passion is not spiritual force, but friction between the soul and the outside world.[26]

—*Hermann Hesse (1877–1962), German-Swiss writer and painter*

Structural unemployment, however, is a bit more serious. For this type, there are jobs and there are workers but the workers don't match the job description either in skills or in location. Economies in the throes of major technological change or sectorial[27] shifts see greater amounts of structural unemployment. For example, if coal mines are closed due to environmental concerns, then coal miners are out of work. However, once they go to the job bank they notice two things. All of the jobs—and there are enough for all of them in sheer numbers—require computer skills that they don't have or are located in diamond mines clear across the country. This isn't going to be a simple matching process between workers and vacancies. These folks need one of two things—either retraining or relocation, both of which are costly in terms of time and money. If a worker is older, the costs may be just too high.

The solution is not to protect the jobs that don't make sense like coal mining jobs. Economies need to evolve to produce what will make people happy—and I don't think pollution or cancers are on the list of happiness-must-haves. There are still options to reducing this kind of unemployment. Governments can sponsor retraining programs, pay for relocation expenses or give early retirement settlements to help reduce the size and impact of this kind of unemployment on the economy and its workers. What a government doesn't want to do is slow down technological change (which causes economic slowdown) but keeps these workers in the coal mining jobs. This kind of policy prevents growth in future standard of livings and attracts young people into jobs they shouldn't be in.

We know that an unskilled labourer or a cook cannot immediately get on with the job of state administration.[28]

—*Vladimir Ilyich Lenin (1870–1924), Russian first premier of the Soviet Union*

Seasonal unemployment implies unemployment that happens regularly during some part of the calendar year. Sectors such as agriculture, construction, or tourism can have a significant seasonal component. This in itself doesn't mean there is a problem. Take, for example, an artist who works for a resort in a beach community. During the tourism season, the artist works long, hard hours but he makes enough money to spend the off-season as "unemployed," creating art. If he is truthful when surveyed, he should say that he is out of the labour force in the off-season. But instead, it might be tempting to answer that he is in the labour force as an unemployed worker—especially if it is easy to get government benefits. Once a government has years of data, seasonal movements in unemployment are quite evident. This kind of unemployment isn't true unemployment, and the government shouldn't try to eliminate it altogether. Statisticians use techniques to de-trend the data of seasonal swings, and this data is known as *seasonally adjusted unemployment.*

---

26. *The Glass Bead Game* (1943).
27. Over the past century, Canada has seen many sectorial shifts, from farming to manufacturing to the service sector.
28. *Will the Bolsheviks Retain Government Power?* (1917).

All things have their season, and in their times all things pass under heaven.[29]
—Ecclesiastes 3:1

The kinds of unemployment mentioned so far are either good unemployment or unavoidable unemployment in a dynamic economy. If you add them all up, economists call this the *natural rate of unemployment.*[30] Once a country gets to its natural rate of unemployment, the government can breathe a sigh of relief. The economy is said to be at full employment. Needless to say, the size of the natural rate is of great interest, and different economists can come up with different answers as to what that number is for any particular country in any particular year. Unfortunately it isn't a constant number, but rather a moving target because it can change if technology changes at different rates or if the government changes the generosity of its unemployment benefits. This little point is important because if a government tries to lower unemployment below this natural rate, it can push the economy into inflation. But more on that issue later in the book.

THE BAD AND THE UGLY

Be not overcome by evil, but overcome evil by good.[31]
—Romans 12:21

Cyclical unemployment or the bad kind of unemployment occurs when you can't match workers with jobs because there just aren't enough jobs to go around. It gets its name from the idea that an economy cycles between good and bad years—between expansions and recessions. In a recession, no amount of searching, retraining, or relocating will get everyone hired because firms aren't hiring—at least not at the current wages in the marketplace.

Cyclical unemployment brings us to a discussion about human capital accumulation. One of the problems with unemployment is the potential depreciation of skills that occurs when people are out of work. In a tight economy, new grads may take any job just to be employed. This could change the grads' intended career paths because they miss out on getting the relevant on-the-job training they need for the next job on the path. (Think people with PhDs driving taxicabs.) Although they are technically not unemployed, they are underemployed, and we don't really know how significant this loss in productivity[32] or output is for national well-being.

We have finally come to the central controversy in macroeconomics. Keynes argued that governments need to spend on programs to get these workers jobs and end the involuntary unemployment. Economists, as represented by Hayek, think that the wage structures need to adjust to get rid of the unemployment. One is an interventionist view and the other is very hands-off. We will look at the underlying arguments for each perspective in order to understand their policy recommendations in Chapter 12, Side Views.

---

29. Douay-Rheims 1899 American Edition.
30. Nobel Prize winners Milton Friedman (1912–2006) and Edmund Phelps (1933–) developed this concept, although Abba Lerner (see the Gossip Column for the entrée) laid the groundwork for this idea.
31. Douay-Rheims 1899 American Edition.
32. For a country, average productivity is equal to (real GDP/worker).

FRUITS OF YOUR LABOURS

To do any good you have got to get down to grips with the subject and in human touch with the audience.[33]

—*Sir Winston Leonard Spencer Churchill (1874–1965), British prime minister*

Employment is the precursor to well-being. It allows people to produce, and if the work is paid, they can use their income to buy well-being. If their employment is unpaid, they can still enjoy the fruits of their efforts and be happy. Some things we can measure and some things we can't, but governments need to take this into account the best they can. The unemployment rate can have good and bad components. Governments need to know and understand the difference if they want to do good or at least do no harm.

Emma tweets:

@EvelineAdomait Work is a good thing because it produces well-being. #happy

David tweets:

@EvelineAdomait Unemployment is easy to measure #mostlyrates

Salim tweets:

@EvelineAdomait I didn't know that unemployment comes in types and some is natural. #cyclicalbad

---

33. *Great Contemporaries*, "Clemenceau" (1937).

CHAPTER 8

Good to Grow

Business is always thoroughly sound and the campaign is in full swing, until suddenly the debacle takes place.[1]

—*Karl Heinrich Marx (1818–1883), German philosopher, economist, sociologist, historian, and writer*

Libby shrieks and announces that the breaker had gone out on the stove and that she needs more time to cook her food. She looks frazzled.

Justin puts his arm around her and says, "No worries. We have lots of time." Libby visibly relaxes and smiles at Justin.

Brooke nods. "Yeah, not a problem for me either. I love these appetizers! Salim, tell your mother that I want the recipes. Really great flavour!"

Salim laughs and responds, "My mom is a great cook. In fact, when she was laid off, she made money for the family by preparing appetizers and selling them to a catering company. She doesn't do that anymore, so I am sure she will share her recipes with you."

"How come she doesn't do that anymore?" Emma inquires.

"Running her own business was fine, but when the economy improved, she got her old job back in accounts receivable. She works for a company that imports clothing from Pakistan, and makes more money for a lot less stress."

"I know what you mean," David pipes up. "My dad owns his own business and has about 10 employees. I can't remember a time when he wasn't stressed about either too much work or not enough. When the economy is good he works all the time, and when it's bad he tries to get jobs and worries about having to lay people off."

"All I know is that since my mom's layoff, my parents push school all the time because they want me to get a *good* job as an engineer," responds Salim. "Hopefully, I can get a decent entry-level job once I graduate."

"Didn't Prof. Adomait say that we should make sure we don't graduate in a recession? That we should get good marks so we can keep going to school if the economy is bad?" Emma sweetly chimes in.

Everyone laughs at what seems so uncontrollable and unforeseeable.

AIM FOR POTENTIAL

As enunciated today, "progress" is simply a comparative of which we have not settled the superlative.[2]
—*Gilbert Keith Chesterton (1874–1936), British writer*

Let's take a moment to recap what we know about the real economy so far. It's all about maximizing human well-being, which we know correlates to real GDP per person. This output is produced by people who work in the labour market[3] getting paid with money that shouldn't lose its value due to inflation. In this chapter, we will look at the concept of progress, or positive change, in the growth of real GDP per capita, which we believe implies the advancement of human well-being.

---

1. *Das Kapital*, vol. 3 (1894), was edited by Friedrich Engels and published 11 years after Karl Marx died.
2. *Heretics* (1905).
3. There are other factors of production that also contribute to real GDP growth.

An economy can grow in one of two ways. First it grows in capacity, meaning what was previously impossible now becomes possible. An economy becomes capable to do something it couldn't do before and so has grown. Think of it as giving more space for the economy to grow into. Second, an economy can grow from inefficient to efficiency. In other words, the economy starts by missing the mark and falling short of its potential, but then it starts to make a few changes to end the waste of valuable resources (including unemployed workers) and the economy grows.

Let me illustrate the difference with an analogy. Suppose you are the input (as an author, painter, or songwriter) into the production of some creative output (a book, a painting, a song, etc.). It is possible to raise your potential or grow as an artist by taking instruction from a master in that field. Raising your potential requires that you improve in the skills you bring to the table. But then let's say you go through a lazy phase and produce less output than you could, even though your potential is now higher with the new skills you have acquired. This is inefficient and you know you are not reaching your potential; so one morning you wake up, smell the coffee, and decide to work harder, to the point where the quantity of your work grows again. Both would appear as growth in real GDP, but they are very different stories. We begin this chapter by exploring what determines the potential of an economy, and later we will look at keeping the economy at that potential.

Freedom's possibility is not the ability to choose the good or the evil. The possibility is to be able.[4]

—Søren Aabye Kierkengaard (1813–1855), Danish philosopher and theologian

Every economy has the capacity to produce a certain amount of output (as measured by real GDP) in any given year using the resources it has to work with. I have already written an entire chapter on inputs in *Cocktail Party Economics*,[5] so I won't repeat myself here. Instead, we will briefly look at the major factors of production with an eye on the role governments can play in helping to improve them. Theoretically, if the quality or quantity of these inputs improves, then the productive capacity of the economy also increases from year to year. Potential output is a moving target, which is hopefully ever onward and upward through the march of time. Mathematically, when we plot potential output over many years it should look like a straight(ish) line sloping upward from left to right. For our purposes, you should think of any point on this line as the best we should (but not could[6]) do in that year, given the resources we've got to work with. At every potential level of output, the economy is devoid of recessions, depressions, and inflation. It's an Eden before the fall. Later in the chapter, we will look at the real world, where in any given year we miss the mark and fall short of that ideal. Unfortunately, we do experience the pain of recessions, depressions, and inflation, so we will need to deal with these realities. In subsequent chapters we will try to find the path of redemption and address the possible solutions to these economic problems. (Wow, this all seems quite biblical.)

---

4. *The Concept of Anxiety* (1844).
5. See Chapter 4.
6. We aren't looking for heroic efforts here—just normal and appropriate efforts.

DOING MORE WITH MORE

I give thee all,—I can no more,
Though poor the off'ring be;
My heart and lute are all the store
That I can bring to thee.[7]
—*Thomas Moore (1779–1852), Irish poet and hymnist*

So what do economies normally have to work with on the path to raising their potential? The major inputs include:

1. labour
2. capital
3. land, natural resources, and weather
4. technological change
5. entrepreneurship
6. systems and institutions

Most of the inputs just listed belong to people. Sometimes these inputs belong to different people, but many times the same person can wear multiple hats in the resource market. If a person works for someone, he or she is a labourer; if a person saves and provides financial capital, he or she is a capitalist. Landowners rent their space, inventors invent things and entrepreneurs take risks and start new businesses. It is easy to see how people can wear multiple hats. For example, inventors might start a business using their personal savings and also work long hours for themselves. Essentially, they wear four hats in the economy: inventor, entrepreneur, capitalist, and labour. Maybe someone should get into the hat business!

Many forms of Government have been tried and will be tried in this world of sin and woe. No one pretends that democracy is perfect or all-wise. Indeed, it has been said that democracy is the worst form of government except all those other forms that have been tried from time to time.[8]
—*Sir Winston Leonard Spencer Churchill (1874–1965), British prime minister*

Although it takes individuals to produce the wealth of a nation, individuals live within systems—political, social, and religious. When put into historical context, it seems that governments have the most control over this particular input with the greatest legacy. For instance, democracy is supposed to develop systems "by people for the people" and usually leads to free markets and private ownership of resources. In contrast, a communist system, like that of the Bolshevik Party, began with a slogan of "Peace, bread and land" and led to an economic system of central planning and state ownership. These are very different economic systems, which can change the path of growth potential for their respective economies.

Let's look at the macro issues surrounding the inputs I have listed in turn.

---

7. "My Heart and Lute" in *Bartlett's Familiar Quotations*, 10th ed. (1919).
8. *The Official Report, House of Commons* (5th Series), November 11, 1947.

1. Be-Labouring the Point

The labourer is not a capitalist, although he brings a commodity to market, namely his own skin.[9]

—*Karl Heinrich Marx (1818–1883), German political philosopher, economist, sociologist, historian, and writer*

No matter what system people operate under, most of the productive capacity of a country is connected to labour. The easiest way to measure the output of a worker is average productivity (AP_L). To get that measurement, we simply take the total real GDP (Y) for the country and divide by the number of workers (L) or labour hours worked. This means that

$$AP_L = Y/L$$

which can be rearranged with a little bit of algebra so we can see it from the potential real GDP perspective to be

$Y = L \times AP_L$ (where L is the amount of labour and AP_L is the average productivity of that labour)

There are really only two ways to raise potential output (Y). We either need more workers (L) or the average productivity (AP_L) of a worker must increase. One indicates quantity (more workers) and the other quality (more productive workers). Governments should be concerned with both.

First, let's look at the quantity of labour. In a dynamic economy, we need all kinds of labour to do all kinds of jobs. When events like wars, epidemics, or baby booms impact the demographics of a country, weird things can happen to the number of workers available to do the work.

Much of the poverty in Africa during the AIDS epidemic of the 1980s was due to the death of people in the worker age bracket. For a while, it was the very old and very young who survived. This created further devastation because the economy could not reach a level of output to get the survivors out of abject poverty due to a lack of able-bodied workers. Although it is still socially devastating, an epidemic like influenza, which kills off older people, would have a very different economic impact than what happened due to HIV and AIDS.

FILLING IN THE BLANKS

Remember, remember always that all of us, and you and I especially, are descended from immigrants and revolutionists.[10]

—*Franklin Delano Roosevelt (1882–1945), American president*

Much of immigration policy in richer countries—the ones everyone is trying to get into—connects the privilege of immigration with labour market deficiencies. Often, governments screen applicants for the labour market characteristics they think are needed to

---

9. *Das Kapital Buch II* (1893).
10. *The Public Papers and Addresses of Franklin D. Roosevelt* (1938).

create economic growth. For example, after World War II, starting in 1947, Canada actively recruited Dutch farmers through the Netherlands Farm Families Movement. However, this kind of policy can be a political minefield, as some might think that foreigners come to our country only to take our jobs away from us,[11] and is really a zero-sum game.

Others think that governments don't always know what the labour market really needs or how well foreign workers will integrate into the workforce once they get here. If immigrants become unemployed or underemployed, this is a drag on growth (although those immigrants often have very productive children—moi, for example). The best outcome is for foreign workers to immigrate, create new jobs, and create new real GDP. Fortunately, this has been the historical experience of both Canada and the United States. It hasn't always been neat and tidy, however. In the USA, illegal immigrants have been given amnesty[12] precisely because it would be bad for the economy if they went "home."

Where did you come from, baby dear?
Out of the Everywhere into here.[13]
—*George MacDonald (1824–1905), Scottish writer and pastor*

In many developed countries around the world, fewer young people work to support a larger population of older people who live long into retirement. This is called an *inverted population pyramid*, and this situation should concern governments because it could potentially be economically unsustainable. This can happen fairly quickly. For instance, China, with its one-child policy (often a son), has become a ticking population time bomb. When all those children grow up and get into the workforce they must support a much larger population of elderly parents or even grandparents. (There is also the problem of the disproportionate number of males to females, which makes it more difficult to keep the family line going with the next generation of children to carry the economic load.)

Countries with baby-boomers also have a version of the same problem because boomers are having smaller families and not replacing themselves in the population. Their governments, who recognize where they are headed, may try to influence the fertility of a population by giving tax incentives to families to have additional children. Governments may also target a younger demographic for immigration to obtain a worker pool that will help support the retired population.

THE QUALITY OF EDUCATION IS STRAINED

Books are the true levelers. They give to all who will faithfully use them the society, the spiritual presence, of the best and greatest of our race.[14]
—*William Ellery Channing (1780–1842), Unitarian theologian and preacher*

The second aspect of labour is the quality of worker, which can be increased to improve productivity. Human capital, or the skill level we possess, is usually acquired through education or experience. Governments influence human capital when they do such things

---

11. I recall my dad telling me stories about the hostility toward his family upon arrival. My grandfather purchased a farm using the wages of the oldest three boys (my dad was the oldest at 16). They became hired hands to local farmers. Eventually, all three boys bought farms.
12. http://www.usamnesty.org/.
13. Song in "At the Back of the North Wind."
14. *Self-Culture* (1838).

as decide the level of education to which they are willing to allocate funds. Because an educated workforce is a more productive workforce, all developed countries provide free education through to the end of secondary school. In many countries, governments also partially fund post-secondary education to varying degrees. There exists a lot of debate on the appropriate level of education to fund because of the trade-offs between the quantity and quality of a worker. The longer individuals are in school, the less time they can be in the workforce (quantity), but the greater the human capital they acquire (quality). Governments need to decide what is optimal, and there are a lot of differences between jurisdictions. Sometimes governments shift gears from an academic setting to workplace programs. These include internships, apprenticeships, and on-the-job training or retraining programs that are thought to keep the workforce current in a modern economy.

In his book *The Great Stagnation*,[15] Tyler Cowen points out that America went from a less than 7% secondary school completion rate in 1900 to more than 80% in the late 1960s. He calls this historical event the "low-hanging fruit" in the creation of prosperity. In other words, Cowen feels that one of the easiest things a country can do to be prosperous is to educate its people across the board. We would therefore expect to see less-developed countries that increase their level of education to also experience a similar explosion of growth in output. However, for the already developed countries, we won't see the dramatic increase in potential by focusing on education. That is because we are already highly educated. That kind of growth only occurs in a situation where we go from a very low education level to a very high level. We in developed countries can only hope to maintain our current potential and prevent decline if we continue to educate our children at high levels. It looks like growth will have to come from sources other than improvements in educational attainment.

When it comes to workers, education isn't the only policy in town that affects potential. In order to function properly, labour also needs to be healthy. Keeping people healthy is not that difficult in developed countries, but in poorer regions, things like nutrition, a low rate of sickness, and a safe work environment[16] aren't givens. Obviously when workers are sick or injured, they aren't productive. Typically, when countries get richer they address these health and safety issues to maintain high levels of productivity; however, sometimes new problems can arise due to the nature of an efficient production processes. As we saw in our last chapter, Prof. Layard pointed out that things like psychological, emotional, or mental health problems impact a country's ability to produce effectively. Depressed workers take off more sick days, which decrease their productivity and lowers GDP.

For those of us in developed countries, it appears that efforts to increase the quantity and quality of labour aren't going to help us make great strides in economic growth. Things are good and it is hard to increase human capital beyond levels we currently enjoy. Furthermore, the politics of fertility and immigration are pretty sticky, so governments can't really move quickly in this area. It is therefore time to look at another input to see if it can do the job.

2. You're Such a Capitalist

Capital has its rights, which are as worthy of protection as any other rights. Nor is it denied that there is, and probably always will be, a relation between labor and capital

---

15. *The Great Stagnation: How America Ate All the Low-Hanging Fruit of Modern History, Got Sick and Will (Eventually) Feel Better* (2005).
16. Known as workplace "health and safety."

producing mutual benefits. The error is in assuming that the whole labor of community exists within that relation.[17]

—*Abraham Lincoln (1809–1865), American president*

Perhaps the source of growth is coming from physical capital rather than human capital. For GDP accounting purposes, capital is physical—buildings, machines, and inventories. The best thing about capital is that it makes labour more productive and thereby grows the economy. Wealthy countries usually have fairly high-tech-based production. However, the acquisition of physical capital (high or low tech) requires that business owners use some of their income to buy the capital that will improve their production instead of using the income to buy consumer products. Now if these companies don't have the funds, then other people can provide from their savings in the form of a loan to the business for capital purchases. Either way, somebody needs to be saving in order for business to borrow and invest. Investment is directly linked to savings, with a domino effect on growth. More savings by households should lead to more business investment, and more investment to higher labour productivity, and higher productivity to economic growth. Let's follow the money shall we?

HOW DO I SAVE, LET ME COUNT THE WAYS

But why do people save in the first place? People save from their income because savings gives the promise of future consumption. It is really just delayed gratification: save now so you can buy later. The instruments for saving take many forms: stocks, bonds, bank accounts, and so forth. The pieces of paper or the digital statements that people get represent their savings, and savings can do much from an economic perspective. These savings are usually in financial institutions[18] that transform the savings dollars of households into loans for the physical investments by a business. Economic laypersons just skip a step when they call their savings "their investments" because investing sounds sexier than saving. To the economist, the household saves and the firm[19] invests, with the savings dollars equal to the investment dollars.

The connection between people's savings and business investments is an important one, especially when governments form economic policies and regulations to stimulate economic growth. Developed countries often give preferential tax treatment to savings precisely because of the saving–investment linkage. For example, by providing registered savings plans or tax-free bank accounts, governments reward individuals who save because their interest income is either taxed later in retirement when their overall income is lower or these accounts are not taxed at all. Governments can also do such things as not tax a certain amount of capital gains income on stocks or property. All of these tax policies encourage the citizens of a country to save so that funds are available for business investment. The poor, who generally do not save, may view this preferential tax treatment as unfair if they don't see the connection to growth, but, in truth, this connection is essential.

---

17. First State of the Union address (1861).
18. Financial institutions are called *financial intermediaries* and include commercial banks (loans and mortgages) and investment banks (stocks and bonds).
19. Economist often speak of the "Theory of the Firm."

IN GOVERNMENT WE TRUST

You may be deceived if you trust too much, but you will live in torment if you do not trust enough.[20]

—*Frank Crane (1861–1928), American minister, motivational speaker, and writer*

In order for all of this to function well, savers have to trust investors. After all, savers only have a piece a paper as proof of the transaction—investors, on the other hand, have the use of their hard-earned savings. Governments are uniquely able to provide a certain level of certainty for those doing the saving through the legal system. People want to know that when they put their wealth in a financial institution as savings or "investments," the funds not going to be deliberately jeopardized. Governments can regulate to ensure that there is some measure of honesty and integrity from those using the funds for their businesses by requiring disclosure statements, regulating due diligence requirements, and prosecuting those who engage in white-collar crime. What they can't guarantee is how much savers can expect as a "normal" return on their investments.[21]

The only road, the sure road—to unquestioned credit and a sound financial condition is the exact and punctual fulfilment of every pecuniary obligation, public and private, according to its letter and spirit.[22]

—*Rutherford Birchard Hayes (1822–1893), American president*

On the business side of the saving–investment connection, governments can encourage businesses to actually invest the savings available in buildings and equipment through tax incentives. This use of the savings dollars is preferable to having consumers borrow the funds and accumulate credit card debt. When businesses are allowed to write off equipment purchases and to depreciate their existing capital, they reduce the taxes they would normally have to pay. This tax policy decreases the opportunity cost of buying the physical equipment, and so in theory the business should buy or invest more and create more economic potential.

3. Natural Resources: Blessing or Curse

Behold I set forth in your sight this day a blessing and a curse:[23]

—*Deuteronomy 11:26*

Here is the good news for economic growth: normally when countries possess and invest in their natural resources, it's a good thing. Natural resources provide a comparative advantage in production and become a source of employment and national income. However, there are also some possible downsides to relying on natural resources.

In most cases, natural resources take a lot of capital to extract—more than a normal business. Offshore drilling, for example, needs a lot of specialized equipment to actually build the offshore platform. Once built, they usually fly workers to and from the site and

---

20. As quoted in *Business Education World*, vol. 15 (1935).
21. I highly recommend that you read Chapter 12 in *Cocktail Party Economics* if this seems confusing to you.
22. Speech at New England Society Dinner, Brooklyn, December 21, 1880.
23. Douay-Rheims Bible 1899 American Edition.

often operate heavy equipment in a treacherous environment. The sheer size of the initial investment can make it difficult to develop the resource and generate growth. On top of the cost of the project itself, a country can have vast untapped mineral, oil, or forests, but if the country doesn't have the transportation or hydro infrastructure to operate effectively, then the natural resources sit idle. Foreign investment can play a part in getting these natural resources to market if the investment isn't possible from within the country, but these foreign investors will want the legal-political infrastructure guarantees about the relative safety of their investments. Politically unstable countries will have more difficulty realizing growth because of the cautious nature of investors.

Not only that, if the political system of the country with natural resources allows for widespread corruption, then those natural resources can produce wealth, but it becomes concentrated in the hands of a few and does not improve the lives of ordinary citizens. In fact, the discovery of a lucrative natural resource can make a poor country even more vulnerable to corruption because it can concentrate the potential wealth in a geographical region small enough that it can be controlled by a few people.

There may be a less sinister story about why natural resources can prove to be a curse rather than a blessing. It's possible that the existence of a "goldmine" of a resource leads to government bureaucracy and mismanagement because that resource is seen as a national treasure that must be protected. Governments do not necessarily make good business decisions if they run the business themselves, or if the resource is extracted by the private sector, they can easily raise the costs by unnecessary regulation and interference. Either direct or indirect involvement of government can slow growth.

As to diseases, make a habit of two things—to help, or at least, to do no harm.[24]
—Hippocrates of Kos (460 BC–377 BC), Greek physician

Even in a free-market economy, countries that depend on natural resources tend to experience an appreciating[25] currency as the world demands their currency to buy those natural resources. A higher price for the currency causes the non-natural-resource sectors to find it difficult to sell their goods abroad. For example, manufactured goods are now more expensive to foreigners when both the price of the product and the appreciated currency are taken into account. This is a phenomenon known as the Dutch Disease, coined by the magazine *The Economist* in 1977 because of the decline in manufacturing after the 1959 discovery of a large natural gas field in the Netherlands.[26] Manufactured goods could no longer compete on the world stage once the Dutch guilder appreciated.

If some countries have too much history, we have too much geography.
—William Lyon Mackenzie King (1874–1950), Canadian prime minister

In Canada, the Dutch Disease has become a geo-political hot topic. Alberta's oil-based economy has been blamed for the decline in manufacturing in Ontario and Quebec.

---

24. *On Epidemics*, translated by Francis Adams (1849).
25. If the exchange rate is a flexible (or floating) system, then currency traders use the words *appreciation* and *depreciation* to show what happens to the value of a currency. Appreciating means the currency is rising in value vis à vis another currency. If the exchange rate is fixed (or pegged), then currency traders use the terms *revalue* or *devalue* to show what happened to the relative worth of the currency. A devaluation of the currency means the new fixed rate is lower vis à vis another currency than before.
26. It turns out that in Dutch circles, the gas field and I were born in the same year.

The discussion falls on a right–left divide because politically Alberta has a right-wing conservative government whereas Quebec governments are more left-wing. Economists Jack Mintz and Matt Krzepkowski[27] refute the severity of Dutch Disease in Canada, saying that manufacturing has been in decline for at least 30 years and the dollar has been all over the place during that time period.[28] Overall, the existence and extraction of natural resources has increased the standard of living in Canada, although the benefits are uneven across the country. The most striking example of economic growth is Newfoundland, which became a "have" province because of the development of its natural resources.

WEATHER FORECAST

Nothing—so it seems to me . . . is more beautiful than the love that has weathered the storms of life.[29]

—*Jerome Klapka Jerome (1859–1927), English author*

The weather, and its extremes, can change the productive capacity of a country. When the real GDP includes such things as grains, fruits, and vegetables, the vagaries of sun, rain, and frost can lead to bumper crops, normal yields, or complete disasters. Speaking of disasters—floods, tsunamis, earthquakes, hurricanes, forest fires, and tornadoes can wipe out factories, natural resources, and transportation systems along with workers. So what can governments do? Well, they can't control the weather, but prosperous countries do seem to reduce the impact of the fallout. Just compare the death toll of something like a flood in a rich country versus in a poor country. Rich countries have better building codes, emergency response systems, and cleanup mechanisms to deal with nature's rage. Our well-developed insurance markets also help businesses to rebuild and produce again. But none of the factors mention so far seems to give us much hope for sustained growth, which is why people often think in terms of limits to growth. Time for the silver lining in the cloudy sky.

4. Technologically Adept

The reasonable man adapts himself to the world: the unreasonable one persists in trying to adapt the world to himself. Therefore all progress depends on the unreasonable man.[30]

—*George Bernard Shaw (1856–1950), Irish writer*

Neither Karl Marx nor the Reverend Malthus[31] saw the impact technological inventions would have on economic growth. Technological advancement has been the X-factor that has changed everything in quite revolutionary terms—the Industrial Revolution, the green revolution, and the digital revolution. The developed world has enjoyed unbelievable growth in real GDP through life-changing inventions: indoor plumbing, electricity,

27. http://www.huffingtonpost.ca/2013/03/05/dutch-disease-alberta-ontario-quebec_n_2812298.html.
28. A recent paper by Stephen Gordon supports this finding; see http://policyschool.ucalgary.ca/?q=content/canadian-manufacturing-sector-2002-2008-why-it-called-dutch-disease.
29. *The Passing of the Third Floor Back* (1908).
30. *Maxims for Revolutionists* (1903).
31. Rev. Malthus wrote "An Essay on the Principle of Population" (1798), in which he argued that the subsistence level was inevitable because population growth would outstrip the growth in agricultural products. This is known as the Malthusian catastrophe.

labour-saving household appliances, automobiles, robotics, and the Internet. Try to imagine your life without your cell phone or your home without a toilet connected to indoor plumbing (although in many parts of the world there are more households with cell phones than toilets[32]). Inventions and innovation enhance the productivity of the inputs that we already have. Our future growth now relies on the seemingly limitless supply of knowledge-based technological improvements.

Invention and innovation give birth to capital, which in turn makes labour more productive (although some biomedical inventions might actually make people more productive directly). This is why most governments support education and research in the areas of science, technology, engineering, and mathematics, or STEM subjects for short. Those same governments also provide research and development (R&D) tax credits to support new inventions developed by the likes of pharmaceutical, fuel cell, or computer companies.

With new inventions come patent laws, which can be a blessing or a curse. Patents give temporary monopoly power to the inventors for some specified time. This provides an incentive for them to continue inventing because they receive financial benefits for their efforts. However, the true benefits of an invention are only realized once it gets into the public domain and becomes more widely adopted. Governments have to decide how long a patent should last and balance the incentive for business with the benefits to the wider public. For example, once a drug loses its patent, more affordable generic drugs become available to the public, which increases human well-being overall.

5. Entrepreneur[33] or Undertaker

Applaud us when we run, console us when we fall, cheer us when we recover.[34]

—*Edmund Burke (1729–1797), Irish political philosopher and politician*

In the 1700s, economist Richard Cantillon invested (read "saved") in John Law's[35] Mississippi Company.[36] He was the first person to define an entrepreneur as a businessperson who faces uncertain revenues but certain costs. In other words, entrepreneurs are the risk takers in any business venture. With these great risks, however, there can also be great rewards for them. Entrepreneurs combine all of the other inputs together to actually get a product to market. Without them, resources would be idle. Governments help create the legal and bureaucratic framework that makes it easy for entrepreneurs to start up a business. Of course they can also make it hard by creating too much red tape[37] or incomprehensible processes to legally operate.

---

32. This is partly because indoor plumbing requires more local infrastructure in terms of municipal sewage systems than cell phones, which only require local cell towers.

33. French for "undertake."

34. Speech at Bristol Previous to the Election (6 September 1780).

35. See the gossip column in Chapter 4, Money Is as Money Does.

36. Cantillon got out before the crash and made a fortune. This didn't make the losers very happy, and he was harassed with lawsuits and threats on his life. His home was burned to the ground, and it is assumed he was murdered in 1734. It is also possible he staged his own death to put an end to the harassment and lived the remainder of his life under the name Chevalier de Louvigny.

37. The term *red tape* appears to date back to the 1600s. Charles V used red tape to distinguish important dossiers that needed to go to Counsel of State from lower-level administrative issues, which were bound in ordinary rope and didn't need to go to the council.

FINANCIAL BACKERS

Getting along with women,
Knocking around with men,
Having more credit than money,
Thus one goes through the world.[38]

—Johann Wolfgang von Goethe (1749–1832), German writer, scientist, philosopher, and politician

Normally business owners do not have enough financial capital to adequately fund a start-up, so they need to raise funds. (Start-up is usually the most difficult time to get financing because commercial banks don't really want to lend to people for risky ventures, and almost by definition a new business is risky. Venture capitalists provide a great service in this segment of the market.) Even when a business is up and running, owners need access to funds to operate efficiently because they don't usually get revenue in regular installments even though they have a regular payroll to meet. Here banks provide much needed products such as business loans or lines of credit. In richer countries, well-developed capital markets[39] make it possible to obtain all kinds of different financing arrangements that make it much easier to start and run a business.

However, in many developing countries, the banking sector isn't so well developed, which slows down growth. A recent innovation to get start-up funds into the hands of entrepreneurs in poorer nations is called *microfinancing*, particularly in the form of *microcredit*. As the name *microcredit* says, the financing comes in the form of credit[40] of small business loans. This loan is approved for the expressed purpose of starting up a small business. Microcredit[41] empowers local entrepreneurs (particularly women) to operate a new business and repay those loans. Personally, when I give to aid projects in developing countries, I like to see this as a component because it provides a means to finance entrepreneurs who are so vital to a vibrant economy. I also love to see women empowered through these microfinancing programs because it raises their status in their communities, where they are usually among the most vulnerable and reliant upon others for their well-being. Microfinancing has proven to be a useful tool to get new businesses started and a boon to developing countries. Hopefully, the institutions within those countries will evolve enough to have well-functioning capital markets and not need this form of aid any longer.

6. Institutionalized

Individualities may form communities, but it is institutions alone that can create a nation.[42]

—Benjamin Disraeli (1804–1881), British prime minister and writer

People are social and so live together in societies. Because people need to learn to get along, societies set up systems of governance and institutions,[43] which structure the lives

---

38. Claudine von Villa Bella (1776).
39. "Financial markets: An engine for economic growth" (July 2013), http://www.stlouisfed.org/publications/re/articles/?id=2388.
40. Financing could be other than equity or debt but credit is always debt.
41. Economist Muhammad Yunus (1940–) won the Nobel Peace Prize for the idea of microcredit and microfinancing.
42. Speech at Manchester (1866).
43. Economic historian Douglass North (1920–) won the Nobel Prize in Economics for connecting economic and institutional change.

of ordinary citizens so that things run smoothly. These systems can be formal, through the constitutions and courts of the land, or informal, through the customs and traditions of the people. Some systems are better than others at promoting growth in the economy and well-being among the citizenry.

Economist Daron Acemoglu showed that the economic differences in the colonies of North America and of Africa are rooted in the institutions that were formed by the contrasting motives of the particular colonizers. In Africa, for instance, the level of infectious diseases made it inhospitable for Europeans to set up shop there, and so they approached this continent as an absentee landlord: Extract natural resources as quickly as possible and get out of town. On the other hand, in North America, the Europeans found a potential home away from home, which motivated them to create institutions that turned out to be more congruent with long-term economic growth.

Laws around property rights become an important institutional factor for long-term growth. If you are going to build a home to live in, you want to know that you own it with "all of the rights, privileges and obligations herein." Seemingly simple differences in the legality and enforcement of property rights changes whether research dollars are spend on R&D in North America or in China, whether native peoples living on reserves maintain their homes, or whether homeowners hire armed guards with machine guns at the entrances of their residences as they do in some parts of Latin America. Clearly, defining ownership of both intellectual or physical property and enforcing their protection provides a secure environment on which to build an economy.

Political institutions are a superstructure resting on an economic foundation.[44]
—Vladimir Ilyich Lenin (1870–1924), Russian premier of the Soviet Union

Add to this how a government handles laws, policing, courts, government red tape, government regulations, international relations (especially through trade agreements between counties), cultural and religious beliefs, bribery, corruption, political patronage, lobbyists, and pork barrels,[45] and you can see that economies can look very different from each other even though the underlying mechanism of economic behaviour is very much the same. You see, people still respond to incentives, evaluating the relevant costs and benefits of any decision. Governments, by how they handle all of the things just mentioned, change those incentives, thus causing people to change their behaviour in the economy.

GOSSIP COLUMN: JOSEPH SCHUMPETER

Joseph Schumpeter (1883–1950) was born in Moravia[46] into a bourgeois family. His father owned a textile factory, but he died when Joseph was only four years old. His mother moved the family to Vienna, where she met and married an aristocratic general. This change in social class meant that Joseph attended an exclusive private school. The experience changed him as he adopted the ways of his classmates and appeared to others as part of the aristocracy. The combination of brains and opportunity opened the door for him to attend the University of Vienna, a prestigious school

---

44. *The Three Sources and Three Constituent Parts of Marxism* (1913).
45. Government spending meant to buy support from the constituents for a particular politician.
46. Part of the Austro-Hungarian Empire, which is now part of the Czech Republic.

at the time, to study economics. Once he was done at Vienna, he lived in England, and during this time married a woman 12 years older named Gladys Ricarde Seaver. The marriage was very unhappy and they separated after six years.

He then left Britain to become a financial advisor to an Egyptian princess, and while in Egypt wrote his first book on the nature of economic theorizing, which led to his first job as a university professor. Three years later, his next book *The Theory of Economic Development* launched his career as a serious academic. As fate would have it, after WWI, academia gave way to public policy when he took on the roles of advisor for the German government and finance minister for the Austrian government. These roles were held briefly and without real effect on these respective economies. He then became the president of the Biedermann bank but these were the hyperinflation years and the bank failed. He was personally liable for some of the debt but instead of declaring personal bankruptcy, he paid off his obligations even though it would take a decade.

Despite the financial chaos, he married the daughter of an employee of the apartment building where he grew up who was young enough to be his daughter. He never told people her background but maintained that the year before their marriage she was at finishing school when actually she was working as a maid in Paris. Despite her humble roots, he had been in love with her for five years, and they married when she was 21 and he was in his early 40s. Alas, tragedy struck when she and the baby died in childbirth a year later, just two months after the death of his mother.[47]

He went back to his academic career and left Nazi Germany and Austria to end up at Harvard, where he married for the third time another younger woman. She was the economist (Romaine) Elizabeth Boody, an expert on East Asia economics and politics, who collaborated with Joseph on his book *History of Economic Analysis* (1954), which she edited once he died at the young age of 66 years. She died of cancer in 1953, just 3 years after his death at the even younger age of 55 years.[48] She may have also helped him with earlier writing, but we can't say for sure.[49]

Schumpeter is most famous for his idea of creative destruction. This theory gives a special place to a breed of outsiders known as entrepreneurs, and these entrepreneurs were more than just owners of businesses. These people were the innovators who came up with creative ideas that would destroy existing businesses or if not completely destroy them would severely diminish their importance. These innovative bourgeois entrepreneurs would enjoy temporary monopoly profits until the process and product became routine and the profits became competitive. He believed that these folks were really genetically gifted for this role and were the new elite not because of class but because of talent. Furthermore, these people were his reason for business cycles. Once the entrepreneur created a new invention or innovation, then competitors borrowed to invest. This makes the economy boom. Once the rush to get into the sector is over, the economy cools and heads for a bust until a new entrepreneurial idea comes along. The elite entrepreneur is the force for change and directly contrasts with the Marxian belief that the proletariat is the force for revolutionary change.

Professor Schumpeter maintained that he had three life goals—to be the greatest economist in the world, the best horseman in Europe, and the greatest lover in Vienna.[50] He said he had achieved two of the three goals.

47. Robert Heilbroner, a student of Schumpeter, devoted his last chapter to Schumpeter in the book *The Worldly Philosophers*.
48. http://www.oxfordreference.com/view/10.1093/oi/authority.20110803100447116. http://www.econlib.org/library/Enc/bios/Schumpeter.html.
49. *Joseph Schumpeter: Scholar, Teacher, and Politician* (1992), by Eduard März.
50. http://www.unibg.it/dati/corsi/90014/40787-Economist_Schumpeter.pdf.

THE SINES AND TIMES OF THE LINES

The outstanding faults of the economic society in which we live are its failure to provide for full employment and its arbitrary and inequitable distribution of wealth and incomes.[51]

—*John Maynard Keynes (1883–1946), British economist*

Ok, up to now we have said a lot about how to grow an economy and the role governments can play in raising potential GDP. But what if we fall short of the ideal? Just because an economy has potential doesn't mean that we realize that potential. This leads us to the concept of business cycles. Cycles look like waves that go above and below the potential trend line. See the graph below to get the idea.

Notice from the peaks of the waves that it is possible to be above the potential of the economy. This might seem odd, but we define potential as the normal usage of inputs, not heroic efforts or something extraordinary. Economies can experience heroic efforts at times. But be warned, the negative side effect to this level of activity is inflation. You see, an economy operating at full tilt means that people and machines are working excessively hard and that the level of unemployment is quite low. We all know that machines eventually start to break down and have to be fixed, even if it costs more than normal to get them back up and running. When the economy is red hot, workers get poached away with offers of higher wages and better benefits. During these times, unions negotiate higher wages and often get them because companies can't afford to lose time and profits due to a strike. All of this pushes product prices up, leading to inflation. This phenomenon is called demand-pull inflation because the high demand for goods and services pulls the economy into higher prices.

In contrast, if the cycle is below the trend line then the economy experiences cyclical unemployment, which means that resources that could work aren't working. Not only does this kind of unemployment lead to lost output, but it also causes depreciation of human capital and, if it persists, can lead to the discouraged worker syndrome we talked about before. Long-term cyclical unemployment can permanently decrease economic

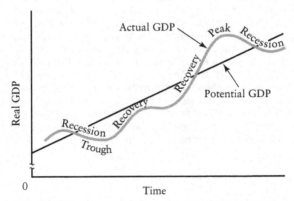

Taken from: *Macroeconomics*, Fourteenth Canadian Edition by Christopher T.S. Ragan.

---

51. *The General Theory of Employment, Interest and Money* (1935).

potential by decreasing the quantity and quality of the workforce. Here is a tip. If you happen to graduate in a recession and you can't find a job in your field, I recommend that you keep going to school to improve your human capital rather than go into the workforce only to find yourself depreciated due to the quality of the work experience.

When an economy is at potential or right on the trend line, unemployment is just low enough to be at the natural rate—not too high or too low to be a problem. In this state, the economy operates at full employment and with no cyclical unemployment. That is why this level of unemployment is sometimes called the non-accelerating inflation rate of unemployment or (thankfully) the NAIRU for short. I know, I know, not every thought needs to be in a name. Think of this as the natural unemployment rate, which can coexist with a stable inflation rate. If the unemployment rate is higher than the NAIRU then the inflation rate must be falling or decelerating. If the unemployment rate is lower than the NAIRU, then the inflation rate must be rising or accelerating. Probably the name[52] should have been the stable inflation rate of unemployment (SIRU), but nobody asked me when it was named.

PICK YOUR POISON

If we are anywhere on the long-run trend line, the unemployment rate is at the natural rate. If the business cycle goes above the trend line, the economy is ripe for excessive inflation. Any time the cycle goes below the trend line, the economy faces recessionary unemployment problems. The distance between the cycle line and the trend line is known as the *output gap*, which records how far off the mark we are—as measured by real GDP dollars. Positive output gaps are inflationary, with escalating prices. Negative output gaps are recessionary, with the ills of unemployment. In the previous graph, we don't see inflation and cyclical unemployment occurring at the same time, which is why economists often talk about the unemployment and inflation trade-off.[53] This means that when governments try to fix inflation they can cause unemployment, while the solutions to unemployment are often inflationary. Staying on the trend line where neither problem exists is a difficult balancing act but, really, that is where we want to be.

CONNECTING THE GAPS

One thing I have learned in a long life: that all our science, measured against reality, is primitive and childlike—and yet it is the most precious thing we have.[54]
—*Albert Einstein (1879–1955), German-born physicist*

The business cycle as seen in the earlier graph is in terms of real GDP cycling above and below the long-term trend line. When off the line, the economy has the problems of inflation and unemployment. Now, we need to connect the size of problems with the actual size of the output gaps or distance away from the trend line. Governments have teams of economists looking for the precise relationship between the various gaps. Let me give you one example.

---

52. Modigliani, Franco, and Lucas Papademos, 1975, "Targets for monetary policy in the coming year," Brookings Papers on Economic Activity.
53. We will deal with the terrible problem of stagflation—unemployment and inflation together—later in the book.
54. Letter to Hans Muehsam (9 July 1951), Einstein Archives.

In 1963, economist Arthur Okun used econometrics[55] to find an empirical relationship between unemployment and output gaps (this relationship is known as Okun's law). Most often, this rule of thumb says that for every 2% deviation from potential real GDP, unemployment is 1% off of the natural rate. For example, if real GDP is 100 million and the natural rate of unemployment is 7%, then an economy producing 98 million has a recessionary gap of 2 million. This is a 2% gap, which means that unemployment is 1% above the natural rate at 8%.

This rule of thumb doesn't necessarily make things much easier for governments in managing the economy. Partially this has to do with the fact that both potential real GDP and the NAIRU are moving targets over time and in order to use Okun's Law, you need to nail down potential GDP and the NAIRU precisely. First, potential output changes when the capacity of the economy changes and the trend line isn't necessarily a perfectly straight line. Second, the natural rate of unemployment changes if any of the (frictional, structural, or seasonal) components of the natural rate of unemployment changes. Furthermore, even if you nail down these numbers, this is a rule of thumb not a "law" like that concerning gravity. The relationship doesn't have to be precisely 2% output gap to 1% unemployment. Nevertheless, this is an important connection and useful information. Governments should try to hit the moving targets.

GOOD GROWTH

The capitalist process shapes things and souls for socialism.[56]

—*Joseph Alois Schumpeter (1983–1950), Austrian economist and political scientist*

We can easily romanticize the past. But make no mistake, those who consider themselves poor in a developed country today enjoy many more comforts than the rich of earlier eras. Advantages like electricity, indoor plumbing, household appliances, and cell phones provide us with a level of quality of life that those in days gone by could only dream about in an afterlife.[57] However, we don't usually compare our lot in life to our ancestors but instead we compare ourselves to our neighbours in the here and now. I think it is good to stop and reflect on the flow of history from time to time. Economic growth provided us with our current circumstances, and it is this same engine that will provide for future improvements in standard of living, as well as the means for raising the fortunes of those less fortunate around us.

In terms of the business cycle, the closer we can stay to the trend line the better. Deviations cause unnecessary hardship, and during the entrée section of this book we will look at what can be done to stay on target. Most economists can agree on the benefits of growth, but for dessert we will look at the controversy surrounding the role governments can and should play in helping us stay on target.

Libby tweets:

@EvelineAdomait It is an increase in the quality and quantity of the inputs that leads to growth. Business cycles swings should be minimized. #growthisgood

---

55. He used data from 1954 to 1962.
56. *Capitalism, Socialism and Democracy*, 3rd Edition (1942).
57. If you are interested in a more in-depth look at growth, read *The Rational Optimist: How Prosperity Evolves*, by Matt Ridley (2010). You can also Google Hans Rosling and the Joy of Stats for a visual presentation.

CHAPTER 9

Taking Stock and Going with the Flows

Think of three Things, whence you came, where you are going, and to whom you must account.[1]
—*Benjamin Franklin (1706–1790), American politician, writer, and inventor*

When the laughing subsides, Justin turns to Libby and asks, "So, how expensive is it to go to grad school?"

"Pretty expensive. Depending on my grades and where I go, it's possible to get some funding from the school as a teaching assistant, but I've been saving from my summer jobs to be able to do this without support from the school. At this point most of it is sitting in savings bonds at the bank."

Brooke jumps in, "I'm going to have to get serious about saving my money if I want to go to law school because I don't think they provide funding and I don't want to take any time off between my degrees. Prof. Adomait says we depreciate in human capital. Besides, I like school."

"I think I'll just break even when I am done with school," says Salim. "Co-op jobs cover my terms but I can't see how it is possible to save. But I think that's fine. I'll have time to save later."

David agrees, "Yeah, you only live once. And I don't see the point of saving now. I want to live a little. In fact, in order to start a business, I'll probably have to go into major debt to make it happen. I'm looking into government programs for start-ups for help."

"So you're planning on becoming a big-shot millionaire?" laughs Emma.

"Hey somebody's gotta be one, and why not me?" David shoots back. "If I'm going to try, I should do it when I'm young and don't have a lot of obligations."

"If you become rich can I marry you?" jokes Emma. "I would love to be wealthy enough that I could concentrate my time on writing a novel."

David rolls his eyes, "Right, sounds like a deal to me!"

Justin and Libby start to laugh as Salim says, "Wouldn't it be weird if any of us actually married each other?"

Brooke jumps in with, "I'm not getting married[2] for a long time, so don't look at me!"

Libby looks at Justin and says, "Yeah, weird—but people do meet at university. Why can't it be in an economics study group? At least we know how to evaluate the costs and benefits of the relationship!"

"Yeah," says Emma, killing herself laughing, "If David and I get married, we are going to invite Prof. Adomait to the wedding as a thank-you for the extra benefits of her course."

David groans and rolls his eyes again.

---

1. *Poor Richard's Almanack* (1755).
2. *Dollars and Sex: How Economics Influences Sex and Love* (2013), by Marina Adshade.
3. Taken from *Capital*, vol. 111 (1894), edited by Friedrich Engels (1820–1895) and published after Marx's death.

IT'S ALL IN THE TIMING

It does not take more time to deal with large figures than with small ones.[3]

—*Karl Heinrich Marx (1818–1883), German philosopher, economist, sociologist, historian, and writer*

To be honest (and I try to be honest), this chapter will feel a bit like "everything and the kitchen sink" because it covers many different kinds of economic concepts (or variables[4]) with the commonality that they have both stock and flow measurements, which are important in understanding how the economy operates. (In the spirit of full disclosure, I have to tell you that this chapter will take a bit of focused attention in order to completely make sense. You might want to go get a coffee.)

I don't want this book to feel like a dictionary, but it would probably be good to give you a basic definition of a stock and a flow and then compare and contrast them with each other. The easiest way to think of an economic stock is to add the word *pile*— stockpile—and then you have the basic idea of a static amount of something. Flows, on the other hand, connote the idea of movement or change. When we have to get to the nitty gritty of actually counting how much is in the stock or how much is in a flow, we need to know that a stock number is calculated at one point in time (pick a point, any point), whereas a flow records numbers between a start and an end date. Stocks and flows are connected because they measure the same economic variable, with flows changing the size of the stock.

Let's look an analogy from nature. A lake on a particular day has a stock of water. The monthly flow of river water feeding into this lake will change the stock value, as will the outgoing flow of stream water leaving the lake during the same month. If the net amount of flows (river water in, minus stream water out) is positive or negative, then the stock of water in the lake on that particular day will be up or down when compared to previous stock values. Normally, stocks are much bigger in magnitude than flows in the scheme of things.

Leaving water aside, there are a plethora of economic variables that have important stock and flow components. This chapter is structured around the key players in the economy and their particular stocks and flows. It turns out that everybody has them. These players include the following:

1. Financial intermediaries, including central, commercial, and investment banks[5]

2. Households of family and non-family composition[6]

3. Firms, which can be incorporated or unincorporated (sole proprietorships and partnerships)[7]

4. Governments, specifically those known as the Department of Finance or the Treasury

5. International counterparts to the first four groups

---

4. There are so many different economic measurements that we will look at that the mathematical term *variable* is probably the best way to cover the breath of ideas.
5. Commercial banks (or retail banks) are the type where most of us do our banking in terms of savings and loans. Investment banks help companies raise capital in the stock market by underwriting the stock offerings and can also help with corporate mergers and acquisitions. Central banks run the monetary policy of the nation.
6. According to Statistics Canada, 85% of Canadians lived in family households in 2011. http://www.statcan.gc.ca/tables-tableaux/sum-som/l01/cst01/famil52a-eng.htm.
7. A little under 90% of Canadian companies are incorporated, whereas this number is over 90% in the USA. "Labour productivity of unincorporated sole proprietorships and partnerships: Impact on the Canada–United States productivity gap," Statistics Canada, http://www.statcan.gc.ca/pub/11f0027m/2011071/part-partie1-eng.htm.

1. Piles of Money

There can be no safer deposit on earth than the Treasury of the United States.[8]
—Thomas Jefferson (1743–1826), American president

Because we measure most aspects of the economy in terms of money, it is worth going back to look at money[9] in the context of stocks and flows. (Stay with me here because this could get somewhat confusing.) The money supply in the economy is a stock made up of the currency in circulation and deposits in commercial banks. When the central bank takes a snapshot of the stock of money in the financial system, it has to decide which types of bank accounts it will include in the money supply and which it will not. Because there are a number of ways to define the stock of money and depending on your choice of bank accounts, we end up with a number of different definitions of money, such as M1, M2+, and M3, to name a few. As the numbers on the right side of M go up, the types of accounts included in that particular characterization of money within the chartered[10] banks get broader. For example, M3 includes foreign currency deposits, which the other M's don't include. The plus signs (+) mean that similar accounts in other financial institutions, such as credit unions or trust companies, get counted as well. Theoretically, the stock of money consists of the total amount of financial "grease" that exists in the system on a particular day, but the details about what constitutes "grease"(or money) depend on what particular economic issue the economist wants to investigate.

The most difficult subjects can be explained to the most slow-witted man if he has not formed any idea of them already; but the simplest thing cannot be made clear to the most intelligent man if he is firmly persuaded that he knows already, without a shadow of doubt, what is laid before him.[11]

—Lev Nikolayevitch Tolstoy (1828–1910), Russian writer and philosopher

This leads us to the quantity theory of money[12] first articulated by Jean Bodin, which states that the total stock of money (M) in the system must equal the total flow of spending on goods and services in the economy (over a time period) multiplied by the number of times each unit of money was used or circulates (during the same time period). Let's look at each component.

The number of times a currency circulates is called the velocity of money (V). Think of it this way. If you have a 5$ bill in your pocket and use it to buy a coffee and dessert, then the bill has been used once. Next, someone comes to the same restaurant and pays

---

8. Letter to Gilbert du Motier, marquis de Lafayette (1825). Jefferson was author of the Declaration of Independence (1776), which occurred in the same year as Adam Smith's *The Wealth of Nations* was published.
9. As an economist, when I say money, I mean something very specific—the money supply. Because money is used to measure other economic variables, people often say things like "I made money last year working at ABC and I invested my money in real estate. I also have money in sitting stocks." Not so. The correct thing to say is "I made income last year working for ABC and I saved part of my income in real estate. I also have part of my wealth in stocks." The use of the word *money* is invariably incorrect in the public sphere. In this book, I have religiously used the term *money* correctly.
10. "Canadian bank balance-sheet Management: Breakdown by types of Canadian financial institutions," http://www .bankofcanada.ca/wp-content/uploads/2012/09/dp2012-07.pdf.
11. *The Kingdom of God Is within You* (1894).
12. An essay by Jean Bodin (1530–1596,) a French law professor as well as a political and economic philosopher, was the first to articulate the quantity theory of money. He assumed that the circulation of money was constant.

for coffee and dessert with a 20$ bill. The vendor hands out your 5$ bill as change to that person, who later uses it to purchase milk. This is the second round of circulation. Cash can change hands many times and has a high velocity or turnover. However, some dollar amounts in bank accounts, such as saving accounts, can sit untouched for quite a while, which means they have a low velocity. As the definition of what constitutes the stock of money (i.e., M1+ or M2+) gets broader, the velocity of those definitions of money drops. Think of it this way, if you have an account that requires you to keep a minimum balance in order to get free chequing, then that minimum balance will probably never leave your account and thus not circulate. This is a low velocity of money.

A shilling changes masters more frequently than a guinea and a halfpenny more frequently than a shilling.[13]
—Adam Smith (1723–1790), Scottish economist and philosopher

The American economist Irving Fisher[14] was the first to formalize Bodin's ideas into an equation. He said that the dollar amount of economic transactions that need to be made with money should be equal to the price level (P) multiplied by the number of transactions (T). A transaction captures the idea of quantity. His equation for the quantity theory of money looks like this:

$$MV = PT$$

(where M is the stock of money, V is the velocity of that stock, P is the price level, and T is the number of transactions over a particular time period)

The left side of the equation contains a stock measure and the right side a flow measure. In words, this equation says that a certain stock of money turning over at a particular velocity[15] is needed to purchase the flow of spending over some particular time period. Theoretically, it isn't a huge leap to replace the total amount of money spent (PT) over any time period with the value of nominal GDP produced in the economy per year. We can do this because the total amount of goods and services produced over a year must have been bought by someone using money or it wouldn't be recorded in the GDP accounts.

We can separate nominal GDP into its components of real GDP and the price level. Real GDP replaces T and is normally given the symbol Y[16] in macroeconomic textbooks. The equation can be rewritten as

$$MV = PY$$

(where nominal GDP = PY, P is the price level, and Y is real GDP)

Now for the implications of this simple equation. We can connect any changes by central bankers to the stock of money with the flow of nominal GDP in the economy. If we assume that the velocity of money is constant,[17] then an increase in the stock of money (M) produces one of two results. It either increases the quantity of real GDP(Y), leading to growth in the real economy, or it leads to inflation (P). These are very different consequences of an increase in the money supply and provide a source of debate between

---

13. *The Wealth of Nations* (1776).
14. American economist (1867–1947).
15. The velocity of money essentially gives the stock of money "movement" to match the flow.
16. Keynes was the first to use the symbol Y for real disposable personal income in the General Theory. Current usage includes a broader idea of real income and disposable income has become the symbol Y_d.
17. Which it isn't, but that is part of the differences between Keynesians and Monetarists, which we will look at later in the book. For now we will just go with the assumption that the velocity of money is constant.

economists. We will add this topic to the stockpile of controversies we will cover in the last chapter of the book. (The pun was intentional.)

NEW MONEY

As a rule, there is nothing that offends us more than a new kind of money.
—*Robert Wilson Lynd (1879–1949), British writer*

We already saw in the first chapter how money is created and destroyed. Every new loan becomes a new deposit somewhere in the banking system and new money is created. If deposits are destroyed, then some of the existing stock of money is destroyed. Now you can think about any changes to the money supply as money flows. The central banks have a key role in this process as they buy or sell short-term government bonds. Recall that the shortest-term forms of government bonds are known as Treasury bills (or T-Bills for short).

When the central bank buys T-Bills from the public on the bond market, the bank puts deposits into the banking system and thus creates money. This is a flow of new money. If, however, the bank sells T-Bills, then it takes deposits out of the banking system, which means it destroys money. The commercial banks then decide how much more money will be created or destroyed because they decide their loan activity. In the first case, they have to extend loans, which creates new deposits (creates more money), and in the second they must call in loans, which decreases deposits (destroys money). The initial action of the central bank gets multiplied by the actions of commercial banks to change the stock of money in the banking system. Both central and commercial banks matter. Central banks buy and sell bonds and commercial banks change deposits by changing loans. Interest rates become part of this story.

INTERESTED?

This interest is the source of his gain.[18]
—*Adam Smith (1723–1790), Scottish economist and philosopher*

One of the reasons people buy bonds is to gain interest. I will give more details about bonds of all kinds when I cover governmental stocks and flows, but this is a good time to take a moment to explain how T-Bills work because of their importance in changing the money supply throughout the banking sector.

T-Bills are short-term government debt instruments[19] with a set face value of $1,000 that sell for less than $1,000, which means that they sell at a discount. The difference between the price of the bond and the redemption[20] value of $1,000 is the return to the investor (read "saver"). Mathematically (and, believe me, sometimes this makes things easier to understand) the return looks like this:

Interest rate[21] = ($1,000 – Price)/Price

(where the numerator is the return on savings paid to the lender and the denominator is the initial outlay)

---

18. *The Wealth of Nations* (1776).
19. There are many different ways to go into debt. If it involves a written contract it is called a debt instrument. These include such instruments as T-Bills, bonds, GICs, CDs, Banker's acceptances, commercial paper, and mortgages or leases.
20. T-Bills are redeemed at some point under a year from purchase.
21. Return in decimals. If you want percent, just multiply by 100.

Note that if the price of the T-Bill changes, then both the numerator (the compensation) and the denominator (the initial outlay) of this equation change as well. When buying and selling occur in the bond market, the price of the bond changes, which implies that the rate of return or market interest rate on that bond has also changed.

DEMAND AND SUPPLY ARE INTEREST-ING

When the central bank sells T-Bills (which we saw decreases the money supply), this also decreases the price of T-Bills in the bond market. In terms of supply and demand, the supply (or sale) of T-Bills has increased, which lowers their price on the market. The difference between the $1,000 face value of the T-Bill and the purchase price widens, which means the interest or rate of return on saving has gone up as well.

If the central bank buys T-Bills, it increases the money supply. The central bank is now on the demand (or buy) side of the bond market and the price of the bonds increases, narrowing the gap between the face value and the bond price. This causes the interest rate or the return on the T-Bill to fall.

If we connect the dots between the changes in the money supply and the interest rates, we see that an increase in the money supply lowers interest rates and vice versa.

MORE INTERESTED?

When a person or business deposits money in a commercial bank, interest is earned on that deposit. The interest rate, then, is the price (or opportunity cost) of holding money because keeping cash on hand means that you give up the additional interest you could earn if you lent the funds instead. When the commercial bank turns around and lends those same funds to other people or businesses, it charges a higher interest rate than what it pays to depositors. The interest rate "spread"—the difference between what the commercial bank pays and what it charges—is the main source of profits for a retail bank.

Normally, when more funds become available in the banking system (because of an increase in the money supply), this also lowers all of the interest rates at the banks, not just the short-term rates as set by the central bank T-Bill activity. The various interest rates posted at your local bank, such as mortgage rates or prime interest rates, are usually connected with each other[22] through various kinds of interest rate differentials. These include the interest rate differences we already saw between deposits and loans, but they also include the spreads between short- and long-term accounts and the premiums between low- and high-risk clients. If the lowest interest rate changes, then all of the other interest rates usually change in tandem. A change by the central bank in the official interest rate usually sweeps through the financial system, changing all other rates of return.

PAYMENTS FLOW BETWEEN ACCOUNTS

Honesty is the best policy—when there is money in it.[23]

—*Samuel Langhorne Clemens (1835–1910), pen name Mark Twain, American writer*

A person lending out his or her savings naturally expects to earn interest as income. Conversely, when the counterparty borrows, he or she sees interest as an expense that needs

---

22. This phenomenon is known as the *term structure of interest rates,* where *term* stands for how long the debt contract is for.
23. Speech to Eastman College (1901).

to be paid. These interest payments flow out of the borrower's bank account into the lender's account. Transfers between bank accounts—because of any market activity—connect the different economic players in the economy to each other. It is time to look at the stocks and flows unique to the various economic players with the understanding that financial intermediaries such as banks or exchanges provide the means for them to connect at all. Let's begin at home.

2. Family Planning

It is impossible to add the stock of money to the flow of saving.[24]

—*Joan Robinson (1903–1983), British economist*

Households[25] earn an income. In terms of GDP accounting, this is a flow. Normally, we talk about annual income rather than other time periods such as monthly (or fortnightly, for that matter) because income taxes are settled yearly. Income taxes are usually collected by the employer and never reach a worker's bank account. We will discuss what governments do with this flow of tax revenue a little later in this chapter. Households can do one of two things with their after-tax wages or salaries:[26] they can spend it or they can save it. What they save and what they spend are also considered flows, and the flow of spending is called consumption. The flow of savings can go to a number of paper assets—such as stocks,[27] bonds, and real assets (e.g., gold and property)—or they can simply deposit the savings in a bank account. There are lots of places to park your savings dollars if you don't want to spend everything you earn. (Although saving[28] seems pretty tough for most people.)

I said before that flows feed into stocks. For households, the flow of savings feeds into the stock of wealth or net worth. There are a couple ways to change the stock of one's net worth. When a family saves, the family's net worth goes up, but if the family makes withdrawals[29] from its savings account and goes shopping for something like a great vacation, the family's monetary wealth declines. (Remember to take lots of pictures, because that is what is left of the trip once it is over.)

"My other piece of advice, Copperfield," said Mr. Micawber, "you know. Annual income twenty pounds, annual expenditure nineteen nineteen six, result happiness. Annual income twenty pounds, annual expenditure twenty pounds ought and six, result misery."[30]

—*Charles Dickens (1812–1970), English writer*

Another way to change the stock of one's net worth is to borrow. Borrowing is a flow that accumulates to generate a stock of debt.[31] As a result, it's possible to have a negative

---

24. *Contributions to Modern Economics* (1978).
25. The word *economics* comes from the Greek *oikos* ("house") and *nomos* ("law or custom"), so the word literally means "rules of the household." I guess the title *home economist* is redundant.
26. When people get their paycheques the amount before deductions is called their *gross pay* and after their *net pay*.
27. Stocks in this case can have both a stock and flow connotation. If the stocks bought and sold are existing shares, then these stocks are really a stock. If, however, a company issues new shares through an initial public offering (IPO) or a secondary or seasoned equity offering (SEO), then these new shares are a flow into the stock market. If a company buys back shares, or goes private, then the flow is out of the stock market and the stock of available shares to trade is down.
28. In 2013, it was a little more than 5% of income, which was a big improvement from the 1.6% savings rate in 2005.
29. This is known as dissavings.
30. *David Copperfield* (1850).
31. "What explains trends in household debt in Canada?" http://www.bankofcanada.ca/wp-content/uploads/2012/02/boc-review-winter11-12-crawford.pdf.

net worth on a household's balance sheet due to debt. Technically, if the stock of liabilities exceeds the stock of assets, then the household can be considered bankrupt.

Let's look at this idea using the asset of a house as an example. When the market value of a house (asset) is worth less than the mortgage (liability), the house is said to be "under water." (So water does come back into the picture as another analogy.) The invention of secured[32] lines of credit makes it easier for a house to go "under water" because the homeowner can borrow against the market value of the home, which reduces the homeowner's equity in the house. Usually this isn't a problem, except if the housing market is actually a bubble and the bubble bursts. Now the house could be worth less than the debt and the house is technically "under water." A couple of bad things could happen next, but let me give you a plausible scenario. The bank might inform the homeowner that his or her line of credit is now frozen. Not only that, depending on the contract, the homeowner may be required to pay off some of the line of credit to get the house into a positive net worth. Banks don't want to evict people, so they offer what appears to be a reasonable repayment plan. But what if you had just come back from vacation with a wallet full of credit card receipts that you had planned to use your line of credit to pay for once the bill came in? Now the homeowner feels like he or she is drowning in debt.

The most deadly kind of debt these days seems to be credit card debt[33] because a person's net worth decreases quickly and imperceptibly as he or she makes impulse buys on things that retain little value after the price tags are removed. Because of the ease with which this debt can be accumulated, people can find themselves in a negative-net-worth situation very quickly. The monthly credit card bill represents a flow and the accumulated total (especially if you habitually don't pay it off every month) represents a stock of debt that, given the very high interest rates on credit cards, is a very expensive stock to maintain.

Nothing is so useless as a general maxim.
—Thomas Macaulay (1800–1859), British politician, historian, and writer

I don't want to give the impression that all debt[34] is bad. It isn't. It depends on the type of asset that the debt has purchased. For example, if a household decides to buy a home or a car, the deal will probably be financed. Normally, lenders such as banks will not extend a loan to potential borrowers with a low net worth, so borrowers for these types of loans either have some money to put down as a deposit or have savings somewhere else on their balance sheet. Borrowing in this way may provide benefits that are worth it. Households may borrow to purchase assets such as a car, which allows them to travel to a job that pays a good income. Or they may borrow for a home, which increases in value over time and also allows them to forego the flow of rent payments. This kind of debt is often prudent depending on the "luxury value" of the item relative to the household's earning potential. Sometimes people have "eyes that are bigger than their stomachs."

---

32. Homeowners use their homes as collateral for the line of credit.
33. "Household insolvency in Canada," http://www.bankofcanada.ca/wp-content/uploads/2012/02/boc-review-winter11-12-allen.pdf.
34. "Household spending and debt," http://www.bankofcanada.ca/wp-content/uploads/2011/02/household_spending_debt.pdf.

HOW OLD ARE YOU?

I should have liked, I do confess, to have had the lightest license of a child, and yet to have been man enough to know its value.[35]
—*Charles John Huffam Dickens (1812–1870), English writer*

The different ages and stages of life can predict if a person is a borrower or a lender. Young people tend to spend more than they earn and therefore must borrow the difference in order to get started out in life. Certainly, going into debt for an education is a good long-term investment in human capital[36]—especially for women.[37] People in mid-life often spend less than they make as they save for retirement, whereas retired people spend more than they make as they draw down their pension funds and other savings in order to support themselves. Franco Modigliani[38] called the pattern of saving based on age the *Life-Cycle Hypothesis of Saving*. This hypothesis basically implies that sudden bursts in income (a big tax return or inheritance) don't necessarily mean big changes in spending patterns. Consumption patterns tend to get smoothed out over time, with households mixing debt, savings, and income in paying for the journey from the cradle to the grave.

LUCKY AND UNLUCKY BREAKS

Unfortunately, we don't always have control of our financial destinies. Sometimes the marketplace can decrease the market value of a person's net worth without him or her doing anything intentional. For instance, during stock market or housing crashes, a family's net worth can crash as well. On the bright side, much of the wealth accumulation of the past 50 years is related to stock market and property gains due to past savings. For the average household, the increase in the value of the home is a major source of wealth.

GOSSIP COLUMN: SIR WILLIAM PETTY

Sir William Petty[39] (162 –1687) was born the son of a tradesman, and by 35 years of age became wealthy and connected to the aristocracy. His descendants would have an inheritance that endured generations because of the fortune he amassed. One of them, the Marquis of Lansdowne, became a British prime minister, albeit for less than one year. So how did Petty do it?

Petty was a bright man who took risks. In an effort to improve his family's clothing business, he earned his passage on a ship to France as a sailor. As luck would have it, he was short-sighted and failed to see a sandbank off the coast of France, endan-

---

35. *A Christmas Carol* (1843).
36. http://www.statcan.gc.ca/pub/11f0019m/11f0019m2013347-eng.pdf.
37. The rate of return on education is higher for women than men because women tend to have fewer outside options for high-paying jobs than men without an education.
38. Franco Modigliani (1918–2003), an Italian-born American economist, won the Nobel Prize for his contributions to the theory of saving in households and corporate finance in business.
39. *The Genesis of Macroeconomics: New Ideas From Sir William Petty to Henry Thorton*, by Antoin E. Murphy (2009).

GOSSIP COLUMN *(CONTINUED)*

gering the ship. The captain was so angry that he had Petty flogged and in the process broke one of his arms. Of no value as a sailor, he was put ashore to recover in Caen on the coast of Normandy. There he impressed the Jesuits, who subsequently admitted him to the University of Caen, where he stayed for one year. He tutored in English and navigation to support himself.

Eventually he went back to England for one year but didn't stay long, as he fled the First English Civil War (1642–1646). He went back to the Continent to study medicine at various European cities, ending up in Paris. He returned to England in 1646 to resume in the family business, but gave up the cloth trade to take up inventing. All of his inventions failed.

Undaunted, Petty went on to an academic career at Oxford, where he became a professor of anatomy. It was here that he resurrected a presumably dead woman during an autopsy before a group of medical students. It seems the fall from the hangman's noose wasn't enough to kill her and Petty saved her life. The woman had been accused of having an abortion, but Petty was able to prove that she suffered a miscarriage instead and ended up saving her from a repeat hanging. His students were so impressed by it all that they pooled some money together to give her a dowry so that she could marry a husband. (This is like every feminist issue in one story!)

In 1651, Petty took a leave of absence from Oxford to become a physician in Cromwell's army, but it wasn't medical care that Petty is most known for. Cromwell needed money to pay his soldiers, and he decided to pay in confiscated Irish lands. This required a survey, and Petty, with a little help from some of his friends, including demographer Captain John Graunt,[40] submitted a tender for the position. Petty was 31 years old when he won the contract, which began in December of 1654. It took less than a year and a half to complete the Down[41] Survey—completed in March of 1656—a logistical miracle involving a team of a thousand assistants applying the principle of division of labour that Petty had observed in the Dutch shipyards. At Petty's suggestion, these workers were paid with the funds generated by a tax on soldiers' pay amounting to one cent for every three acres surveyed.

Now to the part of the story where Petty becomes rich. While waiting for the survey to be completed, the soldiers were given debentures that gave them the right to buy the confiscated land upon the completion of the survey. Many of the soldiers sold their debentures at significant discounts to Petty and other officers because they were short of cash, substantially increasing Petty's net worth. When Petty was paid for his work, he purchased choice land all over Ireland. He also got royalties from publishing a book in 1685, which contained maps of the area he had surveyed.

Needless to say, the folks whose land was confiscated weren't too happy, so disputes came with the territory. One in particular led to a challenge of a duel. Near-sighted Petty, ever quick on his feet, agreed to the duel but only if the place was a dark cellar and the weapon a carpenter's axe, which would level the "fighting field," so to speak. This rebuttal made a mockery of the challenger and the fight never happened.

Once he became wealthy, Petty understandably wanted to remain that way and became obsessed with reducing his tax burden. He argued that the Crown should tax wealth, income, and consumption to extend the tax base beyond the traditional prop-

40. A haberdasher by trade, which may be why clothier Petty knew him. He is most famous for his book *Natural and Political Observations Made upon the Bills of Mortality* (1662), which used simple statistical methods to estimate the population of London. His work was meant to be an early warning system to save the city from the bubonic plague. Unlike Petty, who managed to stay on the right side of the politics as he was favoured by both Cromwell and after the restoration Charles II, he was accused of participating in the Great Fire of London and lost his employment. He died at the age of 53 of liver disease and in poverty in 1674.
41. The survey was "set down" in detailed maps.

erty taxes. This led him to write[42] about the distinction between wealth as a stock and income as a flow. He also connected national expenditure with national income and is considered an early thinker on GDP accounting. Petty, by drawing a distinction between income and wealth, treated labour as a form of (human) capital[43] and labour income as the return on that capital. He found that, even in cold monetary terms, the value of England's stock of wealth in the form of its labour was much larger than the value of its stock of wealth in the form of gold, which was the only thing many people of his time regarded as national wealth.

In his thinking about gold, and its relationship to income and wealth, he developed an estimate for the money supply and the velocity of the circulation of money.

Most of his writings were published after his death and influenced the economic thinkers of the eighteenth century. Petty favoured data-driven analysis over flowery arguments, and economics started to move in his direction.

3. Corporate Statements

The rule of my life is to make business a pleasure and pleasure my business.[44]

—*Aaron Burr Jr. (1756–1835), vice president of the United States*

The stocks and flows of publically traded companies are easy to see because they must produce financial statements as part of their disclosure requirements for the stock exchange. Privately held companies will still produce these statements for internal use and for tax purposes but their stocks and flows are somewhat secret. These accounting documents include the following: income statements, cash flow statements, and balance sheets.

Income statements capture the flows of revenues, expenses, and profits for a particular time period. The most common period is yearly. Cash flow statements are similar to income statements except they only account for dollar amounts that actually go in and out of bank accounts and don't include any income or expenses that are accrued on the books to be dealt later in terms of actual payment. The balance sheet accounts for the stock of assets and liabilities along with owners' equity as of the company's year-end date.

When bookkeepers or accountants do annual statements, they feed income statements (flows) into balance sheets (stocks). Here are a couple of examples. A new equipment purchase (flow) becomes an asset (stock) on the books. Excess profits (flow) that aren't distributed to shareholders are called retained earnings (stock) on the balance sheet. Interest payments (flow) are an expense on the income statement that matches the liability of a loan (stock) on the balance sheet. Essentially, a bookkeeper's job is to keep track of the company's stocks and flows. (I'd rather have a root canal than do this for a living.)

---

42. His publications include: *A Treatise of Taxes and Contributions* (1662), *Political Arithmetic* (posthum.; approx. 1676, pub. 1690), *Verbum Sapienti* (posthum; 1664, pub. 1691), *Political Anatomy of Ireland* (posthum.; 1672, pub. 1691), and *Quantulumcunque Concerning Money* (posthum; 1682, pub. 1695)
43. Canada does not include the value of labour in the National Balance Sheet. http://www.statcan.gc.ca/tables-tableaux/sum-som/l01/cst01/econ02a-eng.htm.
44. Letter to Pichon, reported in *Wit and Humor of Bench and Bar* (1899), by Marshall Brown. Burr is famous for killing Alexander Hamilton in a duel.

INVESTMENTS OF NATIONAL IMPORTANCE

People who count their chickens before they are hatched act very wisely because chickens run about so absurdly that it's impossible to count them accurately.[45]
—*Oscar Fingal O'Flahertie Wills Wilde (1854–1900), Irish writer*

From the perspective of economic growth for a country, the most significant of the stocks and flows is the capital stock and the corresponding flow of investments that business makes. Here we use the word *investments* correctly because businesses buy the physical capital that will generate future income for themselves and their country. In terms of real GDP accounting, this year's investment becomes part of next year's capacity or capital stock. Capacity is so important that even though capital investment isn't a final good or service, we account for it as part of the year's real GDP flows.

The nation's capital stock can grow because of new spending on physical capital, but it can also decline due to the depreciation of existing capital. Buildings or machines depreciate—they wear out or break down—but we don't always have an exact value for how much is actually lost. In Canada, the proxy for the dollar value of depreciation is the Capital Cost Allowance (CCA) found on business tax returns. The CCA allows businesses to reduce their tax bills because depreciation is treated as an expense on the income statement (although not on a cash flow statement because depreciation is accrued on the books and doesn't move in and out of a bank account). The CCA gives an approximate value for how much the existing capital stock has lost in value. This amount is approximate because the government sets the limits on how much a company may depreciate, and this amount may not actually match the actual depreciation of the physical capital. However, approximate is better than nothing.

Architecture is life, or at least it is life itself taking form and therefore it is the truest record of life as it was lived in the world yesterday, as it is lived today or ever will be lived.[46]
—*Frank Lloyd Wright (1867–1959), American architect*

In terms of GDP accounting, we consider new commercial or industrial construction as investment. It isn't hard to understand why a new factory would be a business investment because it can provide more space to expand, a better location to make it easier to sell and transport goods, or specific facilities that will improve performance.

But what about new homes? When homeowners get construction companies to build new houses, the record of those purchases is not found under consumption. For purposes of GDP accounting, statisticians record the transaction as part of an investment made by the construction company. New homes are a flow adding to the housing stock of the country. Housing starts—the requests for permits to build new homes—give us some idea about the anticipated flows into the stock of houses, which is why this activity is reported regularly in the news. Houses can also be torn down, which decreases the housing stock. They also depreciate, which is why we always have a thriving home renovations market. This flow of renovations works to maintain the capital stock at current levels.

---

45. Letter from Paris (May 1900).
46. *An Organic Architecture* (1970).

The strength of a nation, especially of a republican nation, is in the intelligent and well-ordered homes of the people.[47]

—*Lydia Huntley Sigourney (1791–1865), American writer*

Now let's compare the case of buying of a newly constructed home versus the purchase of an existing house in terms of the flow of GDP. In the latter case, there is no change in the housing stock because it was built in previous years and counted toward that year's GDP. The price of an existing[48] home is not included in the investment component of GDP because all that changes is the name of the owners on the title of the property. The services (e.g., legal fees, commissions, and hook-up charges) and the goods (e.g., paint, new carpets, and other types of decoration) associated with house deals are counted toward GDP, but they are classified as consumption rather than investment.

Besides buildings and equipment, inventories are another form of business investment. Inventory investments are costly to businesses, and most would like to minimize the amount of stock on hand. Yet inventories help firms to deliver goods and services to their clients in a timely manner. It turns out that this category is the most volatile and the most telling about the state of the economy. At the beginning of economic upturns, inventories on hand decline because of increased sales, but when the economy slows down, inventories build up and stay on the shelves or in the warehouse. Businesses use inventory control systems to manage production schedules and get the stockroom back to normal levels. The change in inventory is a flow but the inventory on hand is a stock.

RETAINED EARNINGS

All business investment is financed with somebody's savings. The households we looked at earlier contribute to the flow of savings that is lent to businesses through capital markets. But, believe it or not, a major source of savings comes from the businesses themselves through retained earnings. What I mean is that in the flow of income to companies, they keep some profits in their businesses rather than distributing them to the owners through dividends.[49] They do this because the shareholders believe that their savings can make a better return in the company than in their personal possession. When businesses don't have great projects to invest in, they usually distribute the profits through dividends to their shareholders and let them find other places to "invest" their savings in.

4. Public Fun-ds

Government, in the last analysis, is organized opinion. Where there is little or no public opinion, there is likely to be bad government, which sooner or later becomes autocratic government.[50]

—*William Lyon Mackenzie King (1874–1950), prime minister of Canada*

The stocks and flows of government are similar in type to those of households and businesses, but there are usually many households and businesses and very few governments

---

47. Reported in *Dictionary of Burning Words of Brilliant Writers* (1895), by Josiah Hotchkiss Gilbert.
48. In fact, the cost of anything "used" is not included in GDP in any category. Only the value-added costs of the services needed to make the sale are included.
49. Dividends are payments per share of the profits of the company.
50. *Message of the Carillon* (1927).

in a country. This makes government stocks and flows vulnerable to misplaced analogies. You can't just say that because an action by a household is prudent, the same action is also prudent for a government. The impact of a government stock or flow is actually more significant than that for a similar type of stock or flow for a household or a business.

To begin with, governments of all levels[51] produce annual budgets so their constituents know their plans, providing public accountability. In Canada, for instance, the release of the federal budget is presented with great fanfare during a Throne Speech.[52] This ceremony even includes strange rituals, like the one where the federal minister of finance must purchase a new pair[53] of shoes. Think of budgets as precursors to income statements that record the year's activities once the budget year is over. The two salient features of a government budget are income and expenditure projections, basic components of the government's fiscal[54] policy. Let's look at the revenues and expenditure sides of the budget separately.

TAXATION WITH OR WITHOUT REPRESENTATION

Our new Constitution is now established, and has an appearance that promises permanency; but in this world nothing can be said to be certain, except death and taxes.[55]
—Benjamin Franklin (1706–1790), American politician, inventor, and writer

Taxes are an important flow of revenue to the government. These taxes can include income taxes, property taxes, sales taxes, corporate taxes, export taxes, and tariffs on imported goods. Taxes are used primarily to redistribute income among the population, creating more income equity, and as a source of funding for government spending on programs of national importance. I know that most people hate paying taxes, but the hard truth is that countries without a well-developed tax system experience many problems that I would imagine you would want to live without.

In order for a tax—no matter what type—to be acceptable to the electorate, it usually needs some underlying principle of fairness that connects the taxes paid to the ability of the taxpayer to pay them. The best way to do this is to tax either the person's flow of income or the stock of wealth in some proportional way. Let's look at income-based taxes first.

Proportional tax system—With a proportional tax system or constant tax rate, it wouldn't matter if people make $100 or $100,000 because the percentage would be exactly the same for the richer citizens as the poorer ones. Sure, the richer citizens would pay more because they make more, but the proportion would be constant through all the income levels.

Progressive tax system—Here the tax rate increases as you move up the income scale. In this system, a person who makes $100 would pay a lower percentage out of his or her

---

51. These levels can be federal, provincial/territorial/state, and local.
52. Canada is a federal constitutional monarchy. The Governor General is the Crown's representative and reads the speech from the throne to parliament.
53. This tradition may have started in 1868 with Sir John Rose's first budget, and many provincial counterparts have also followed the tradition. Not every minister has followed the tradition. New shoes symbolize "something new" or a new direction.
54. *Fiscal* refers to financial matters; thus companies will have a fiscal year end marking the end of the flow period.
55. Letter to M. Leroy (Nov. 13, 1789), *Complete Works*, vol. 10, ed. John Bigelow (1887–1888).

income in taxes than the person who makes $100,000. For the same level of government tax revenue, the richer person will pay even more tax dollars than he or she would have under a proportional tax system, so understandably, rich people often prefer a proportional tax rate. Canada's income tax system, for instance, is a progressive tax rate system with a higher percentage tax rate for higher tax brackets. Tax brackets are just ranges of incomes on which certain marginal tax rates apply. For example, if you happen to make $100,000 and the system has two tax brackets of $50,000, then the first $50,000 of your income will be subject to a lower tax rate of perhaps 10% and for the second $50,000 you pay a higher rate of perhaps 20%, for a total tax bill of $15,000, or 15% on average. With a proportional tax rate, you don't need tax brackets because one size fits all of the $100,000.

Creeds matter very little . . . The optimist proclaims that we live in the best of all possible worlds; and the pessimist fears this is true. So I elect for neither label.[56]
—*James Branch Cabell (1879–1958), American writer*

It is possible for tax rates to be so progressive that some folks have negative taxes (although most of my high-income friends view all taxes as negative). This means that at some level of income you don't pay taxes at all but instead receive subsidies. This usually occurs if a person is on the low end of the income continuum. For example, welfare, employment insurance (EI), old age security (OAS), and student grants are all given out to low-income individuals. These programs represent an income transfer from one group of citizens to another group, which reduces the income that governments in the middle get to keep. Also for GDP purposes, income redistribution isn't accounted for as government spending but is included in consumer spending. After the redistribution of income, the mix of consumer goods and services bought with that income would change if poorer and richer people buy different things.

Flat tax system—This tax is similar to proportional taxes in that the rate of tax is constant once you are paying taxes, but it is also similar to progressive taxes in that the average taxes paid goes up as income increases. Essentially a flat tax has two rates—zero or no taxes for income that is exempt,[57] and a flat tax on any income after the exempt level of income. To see how this works, we can calculate the taxes paid by two individuals with different incomes who are both allowed $10,000 in exemptions but are then taxed at a rate of 10% on any income over this amount. Suppose the first person earns $50,000 and the second earns $100,000. This means that the first individual will pay taxes on $40,000, or $4,000, and the second on $90,000, which equals $9,000. The average tax rate paid by the lower-income person is 8%, and the higher-income individual pays 9%. Technically, the marginal tax is flat at 10%, but the exemption makes the average tax rate variable depending on the income level.

Regressive tax system—This means the tax rate falls as income brackets increase. In Canada, sales taxes are regressive because a sales tax is only charged on consumption and not savings. Because poorer people consume more of their income than richer folks do as a percentage, the poor bear more of the brunt of sales taxes even if richer people pay more in actual dollars. Let's look at two individual with different income levels to

---

56. *The Silver Stallion: A Comedy of Redemption* (1926).
57. Some policy analysts argue for a guaranteed income supplement to everyone that gets taxed away once income increases.

see what I mean. Suppose one person makes $50,000 and another makes $100,000 per year. Suppose the first person spends $40,000 and the second $60,000 on consumption over the same period. Assuming an easy-to-calculate sales tax of 10%, the government raised tax revenue of $4,000 from the first individual and $6,000 from the second. In terms of tax per dollar of income, the lower-income individual pays $4,000 out of $50,000 or 8%, whereas the second pays $6,000 out of $100,000 or 6%. Notice that the second person pays more in dollars but at a lower tax rate. To rectify the inequity, Canada compensates low-income individuals with sales tax rebates because of the regressive nature of sales taxes once they file their income tax returns.[58]

TAXING WEALTH

Death and taxes and childbirth! There's never any convenient time for any of them![59]
—Margaret Munnerlyn Mitchell (1900–1949), American author

Some might argue that property taxes should be a payment for the flow of municipal services—policing, fire protection, road and sidewalk maintenance, snow removal, schools, garbage collection, and more, depending on the community you live in. But as a tax system, their purposes may be broader than just cost recovery for the benefits of services rendered. Property taxes are also designed to be proportional in nature, with those who own expensive houses (stock) paying more in property taxes than those owning cheaper homes. The theory is that wealth and house quality are correlated. This correlation isn't perfect, as Warren Buffett likes to point out with his relatively modest home. Nevertheless, this is why those who own big houses with lots of bathrooms, multiple garages, a pool, and other amenities pay more property taxes than their less luxurious counterparts in the same community, even if they don't actually use more services.

Some countries, such as Britain and the United States, have estate (or death) taxes. This means as wealth is passed on from one generation to the next, the government taxes a portion of the net worth (stock). Canada abolished estate taxes in 1972, and only the deceased's income (flow)—including interest and capital gains—is taxed when the deceased's executor files the final tax return.

CORPORATE TAXATION

When I am abroad I always make it a rule never to criticize or attack the Government of my country. I make up for lost time when I am at home.[60]
—Sir Winston Leonard Spence Churchill (1874–1965), British prime minister

So far we have only looked at personal income taxes, sales taxes, property taxes, and estate taxes. It is time to look at corporate taxes and find out why they shouldn't be the political hot potato that they are. Recall the idea of a circular flow for a moment. Suppose we have a closed system where all the workers and firms exist in a single country and there is no connection to the outside world. In this world, all the firms are owned by

---

58. It is worth filing an income tax return even if you make very little income just to be eligible for these rebates.
59. *Gone with the Wind* (1936).
60. *In the House of Commons* (April 18, 1947).

domestic shareholders who are members of households and hire workers who also are members of households. For this economy, it doesn't matter whether you tax the households on their personal income or the companies based on their production, because the effects would be the same. In this closed system, everyone one works for a domestic company and every company produces for the domestic market. Let's follow a particular person through the circular flow of income and products and see why it doesn't matter which part of the flow you tax.

Americans are apt to be unduly interested in discovering what average opinion believes average opinion to be; and this national weakness finds its nemesis in the stock market.[61]
—*John Maynard Keynes (1883–1946), British economist*

Suppose we take the case of what economists call a "representative agent." This person is an "average" person whom I will call an average Joe, but with a slight twist on the term *average*. Not only is he an average worker making an average wage, but he is also an average saver because he owns the average number of shares in the company he works for. To see why it doesn't matter if we tax Joe or his company, let's pay Joe. First, he earns a wage and second he gets a dividend on the company's profits. If the company pays the tax, this would leave less income to pay out in wages and dividends to Joe, who we will assume doesn't pay any tax because it was paid by the company. If the company doesn't pay the tax, then more income comes to Joe before tax but it is taken away at the personal tax level if we want to keep government revenues the same. At the end of the day, the amount of after-tax dollars should be the same to Joe. All that changed was who sent the cheque to the government—the company or Joe. In a closed system, even if the company writes the cheque, it is really Joe who is paying.

However, we don't live in a closed system. We live in a world where businesses can shop around to find a country with low corporate taxes and generous business subsidies. In this case, which side gets taxed—the company or Joe—matters, and it all depends on who can more easily move or change countries to avoid the taxes. Countries usually welcome businesses more readily than they welcome immigrants, so companies can move their business operations more easily to other tax-friendly countries than households can. Low corporate taxes provide an incentive to keep local companies in a country or to attract foreign firms to a country. Those businesses provide employment for local workers who can't necessarily follow the jobs out of country. This is why governments usually set corporate tax rates much lower than personal tax rates. (They might even raise more tax revenues as a result.) In a global economy, as opposed to a closed economy, who gets the tax bill does matter.

FAITH, HOPE AND CHARITY

But you, brethren, be not weary in well doing.
—*2 Thessalonians 3:13*[62]

The government also provides tax incentive to individuals or companies when it believes some services or products are better provided by the private sector instead of the

---

61. *The General Theory of Employment, Interest and Money* (1935).
62. Douay-Rheims 1899 American Edition.

government. For example, charitable giving allows households to reduce their tax bills when they give money to organizations that do good works. These are usually services that the government doesn't want to administer directly because the private sector can usually do the work at a lower cost than the government. It could also be that, for political reasons, governments don't want direct involvement in certain areas—the work of faith-based charities is one example. The government then provides tax breaks to contributors but has strict guidelines for the type of work charities can be involved in. Organizations can easily lose their charitable status if they stop doing the "good works" they said they were doing[63] or get involved in areas not deemed appropriate to charitable work.

INCOME PROJECTIONS

If you make the same guess often enough it ceases to be a guess and becomes a Scientific Fact. This is the inductive method.[64]

—Clive Staples Lewis (1898–1963), Irish author and scholar[65]

Even though the government legislates tax rates and subsidy levels, the actual amount of revenues a government expects to get is a bit of a guess—revenues are equal to the average income tax rate multiplied by the actual national income, which isn't known when the budgets are set.

In notation, it looks something like this:

$T = tY$

(where T is total tax revenue, t is the average income tax rate,[66] and Y is national income as measured by nominal GDP. If this is a budget, then national income is a forecast.)

Often governments will deliberately underestimate the forecasted income for the year. That way when the actual numbers come in, things look better than expected. More than that, if the economy happens to falter, then they have some room to accommodate. Either way, the government ends up looking competent, which is very good for public relations.

BIG TIME SPENDERS

Never ask of money spent
Where the spender thinks it went.
Nobody was ever meant
To remember or invent
What he did with every cent[67]

—Robert Lee Frost (1874–1963), American writer

When it comes to the topic of government spending, it would be really easy to go down lots of rabbit trails (or perhaps I should say "rabid," given the high emotions involved).

---

63. Much of the war on terror looks to see if religious organizations with charitable status are really sending money to humanitarian causes as opposed to terrorists groups. http://pointdebasculecanada.ca/articles/1478.html.
64. *Pilgrim's Regress* (1933).
65. His death on November 22, 1963, was overshadowed by the assassination of JFK.
66. This is measured in decimals rather than in percent. For example, 15% is equal to 0.15 in decimals. Percent is a number relative to one hundred but the decimals are relative to one.
67. *The Hardship of Accounting* (1936).

This is the stuff of rant radio and flame war blog posts, and so I just want to give you the big picture and leave others to battle over the gory details.

If you look at the expenditures of a government, they mainly fall into the following broad categories:

1. *Public-sector services offered completely by the government*: Here the government hires the people and provides the services. Usually this means there are departments or bureaus managed by public servants or bureaucrats. Some examples include the departments of defense, finance, justice, natural resources, and oceans and fisheries, to name a few.[68] I think you get the picture, though. Each of these departments prepares budgets, hires staff, and produces public services. Some of their budgets may include services from the next two categories.

2. *Public-sector funding in partnership with non-governmental organizations*: This spending goes to any organization that gets additional funding from non-governmental sources. Post-secondary education is a good example of this because funding comes from student tuitions, donors, and the government. Many arts organizations, such as those producing symphonies, ballets, and operas, would not survive without government grants even though they charge admission and solicit private-sector donations.

   The degree of oversight by the government varies depending on how important this sector is to the public good. For example, the provincial ministry of education heavily regulates allowable tuitions, rules about ancillary fees, and processes around assessing learning outcomes. I don't think the opera gets quite the same level of governmental input.

3. *Public-sector contracts to private-sector companies*: Here governments completely contract out the work but foot (most of) the bill. Some examples include doctors, garbage collection, construction projects of all kinds, and the running of prisons. This is done if the government believes that these services can be provided by the private sector at the same level of quality but at a lower cost. Usually the providers of these services cannot avoid oversight because the government is still accountable for the money even if the government doesn't directly provide the service.

BALANCING THE BUDGET

Let every public servant know, whether his post is high or low, that a man's rank and reputation in this Administration will be determined by the size of the job he does, and not by the size of his staff, his office or his budget.[69]
—*John F. Kennedy (1917–1963), president of the United States*

It's time to bring revenues flows and expenditures flows back together to make a budget (flow). Just to make it clear, let's put it into notation, shall we?

---

68. Department of Finance Canada, http://search-recherche.gc.ca/rGs/s_r?st=s&s5bm3ts21rch=x&num=10&st1rt=0 &langs=eng&cdn=finance&q=spending.
69. State of the Union Address (January 30, 1961).

$B = T - G$

(where B stands for budget, T is net tax revenue, and G is net[70] government spending)

Recall that $T = tY$

(where t is the average income tax rate and Y is national income)

Therefore, this can be expanded to $B = tY - G$

(where t and G are fiscal policy instruments at the disposal of the government to make changes to the economy, Y)

This equation has three possible outcomes for the government budget (B). If B is:

1. Zero—then the government is running a balanced budget.

2. Positive—then the government is running a surplus and is saving.

3. Negative—then the government is running a deficit and is borrowing.

The first two cases are self-explanatory because they look similar to those we have seen before in the cases of households and businesses. The third case, a deficit, is a bit different because of the particular way that governments borrow. Unlike other economic players who heavily rely on commercial banks, the government issues bonds of various types[71] to raise the funds to spend. These bonds include three types, listed in increasing order of importance:

1. *Savings bonds*: Canada savings bonds (CSBs) are very much like guaranteed invest-ment certificates (GICs) sold by commercial banks to the public. Savings bonds are sold through banks on behalf of the government or through company payroll deduc-tions, to individuals who use them as a form of savings. These bonds are not traded on an open market. Instead, individuals must cash in their CSBs at their place of pur-chase. These bonds can be bought in relatively small units[72] with rates guaranteed for the first year, after which the bond interest moves with market interest rates for the remaining nine years to maturity.

2. *Treasury Bills (T-Bills)*: We have already looked at how these bonds work, so I will just compare T-Bills to CSBs. These bonds mature in less than one year, so they turn over quickly and are sold in bigger lots,[73] mostly to institutional buyers such as banks, pension funds, and mutual funds through over-the-counter bond dealers. When the prevailing interest rate changes, it affects the market value of the T-Bill—but you already know that.

3. *Bonds (or debentures)*: More than 60% of government debt is in this form. Similar to T-Bills, bonds are sold through the bond market mainly to institutional buyers in larger lots of bonds. The minimum amount to get into this market is $5,000; however, institutional buyers will often purchase these into the millions. These bonds are more than one year in length with a $1,000 face amount on each bond as well as two coupons attached per year. These coupons are for a fixed amount of dollars and are

---

70. Some government services may have fees to cover part of the cost. Some examples include campsite fees at provincial parks and documentation fees for passports, health cards, and licenses of all kinds.
71. "Consolidated federal, provincial, and territorial general and local governments, financial assets and liabilities," Statistics Canada, http://www.statcan.gc.ca/tables-tableaux/sum-som/l01/cst01/govt07a-eng.htm
72. They come in denominations of $100, $300, $500, $1,000, $5,000, and $10,000.
73. Minimums are $5,000 for three months to a year and $25,000 for one- or two-month T-Bills.

paid semiannually when the coupon is "clipped," or removed from the bond, to be cashed in. The face is redeemed at the very end. For example, the cash flow on a 10-year bond with $30 coupons is: 20 coupons of $30 every six months and the $1,000 face amount when the bond is redeemed. That means the final period will have a cash flow of $1,000 + $30.

Bond prices change due to interest rate changes in the same way that T-Bills do. For example, if interest rates rise then the market value of the $1,000 face and the fixed coupon falls on the bond market. The cash flow isn't worth as much if an investor (read "saver") can buy an alternative savings vehicle that generates more interest for the same initial outlay. This cash flow needs a lower initial outlay to be worth it, and the market forces the bond price to drop in value enough to be equivalent to its interest-bearing competitors.

ALL DEBT IS CREATED EQUAL—WITH SOME MORE EQUAL THAN OTHERS

A national debt, if it is not excessive, will be to us a national blessing.[74]
—Alexander Hamilton (1755 or 1757–1804), American politician[75]

Similar to households or businesses, if governments run deficits it leads to debt. However, there are some major differences. First, people eventually die. Countries usually live on. This means that countries can pass the debts to the next generation. This isn't true for households, which cannot pass on a negative net worth. The least that is possible to inherit from an ancestor is nothing.

Second, governments can fund projects that may have big positive spillover effects on everyone collectively, which individuals may have no incentive to fund privately. These spillover effects may be long term with benefits lasting through many generations. For instance, governments initiate larger projects such as transportation infrastructures (roads, bridges, airports, seaports, etc.), a well-equipped military (pacifist wouldn't normally agree with this category, but I would imagine they are fine with military personnel helping during times of natural disasters, or search and rescue), health programs such as vaccines (to prevent epidemics), education (to promote economic growth), laws (for justice), and so on. These are not programs that individuals can do alone or even want to do at all. Many of these projects have huge start-up costs that current taxation cannot pay for but will certainly outlive the generation that commissioned them. Just as debts are passed on to future generations, so are the assets they create. This kind of debt lays the groundwork for future growth and prosperity. If cities are shortsighted and do not create the infrastructure, such as public transit, to promote growth due to the aversion of debt, future generations, looking back, may not thank them as they suffer through intolerable congestion or the now more complicated construction to bring the system up to snuff.

---

74. *Letter to Robert Morris* (April 30, 1781).
75. One of the Founding Fathers of the USA and killed by Burr in a duel over comments made by Hamilton in a political race that Burr lost.

There is lots of controversy over the acceptable level of debt a country should have, but I will leave that discussion for later in the dessert chapter. For now, I just want to mention that one measure that is used to evaluate debt levels is the debt-to-GDP ratio. This is essentially a stock-to-flow ratio that tries to determine if the country has enough income to afford the level of debt it is under. (This is very similar to a household debt-to-income ratio that banks often use to determine if the household can afford to take on more debt.) One thing is for sure, the topic of government debt raises a lot of political rhetoric, especially if that debt comes from international lenders.

5. Foreign Funds

Dollar for dollar, in or out of government, there is no better form of investment in our national security than our much-abused foreign aid program.[76]
John Fitzgerald Kennedy (1917–1963), President of the United States

Foreign trade, access to financial capital, and a productive workforce are crucial for economic growth. That is why each country has departments dedicated to the task of opening doors and creating trade agreements, managing immigration, and monitoring international capital flows. Specifically, once the door to free trade opens for a country, we see trade flows that become part of the national income flows and that bring with them international financial flows in terms of savings and loans. Our next chapter will look at these flows in some detail.

Right now, I just want to make a couple of comments about the role of aid and debt for developing countries because it is such a hot topic and can help us understand how flows of aid from well-to-do countries can impact the stock of well-being in the recipient countries. It can also highlight the role that a stock of debt can have in the flow of economic growth.

Rich countries provide aid to poorer ones for a variety of reasons. In most cases it's humanitarian, often because of a crisis like a flood, tsunami, epidemic, or famine. It may also simply be part of a longer-term plan to promote development in a poorer country that will benefit not only the country itself but all those around it, providing the prosperity need to create stability in a region. Aid can originate from charitable giving by households or companies (which may link it to their products) or from governments directly. There really is such a thing as the kindness of strangers.

There is always a lot of controversy about foreign aid, and we are not going to go into the details here. The main objection, though, is that it doesn't seem to do a lot of long-term good despite good intentions. People point to such things as systemic corruption, political ineptitude, continued reliance, and bureaucracy as reasons to avoid it all together. Historically, this led to some high-level international meetings, which began in 2002 with the United Nations conference in Monterrey (Mexico) through to the Global Partnership for Effective Development Cooperation[77] in 2012 in South Korea. Many of the participants are part of a global movement[78] afoot to try to increase the effectiveness of international aid.

---

76. This quote was meant to be said at the Trade Mart in Dallas, Texas, on November 22, 1963.
77. http://effectivecooperation.org/.
78. http://www.oecd.org/dac/effectiveness/busanpartnership.htm.

If there is no struggle there is no progress. Those who profess to favor freedom and yet deprecate agitation, are men who want crops without plowing up the ground, they want rain without thunder and lightning.[79]
—*Frederick Douglass (1818–1895), African American abolitionist and writer*[80]

There are two opposing views about the value of aid, which are represented by economists Jeffery Sachs[81] and William Easterly,[82] that are helpful in understanding the complexity of poverty in terms of stocks and flows.

On one hand, we have Sachs, who is positive about the role international aid can make even though he is critical about the underfunding of aid, the unhelpful and unrealistic strings that get tied to the aid, and the unacceptable level of indebtedness of the poor countries on the receiving end of aid. His main idea is that economic growth can be compared to a ladder. Tragically, poor countries can't even get to the bottom rung to start the climb. Consequently, he spearheaded a movement of debt relief (or debt forgiveness) that would "kick start" a country's growth out of poverty.

On the other hand, Easterly sees aid as another form of colonization. He feels that the history of debt relief has often been negative because of corruption. He argues that aid hasn't worked because it ignores the fact that individuals respond to incentives. He also believes that the road to growth is paved with good governance—that energy and money should be spent stripping away the bad rules that lead to poor choices and replacing them with good institutions that promote good polices, such as clear property rights, anti-corruption, tax reductions on capital investment, free trade, and capital mobility.

Needless to say, although the goals of these two approaches are the same—to increase the wealth of poor nations—the means are quite different. Sachs thinks the flow of aid needs to increase and the stock of debt should decrease, whereas Easterly thinks it isn't about the stocks and flows but about the framework within which they operate. This is an important issue and one that I hope in the very near future has economic consensus.

THE WEALTH (STOCK) OF NATIONS

There are two things that bestow consequence; great possession, or great debts.[83]
—*Reverend Charles Caleb Colton (1780–1832), English minister and writer*

If I had to pick one stock to emphasize as the most important for an economy, it would be the stock of net wealth. The flows that feed into the stock of net wealth are producing, borrowing, and saving. Every economic player can do each of these activities. If we aggregate all of the savings and loans by everyone in a country we get:

Total savings = Household savings + Company retained earnings + Government surplus + Net savings abroad

Total loans = Household loans + Business loans + Government deficits + Net international borrowing

---

79. From a speech delivered in Canandaigua, New York (August 4, 1857).
80. Born Frederick Augustus Washington Bailey as a slave.
81. *The End of Poverty: Economic Possibilities for Our Time* (2005).
82. *The White Man's Burden: Why the West's Efforts to Aid the Rest Have Done So Much Ill and So Little Good* (2006).
83. *Lacon; or, Many Things in Few Words* (1823).

Saving is good because it creates available funds, but (and this might seem odd at first) it is the borrowing rather than the saving of each of these players that leads to economic growth—as long as they are borrowing for the right reasons. Households need to borrow to increase human capital, businesses need to invest in physical capital (buildings and equipment), and governments need to spend on public works if the private sector undercapitalizes in a critical area such as transportation, health, or education. It even makes sense for all of these players to borrow from foreigners if they borrow for these right reasons.

In the next chapter we will look more closely at international markets, as they flow into this conversation.

Justin tweets:

@EvelineAdomait Economic variables have stocks and flows. Flows are where the action is as they change the net wealth of nations. #gowiththeflow

CHAPTER 10

International Cheques and Balances

Never have the nations of the world had so much to lose, or so much to gain.[1]

—*John F. Kennedy (1917–1963), American president*

The good-natured ribbing ends as Emma says, "If there is a recession when I graduate, I think I'll just get a job teaching English as a second language in China. It would be fun to travel and see a bit of the world before I settle into a career here."

"I want to get a job with the Foreign Service or the UN. All I know is that I will need a masters to get anywhere, probably a PhD as well," Libby sighs. "I'll be in school for a while."

Salim appears contemplative, adding, "I would really like to be part of an international organization like Engineers Without Borders[2] before I settle into a real job. I want to help at the grassroots level, but I don't think my parents would be happy about it. They would suggest I work for a multinational company if I say I want to see the world, but I'm not sure I want to do that."

"My dad travels for his business a lot but it isn't very glamorous. He really hates flying and the jet lag whacks him out. He also gets stopped at the border a lot . . . which is annoying," says David. "He's thinking of applying for a NEXUS card just to make his life a little easier." After a pause he adds, "I think I will just start a business here and not try to go abroad."

"I want to go to law school, possibly specializing in international law. A lot of environmental problems like climate change are trans-boundary. I am also interested in environmental regulations and trade patterns," Brooke says as she crunches on the veggies. "A lot of school for me too."

The last to speak, Justin says, "I don't know what I want to do, but I think I'll take a year off and backpack throughout the States. I was born there and I have relatives I can stay with. I'm not ready to get a real job!"

ROAD MAP

Aristippus said that a wise man's country was the world.[3]

—*Diogenes Laertius (probably third century AD), Cilician[4] biographer*

The world is a big place. Once a country goes global, it can't help but affect its domestic economy. When we start thinking about the impact of a global economy, economists usually look at the effects of international trade and international finance, which means a discussion about exchange rates is unavoidable.

When I tell my colleagues that I am adding a section on trade to this book, they always respond with, "But that's really micro." They are quite correct that international trade is a micro topic, but the international finance part seems more at home in a macroeconomics book. I think it's worth keeping the two topics together because, as we will see, they really are connected to each other. However, in keeping with our big-picture outlook, I will focus on the roles that key international institutions and national governments play as countries trade with each other and engage in international borrowing and lending.

---

1. Address before the General Assembly of the United Nations (September 25, 1961).
2. http://www.ewb.ca/
3. *Lives and Opinions of Eminent Philosophers*, Book 2.
4. It is located on the northeast end of the Mediterranean Sea. The capital was Tarsus, where the apostle Paul originated.

TERMS OF TRADE

Since trade ignores national boundaries and the manufacturer insists on having the world as a market, the flag of his nation must follow him, and the doors of the nations which are closed must be battered down.[5]

—*Dr. Thomas Woodrow Wilson (1856–1924), American president*

A country that engages in world trade is called an *open economy*, whereas a country that does not is called a *closed economy*. That seems very straightforward so far. (Here is a case where the vocabulary[6] seems to make sense.) Traditionally, the arguments for or against free trade come out of pure microeconomic theory and can be found in Chapter 5 of my book *Cocktail Party Economics*. In case you haven't read it yet, let me give you the incredibly short version of the argument.

Adam Smith and David Ricardo[7] argued that free trade increases the wealth of nations because every country specializes in what it is good at and then trades those items or services for the specialized products or services of other countries. As this continues, the volume of both imports and exports of all countries increases such that there is more stuff overall in the world for all the countries that trade. Open economies experience "gains from trade" and a higher standard of living, whereas closed ones generally do not.

To be fair, even though trade generally causes gains to all the countries that engage in it, you can't just say, "free trade in any particular item always makes a country better off." There is one major economic exception to this general rule. Sometimes a country needs time before it can start to play with the big boys, and so it needs a measure of protectionism in order to get into the game. This is called the *infant industry* case. The idea here is that countries need time to learn the ropes and so need a kind of economic training wheels in the form of limited protectionism. However, this situation should never become permanent because infants need to grow up to be productive and competitive. I only mention this to say that you shouldn't make blanket statements about free trade. The infant industry case is actually rare, but sometimes it provides the theoretical basis for those who want to use this argument to limit trade for less-than-stellar reasons—in order to make personal rather than country-wide gains—and that is a problem.

Making himself very amiable to the infant phenomenon, was an inebriated elderly gentleman in the last depths of shabbiness, who played the calm and virtuous old man.[8]

—*Charles John Huffam Dickens (1812–1870), English writer*

In most cases, countries that "protect" themselves from foreign imports actually reduce the well-being of the majority of their citizens. A clear example of the unintended consequences of protectionism comes from the Great Depression. Trade had been fairly liberal before this time, but because of the severity of the situation, the U.S. government imposed high tariffs (or taxes) on imported goods, hoping to encourage domestic production. This resulted in angry trading partners that retaliated[9] with tariffs on U.S. goods,

---

5. Lecture, Columbia University (April 15, 1907).
6. A more obscure word to describe a closed economy is *autarky*, which means self-sufficient.
7. See gossip columns in *Cocktail Party Economics*.
8. *The Life and Adventures of Nicholas Nickleby* (1838–1839).
9. This is known as a beggar-my-neighbour policy.

which, in turn, harmed the American export sector. Essentially, as a result, world trade came to a standstill and the effects of the Great Depression worsened.

Revenge is the sweetest morsel to the mouth that ever was cooked in hell.[10]
—Sir Walter Scott (1771–1832), Scottish writer

After the Second World War, it was imperative for the USA to help rebuild Europe and to thwart the spread of communism. Part of the Marshall Plan,[11] officially known as the European Recovery Program, was to encourage international trade. However, that was easier said than done because in order to get the world's countries freely trading with each other, every government had to agree to remove its tariffs at the same time. In 1947, the United Nations facilitated a deal between various countries and the General Agreement on Tariffs and Trade, or GATT, was signed. Following the GATT, every few years nations got together for a round[12] of trade negotiations, which included a reduction in tariffs (except for a few key sectors, such as agriculture) until tariffs ceased to be the significant barrier[13] between countries. In 1994, during the Uruguay round, the GATT became part of the World Trade Organization (WTO). Since the inception of the WTO there has only been one more round—in Doha in 2001—but it stalled, with the occasional fits and starts of hopeful activity. At the time of writing this book there has been no luck on ratifying the agreement.

Free trade, one of the greatest blessings which a government can confer on a people, is in almost every country unpopular.[14]
—Thomas Babington Macaulay (1800–1859), British writer, historian, and politician

Despite the failure of the Doha round to conclude, the WTO still provides a framework for subgroups to negotiate as trading blocs. For example, the North American Free Trade Agreement (NAFTA), a free trade area between the three North American countries of Canada, Mexico, and the United States, allows freer[15] movement of goods and services between them. These three countries can each negotiate separate and different agreements with other countries or regions. For example, both Canada[16] and the USA were negotiating separate trade agreements with the European Union (EU) in 2013. Speaking of the EU, the EU started as a trade bloc called a Customs Union, which means that each country trades freely with each other and treats all outsiders the same way.[17]

---

10. *The Heart of Midlothian* (1818).
11. Named after Secretary of State George Marshall. The USA provided funds to help European countries rebuild.
12. GATT had a total of nine rounds, each named after the city it occurred in. Each round remained open until the next round began but the last round in Doha never closed because it was never ratified. The number of countries participating in each round differs because there is a membership process.
13. However, all is not completely positive, and governments shifted to non-tariff barriers (NTBs) to protect domestic businesses from imports. These included subsidies, quotas, rules, and regulations. The WTO does address these issues as well.
14. *Essay on Mitford's History of Greece* (1824).
15. This is not completely free because of rules of origin. Free trade zones don't want outside countries to find the lowest-tariff country to enter the zone, and therefore if one free-trade country wants to sell to another in the zone, it must give proof that the product originated in its own country. Any part of the product that originated outside of the country is subject to tariffs. Once a product gets complicated with many parts, rules of origin are effectively a trade barrier because of the expense to prove origins.
16. CETA is the Comprehensive and Economic Trade Agreement.
17. They don't need to worry about rules of origin.

Today the EU is tightly integrated as an economic and monetary union with a common currency known as the euro.[18]

The GATT has been a powerful force for encouraging trade between countries because it outlined a couple of cornerstones for trade that still apply today. They are as follows:

1. Most-favoured nation (MFN) treatment—This says that if a country has MFN status with another nation, then any removal of trade barriers offered by a particular country to a third country must be automatically offered to those with MFN status even if they aren't part of this particular trade deal. This status always guarantees the best trade treatment for all members, and all members of the WTO have this status with each other.

2. National treatment[19]—Once a product from another country gets inside the country, it must then be treated the same as any domestic product in the same category with respect to taxation or regulations. For example, a foreign car cannot be subjected to tougher environmental or safety regulations than its domestic equivalent.

EXPANDING THE "PRODUCTS"

Whether a transaction be fair or fraudulent is often a question of law: it is the judgment of law upon facts and intents.[20]
—*William Murray, known as Lord Mansfield (1705–1793), British judge and politician*

Back in the day, trade used to be simpler and defined by tangible things such as resources and physical products. However, technology changed all that, and trade now includes such things as consulting, computer programming, cell phone service, and medical services such as x-ray diagnosis provided over the Internet. Thus, the WTO incorporated a General Agreement on Trade in Services (GATS) that broadened the scope of the WTO, which also increased the controversy. Many feel that their sovereign rights as a nation are jeopardized when foreign entities perform key services for profit—especially in the area of the public service, including national defense, telecommunications, and healthcare.

Trade works well as long as everyone behaves properly and trusts each other. It doesn't work so well when one party feels like another is stealing from it. Technology has made production much easier but has also made things easier to steal. Pirating a shipment of grain is much more difficult than stealing a patent or digital music. The WTO addresses these issues with the Agreement on Trade Related Aspects of Intellectual Property Rights (TRIPS), which also thankfully clarifies and provides the framework for developing countries to have access to essential medicines without infringing on patents in the developed world.

---

18. Trading blocs in ascending order to integration: (a) preferential trade areas, (b) free trade areas, (c) customs union, (d) common markets, (e) economic unions, (f) monetary unions, (g) customs and monetary unions, (h) economic and monetary unions.
19. More broadly, national treatment is a cornerstone of international law and applies to all kinds of treaties, not just trade agreements.
20. *Worseley v. Demattos* (1758), *The Dictionary of Legal Quotations* (1904).

AGRI HOLD 'EM

Patience and shuffle the cards.[21]
—*Miguel de Cervantes Saavedra (1547–1616), Spanish writer*

During GATT, the most-favoured nation (MNF) principle caused tariffs around the world to drop quickly. Once a pair of nations negotiated a lower tariff, the deal was automatically passed on to the other GATT members through this provision without multilateral negotiations. The only sector not to enjoy this trade liberalization was agriculture because of the political and social pressures[22] in the USA to protect domestic farming at the inception of GATT in 1947. This exception of agriculture still haunts trade negotiations.

The Doha round stalled because the developed countries wanted to protect their domestic agriculture while developing countries wanted more liberalization in this sector. One of the ways a poor country can break free of poverty is to engage in the trade of goods and services where it has a competitive advantage. Protectionism by rich nations makes this very difficult because a poor nation is most likely to have a natural advantage in agricultural goods because of cheap labour and availability of land. However, the agriculture lobby in developed countries is strong. They use emotionally charged phrases like "food security" to solicit public concern, which in the end puts poorer countries at a disadvantage—countries that actually do have real food problems like the hunger and malnutrition associated with poverty. To make things worse, many poorer countries tax food production because it is the main source of government revenue. In contrast, rich countries subsidize food production or limit cheap imports. The poorer nations just can't compete, to their detriment, making trade liberalization (or the lack thereof) very much an international development issue. Too bad we can't just "rewind" to 1947 and this time "be kind" to future poorer countries.

Even between rich nations, agricultural trade is fraught with every form of protectionism you can imagine. For example, Canada maintains a supply management system[23] for dairy products with a quota on the total amount of dairy products imported.[24] Once the quota is reached, the tariffs go over 200%! This keeps American and European milk products out of the country, which, unfortunately for me, includes cheese.

Despite the failure to come to a general agreement since Doha, talks to reach specific agreements between countries or regions abound. However, even smaller agreements take a long time and sometimes stall because no one wants to give up anything in order to get something in return. Unless these countries are completely complementary in that they don't produce what the other makes, this will prove difficult to do. And just to reiterate the point, agriculture is always a sticking issue. Nevertheless, governments work hard to negotiate open markets for their exporters and try to keep the politically powerful import sector from losing very much.

---

21. *Don Quixote* (1615).
22. "Agriculture in the GATT: A historical account," by R. Sharma, http://www.fao.org/docrep/003/x7352e/x7352e04.htm.
23. Supply management is a quota system that restricts the quantity produced. This raises the price. If cheap foreign milk could enter the market then the price would be driven back down again.
24. http://www.thecattlesite.com/articles/2750/dairy-trade-flows-between-the-us-and-canada.

Once agreements are signed, the WTO provides dispute-settlement mechanisms that allow countries whose rights have been infringed upon in a trade agreement to get a resolution. The WTO also reviews the trade polices of governments around the world.

Courts do not exist for the sake of discipline, but for the sake of deciding matters in controversy.[25]

—*L. J. Bowen,* Cropper v. Smith *(1884)*

The WTO will be busy for years to come, helping the world engage in more trade.[26] Since 1950, the growth in world trade has exceeded the growth in world GDP[27] except in the years 2001 and 2009. Generally, over that time, both trade and GDP have increased, but we shouldn't get too confident about this trend. It can easily go down, as we saw in 2009—the year that took the brunt of the financial crisis of 2008. In 2009, world GDP and trade growth both became negative, with trade declining 12% and GDP 2%. Trade and GDP cycle together, and in terms of creating wealthy nations, trade is certainly part of the prosperity story.

FRIENDS AND RELATIVES

Fate chooses our relatives, we choose our friends.[28]

—*Jacques Delille (1738–1813), French poet and translator*

International trade is of particular importance to Canada, partially because of how much land we have relative to our population. Economists classify Canada as a small, open economy with over 40% of GDP related to trade. This ratio is second only to that of Germany, a large, open economy, whose ratio is more than half of its economy. (The moniker "small" has to do with the amount of real GDP, not our geography.) Due to our latitude, the majority of Canadians live lined up along the U.S. border, and approximately 80% of our trade flows north and south. From the U.S. perspective, trade only counts for less than 20% of U.S. national income, of which Canada is just a part. (In fact, often when economists model the USA, they choose large, closed-economy models.) It is no wonder that trade is relatively more important to Canada than to the USA.

This kind of unequal trade relationship can have tangible consequences for the smaller trading partner. For instance, when the USA changes security measures by having more stringent border-crossing rules or passport requirements, it becomes a trade issue for Canada when our trucks are held up at the border in their travels up and down the continent. Because trade is so much more important to Canada than to the USA, it is usually the Canadians who trek down to Washington looking for ways to keep the flows flowing between our two nations. Once these kinds of trade blockages occur, trade lobbyists start looking for solutions, such as the NEXUS card, which allows low-risk travelers to be preapproved at border crossings for easy access between Canada and the United States.

Special-interest groups often focus on the flood of imports (IM) that happens with trade liberalization, but trade agreements increase the volume of exports (X) as well. In the

---

25. *The Dictionary of Legal Quotations* (1904).
26. http://www.wto.org/english/res_e/statis_e/statis_e.htm.
27. http://www.wto.org/english/res_e/statis_e/its2012_e/charts_e/chart01.pdf.
28. *Malheur at Pitié* (1803).

end, net trade (X – IM) can stay very similar from a national accounting perspective. But things have changed. Remember that it is consumption that ultimately increases our standard of living—this means that the increase in imports makes us happier. We happen to pay for that happiness with our increased exports or by borrowing, which leads us to the topic of international finance.

INTERNATIONAL FINANCE

The importation of gold and silver is not the principal, much less the sole benefit which a nation derives from its foreign trade.[29]

—*Adam Smith (1723–1790), Scottish economist and philosopher*

Capital flows are the monetary record[30] of international trade. In times past, people paid for imports and exports with gold, which was essentially a world currency. Now countries have their own individual currencies, and whenever the trade of goods and services takes place, the participants must also buy or sell currency on the foreign exchange[31] market in order finish the deal. For example, suppose I, an author, export my book to my American brother-in-law Mario who is in the ice cream business. Mario must pay for it with Canadian dollars, which he purchased on the foreign exchange market through his bank by selling his American dollars. For most of us, this goes on in the background, but you can always see the exchange on your bank or credit card statements. This payment is deposited into my Canadian-dollar bank account. Now suppose I want to import ice cream from Mario using the funds in my bank account. I must now sell my Canadian dollars and exchange them for U.S. dollars in order to purchase the ice cream. In effect, the exporting of books pays for the imported ice cream facilitated by currency. Therefore, in my country, the Canadian-dollar amount on the book exports will equal the dollar amount on ice cream imports. The same will be true for Mario; only in his records, both the ice cream exports and the book imports will be recorded in U.S. dollars. In the end, the balance of trade between us is zero no matter which currency you measure it in.

I always understood that barter was the last effort of civilization, that it was exactly that state of human exchange that separated civilization from savagery, and if reciprocity is only barter, I fear that would hardly help us out of our difficulty.[32]

—*Benjamin Disraeli (1804–1881), British prime minster and writer*

Trade flows between countries don't always balance perfectly, however. What if the dollar value of the ice cream purchased by me exceeds the dollar value of the books bought by my brother-in-law? (I really like ice cream and so I order a lot, hoping I can figure out how to get this protected item through customs. If I can't, then I am sitting on the

29. *The Wealth of Nations* (1776).
30. "The Balance of International Payments: the current account (trade) and the capital account (finance)," Statistics Canada, http://www5.statcan.gc.ca/cansim/a46?lang=eng&childId=3760101&CORId=3764&viewId=2.
31. The two main interbank foreign exchange (FX) trading platforms are Electronic Banking Service (EBS) and Reuters' Dealing 3000. These systems tend to specialize in particular pairing of currencies. For example, EBS, the platform developed in partnership with the world's largest banks, specializes in the major pairings, such as EUR/USD, USD/JPY, EUR/JPY, USD/CHF and EUR/CHF, and Thomson Reuters Matching specializes in currencies of the commonwealth (AUD/USD, NZD/USD, USD/CAD) and emerging markets.
32. Speech in the House of Lords (29 April 1879), reported in *The Times* (30 April 1879).

U.S. side and eating it all before I enter Canada. Mario only needs to read one book.) Because no one usually gives something to receive nothing in return, we have a problem. The balance of trade is out of whack and I am in a deficit position because I owe more to Mario than I received from him. (He, as my trading partner, is in surplus position.) Let's just look at what changed hands. I have the ice cream and Mario's payment for the book in my account. Mario has my book and a partial payment for the ice cream. I must pay him more for the ice cream, which I don't have in my bank account. I therefore give him an I-owe-you for the remainder to make up for the value of the ice cream I purchased. I am now in debt to Mario,[33] promising to pay him at some point in the future, hopefully when I sell more books to his fellow Americans.

Most I-owe-you obligations take the form of paper contracts. These include debt instruments (bonds, loans, and mortgages) issued by businesses, governments, or individual citizens as well as partial ownership in the form of stocks or shares in a company. Sometimes the piece of paper is a bigger deal because a foreigner takes outright ownership of a business that makes the goods (direct foreign investment). When everything is said and done, the imports must be paid for, either in current exports or in future ones.

The trade flows around the world tell a back story of international debt. A nation running a trade surplus is essentially an international lender because it exported more than it imported, which means that citizens in other countries owe it payment. A country running a trade deficit can run into problems because it is going into debt to import more than it exports. If those debts become unmanageable, then creditors may call in their debts or foreigners may own more and more of the assets of a country. In the era of global terror, these could include assets of national security such as telecommunications, financial institutions, defense, or transportation, which can pose a significant political problem for governments.

Unite for the public safety, if you would remain an independent nation.[34]
—*Napoleon Bonaparte (1769–1821), French emperor and Italian king*

When you add the dollar value of the real flows of exports and imports (X – IM) with the dollar value of financial capital (IOUs), the value should be zero (as long as we have a record of all of the numbers[35]). This combination is known as the *balance of payments* for any country. Now we have two balances to think about:

1. Balance of trade = Exports – Imports (of both goods and services)
2. Balance of payments = Current account (which includes the balance of trade) – Capital account (financial flows) = Zero

So why do pundits talk about balance-of-payments (BoP) surpluses and deficits when the BoP must balance or equal zero? This has to do with third parties that can change the

---

33. To be honest, my brother-in-law would never allow me to pay the debt. It would be considered a gift as would my book to him.
34. "Proclamation to the French People" (June 22, 1815).
35. In fact, the trade numbers are three times the capital numbers. The reasons are the following. Most countries now use netting payment systems—for example, I owe you $10 and you owe me $7. I actually pay you $3 but the value of the transactions is $17. Also, many firms are multinationals that keep track of the flows in-house, and as such we have no record of the transactions. Last, some capital flows are underground. http://www.econlib.org/library/Enc/InternationalCapitalFlows.html#lfHendersonCEE2-093_figure_033.

financial flows between countries. These are the central banks that use the capital account to change the value of their domestic currency vis-à-vis a foreign currency. Their actions are technically included in the capital account and thus it sums to zero. But what if we separate out a central bank's activities and look at the rest of the BoP? Then it is possible for the rest of the BoP to be in either a surplus or deficit position only to have this excess zeroed by some action of a central bank.

So what exactly can these central banks do? Well, they can buy and sell currency or government bonds (usually T-Bills). For example, if you look at the assets of People's Bank of China—the largest central bank in the world, by the way—you will see that its reserve holdings are mainly U.S. government and institutional bonds. The activity of buying U.S. T-Bills and longer-term bonds makes the USA a debtor country to China and represents a capital inflow to the USA. Thus, the rest of the BoP is in a deficit position if you don't count this Chinese financial capital.

Neither abstinence nor excess ever renders man happy.[36]

—Francois-Marie Arouet, pen name Voltaire (1694–1778), French writer and philosopher

The reason China purchased these American financial assets in the first place was to decrease the value of its currency, the renminbi (which is measured in yuan). When the Chinese sell yuan in the foreign exchange market and buy U.S. dollars, they lower the value of the yuan and increase the price of the dollar vis-à-vis the yuan. They use these dollars to buy American assets. Furthermore, the Chinese central bank can create its currency to sell. The lower-valued renminbi makes Chinese exports relatively cheap, and this led to sustained growth in China's real GDP due to exports. Thus the USA has a trade deficit (it is the importer) and a BoP deficit with China because of the actions of China's central bank.

Obviously, the U.S. government isn't completely thrilled with this appreciation of its currency, especially when its own economy is in recession, but the USA can't really become a major buyer of Chinese yuan to neutralize the impact. You see, the renminbi is not a currency other central banks would want to keep on reserve because China does not have a strong bond market and it controls the amount of currency that can be converted to other currencies. The only place the renminbi is really used is in China, but there is some movement afoot to change this. At some point in the future, China would like the yuan to be a world currency like the U.S. dollar and the euro.

The old saying holds. Owe your banker £1000 and you are at his mercy; owe him £1 million and the position is reversed.[37]

—John Maynard Keynes (1883–1946), British economist

From China's perspective, too much of anything, including American assets, can be excessive. The recent financial crisis decreased the value of U.S. bonds, and as such China has lost market value in its reserve holdings. China is currently trying to diversify those holdings, but there is only so much it can do when the USA is the biggest bond market in the world and the primary reserve currency for all central banks.

---

36. *Sept Discours en Vers sur l'Homme* (1738).
37. *Collected Writings: Overseas Financial Policy in Stage III* (1945).

TIME TO TALK CURRENCY

In truth, the gold standard is already a barbarous relic.[38]
—*John Maynard Keynes (1883–1946), British economist*

We have been dancing around the topic of exchange rates using terms like "reserve currency," and now it is time to look at exchange rates in more detail. Specifically, we want to formalize how governments and central banks change the value of the currency either on purpose or as an unintended consequence of their activities.

Let's start with on purpose. As we saw in the previous section, central banks can change the value of their currency with respect to another currency by selling or buying it on the foreign exchange market. In China's case, it sold yuan to purchase U.S. assets. This activity is known as *fixing* or *pegging* the exchange rate, and only central banks can actually do this. To understand the modern take on this activity we need to go back to July of 1944, just after WWII.

TAKE ME BACK

What's past is prologue.[39]
—*William Shakespeare (1564–1616), English writer*

The place is Bretton Woods, New Hampshire, where leaders from more than 40 nations came for the United Nations Monetary and Financial Conference at the spectacular Mount Washington Hotel. (The grand hotel is now a spa and has a couple of golf courses, but I am not sure the delegates had the time to avail themselves of the facilities.) This conference would be the genesis of the International Monetary Fund (IMF), the World Bank Group, and the GATT. These agreements and institutions would help the world recover from the effects of two wars and the Great Depression and move them into the Golden Age[40] of international growth. It should be noted that Lord Keynes was the British delegate to the meetings and played a key role in the negotiations.

The difficulty lies, not in the new ideas, but in escaping from the old ones, which ramify, for those brought up as most of us have been, into every corner of our minds.[41]
—*John Maynard Keynes (1883–1946), British economist*

One of the agreements was a system of fixed exchange rates similar to the gold standard that reigned from 1871 to WWI, when things broke down. I say similar because the Second World War left many countries without gold, so fixing individual currencies to gold wasn't an option. What the Bretton Woods agreement provided was an additional step that explains why the U.S. dollar is now the biggest reserve currency in the world. Every country would fix its currency to the U.S. dollar, and Americans agreed to fix their currency to gold. It was a de facto gold standard.

---

38. *Monetary Reform* (1924).
39. *The Tempest* (1610–1612).
40. Sometimes called the Golden Age of Capitalism and lasted from 1945 to the early 1970s.
41. *The General Theory of Employment, Interest and Money* (1935).

The IMF was established to manage the system and to provide help if countries got into balance-of-payment difficulties. These countries were those whose fixed rate was pegged higher than the underlying free-market rate. In order to keep the currency value up, the country's central bank needed to buy back its currency, which meant it had to sell the U.S. dollars it kept on reserve. If the overvaluation was chronic, then the country would run out of reserves and need help from the IMF. Often the IMF would re-peg or devalue the currency, and once speculators realized that this was the consequence, they would attack a currency by selling it off, causing the country to lose reserves even faster. Once the currency was devalued, the speculators would buy it back for a profit. (They sold high and bought low. It doesn't matter what order you do this in.)

That is gold which is worth gold.[42]
—George Herbert (1593–1633), English poet and orator

The theory behind fixed exchange rates was to create exchange rate certainty and thus facilitate trade. The system lasted for close to 30 years but ended with President Nixon, who de-linked the U.S. dollar from gold. Here's why he didn't really have a choice. The post-WWII era saw unprecedented growth and prosperity. The Marshall Plan worked and the Bretton Woods fixed-exchange-rate system helped because dollars flowed out of the USA into the world. Most currencies were fixed too low relative to their true market value, so central banks needed to sell off their currency and buy U.S. currency to get back to the peg. (This is similar to the China–USA story from earlier in the chapter.) This meant that the USA ran huge trade and balance-of-payments deficits with most of the world. Furthermore, the USA became a debtor nation and filled other countries' reserve holdings and banks with U.S. dollars. In order to increase the domestic money supply at home, the USA printed money, lots and lots of money, such that it didn't have enough gold to back very much of it at all. Once countries (particularly France) realized this, they demanded dollar conversions to gold, and Nixon put a stop to it.

FIXED EFFECTS

The reader of these Memoirs will discover that I never had any fixed aim before my eyes, and that my system, if it can be called a system, has been to glide away unconcernedly on the stream of life, trusting to the wind wherever it led. How many changes arise from such an independent mode of life![43]
—Giacomo Casanova (1725–1798), Italian adventurer and author

The Bretton Woods system is over, but that doesn't necessarily mean that fixed exchange rates are over. As we have seen with the yuan–US$ exchange, it is possible to fix or peg the currency without involving gold. This brings us back to the IMF. After the demise of the Bretton Woods system, the IMF reinvented itself as an organization responsible for oversight and surveillance of the international monetary and financial system. The IMF not only cares about exchange rates, but evaluates the economic policies of member states with the end of promoting global growth and economic stability. During unstable times, or in its dealings

42. *Jacula Prudentum* (1651).
43. *Memoirs of J. Casanova de Seingalt* (1894).

with developing countries, it provides advice and loans. It also sets the conditions for loans to countries that cannot provide collateral but need funds. (You can't just sit through the advice to get to the loans. You actually have to follow it.) These conditions are usually policy reforms within the asking country aimed at reducing that country's economic problems.

One of the things economists learned through the fixed-exchange-rates regime was the fact that a country cannot run inflationary monetary policies if it has a fixed exchange rate with the USA. (This is not true for the reserve country[44] of the USA, whose case we will look at a little later.) As a condition of funds, the IMF[45] could stipulate that countries with rampant inflation needed to maintain a fixed exchange rate with the USA to tie the hands of their central bankers.

Remember that what pulls the strings is the force hidden within; there lies the power to persuade.[46]

—Marcus Aurelius Antoninus Augustus (121–180), Roman emperor and philosopher

To see how this works, let's look at the idea of purchasing power parity, or PPP. Wait a minute, didn't we see this term when we talked about international real GDP comparisons? Right you are. In the context of exchange rate determination, this idea says that if a particular country has a lower price, then other countries will buy and thus appreciate the exporting country's currency until the overall price (adjusted for exchange rate costs) is really the same across the board. They are at parity, so to speak.[47] Therefore, when international comparisons are made, you need to know both the price of the good in the country and the exchange rate before you can decide which country has the cheaper price.

We are, as I have said, one equation short.[48]

—John Maynard Keynes (1883–1946), British economist

So, why does this connect with inflation? The simplest way to see what is going on is with an equation. (I know, I know—I said no math, but this isn't really math. It's more like a relationship in shorthand.)

The PPP equation is:

$$P_{domestic} \times \text{Exchange rate} = P_{USA}$$

P stands for prices (measured as a price index[49]), and the exchange rate is defined as the number of U.S. dollars a unit of domestic currency can buy. If this exchange rate

---

44. The country whose currency is acting as central bank reserves for other countries.
45. The IMF and World Bank became more neo-liberal in their policy recommendations. The policy recommendations for developing countries endorsed by the U.S. Treasury, the IMF, and the World Bank (all of which are based in Washington) became known as the Washington Consensus, a phrase coined by British economist John Williamson in 1989. The recommendations include privatization of public companies, liberalization of trade and capital flows, and macro polices of low inflation and fiscal austerity. The Washington Consensus was most influential during the Reagan/Thatcher period, but the ideas resurfaced in Europe during the more recent sovereign-debt crisis.
46. *Meditations* (161–180).
47. The parity is never perfect, and PPP can't be used to calculate exchange rates because it assumes all of the goods in an economy are traded. However, we know many services within a country are not traded (such as haircuts or manicures) and their prices are important in the local calculation of inflation. However, this theory does help us understand trends in exchange rate movements even if it can't be used to nail down exact exchange rates.
48. *The General Theory of Employment, Interest and Money* (1935).
49. The basket of goods used to create the price index is the biggest issue for PPP. The iPod index and the Big Mac index are examples of PPP for a single good. The OECD uses a basket called the household final consumption expenditure (HFCE), which overlaps significantly with consumption in GDP accounting, to create its monthly PPP comparisons.

increases, then the domestic currency is appreciating. (This also implies that the U.S. dollar is depreciating.)

Let's see what happens if we have a fixed exchange rate. Suppose the central bank within a country outside the USA increases the money supply and this leads to inflation. The goods of this country are now less attractive on the world market because of their higher prices and people stop importing the goods. This leads to a drop in demand for the currency, and the exchange rate, if allowed, will depreciate. The left-hand side of the equation will stay the same, but prices are up and the exchange rate is down.

However, the central bank has agreed to a specific fixed exchange rate and must therefore stop the decline by buying up its currency to boost the currency's value. This act of buying the currency takes money from deposits at banks and puts it into the central bank, and thus out of circulation, and it ceases to be a part of the money supply. Thus, the requirement to maintain the currency means that the initial increase in the money supply was undone in the end. Effectively, a fixed exchange rate removes the ability of a country to manage its own monetary affairs. If a country suffers from excessive inflation, this constraint isn't necessarily a bad thing.

COMMUNICABLE DISEASES

There is a solidarity and interdependence about the modern world, both technically and morally, which makes it impossible for any nation completely to isolate itself from economic and political upheavals in the rest of the world.[50]

—Franklin Delano Roosevelt (1882–1945), American president

Only the reserve country (the USA) can expand the money supply, but this forces other countries to follow suit if they want to maintain the peg. Let me explain. Suppose now that the USA expands the money supply such that it creates inflation and P_{USA} rises. If the exchange rate isn't fixed, then the domestic currency would appreciate to balance out the quation. This means the U.S. dollar has depreciated.[51] However, we have a fixed exchange rate so the domestic country must respond. It sells its currency and buys the depreciating U.S. dollar, stopping its fall. The domestic currency hits the local banks and, voila, new money. This new money could be inflationary, and if it is, then the inflation that began in the USA is transmitted by the fixed exchange rates to countries around the world. Thus, the saying goes, "when the USA sneezes, we catch a cold."

You can see why countries that wanted to insulate themselves from these inflationary effects opted out of the fixed regime even before Bretton Woods was over. This opting out leads us to the other kind of exchange rate regime—the *flexible* or *floating exchange*, which was (and currently is) Canada's approach for most of the postwar period.

Once an exchange rate is flexible, then increases in exports or imports change the value of the currency. A country that exports more will require foreign buyers to also purchase currency. The currency will therefore appreciate. The reverse is true for imports. If we buy from abroad, then we sell our currency, which will depreciate it when compared to the country we are importing from. If a free trade agreement increases both imports

---

50. From the "Quarantine speech" given on October 5, 1937, in Chicago.
51. This is an interesting observation in its own right. The currencies of countries experiencing inflation should be depreciating.

and exports by the same amount, then the exchange rate shouldn't move very much at all. We have now seen how real trade flows can impact the exchange rate, but what about international capital flows?

RELATIVE INTEREST

We draw compound interest on the whole capital of knowledge and virtue which has been accumulated since the dawning of time.[52]
—*Sir Arthur Ignatius Conan Doyle (1859–1930), British writer*

There are two main concerns facing international investors (read "savers") as they decide which country to park their savings in. One is the return on the investment in percent, and the other is the level of risk for that return, also measured in percent. This means we can collapse both risk and return into a single percentage—a risk-compensated rate of return.

From a nation's perspective, the central bank has control over the official interest rate, which is the rate of return on the safest government debt. All domestic financial markets set their rates of return relative to this lower bound. For example, an individual looking to get a loan will be accessed on his or her level of risk and get charged the interest rate that matches that risk premium on top of the official interest rate. Stocks, because they are relatively risky, will make (on average) a much higher rate of return over a decade than the official interest rate set by central bankers. They need to, or no one would buy a risky asset if a safe one makes the same return.

So what has this got to do with exchange rates? Plenty. Although trade may be at the foundation of international finance, capital markets have taken on a life of their own. Now people and institutions go into capital markets around the world to buy paper of all kinds—stocks, bonds, mortgages, and so forth. Savings has also gone global.

The monetary system is essentially a Catholic institution, the credit system essentially Protestant.[53]
—*Karl Heinrich Marx (1818–1883), German philosopher, economist, sociologist, historian, and writer*

This brings us to central banks again. If a central bank decides to increase the official interest rate, then all other rates of return on assets will also go up in tandem within that country. But between countries we have a different story. Central banks can change their interest rate relative to their neighbours. If the rate in country A goes up but country B's rate stays the same, then investors will leave B with its relatively lower rates and move their funds to country A. This means they must go to the exchange rate market to buy and sell currency to make this transaction happen. In this case, the currency of B will depreciate and A's will appreciate. Big savers chase every percentage point they can get, so much of the activity on the foreign exchange market is related to interest rate differentials set by the safe countries of the world. Higher interest rates lead to appreciating currencies. If a central bank decides to use interest rates to deliberately change the country's

---

52. *The Stark Munro Letters* (1894).
53. *Capital*, vol. III (1894), edited by Friedrich Engels.

exchange rate, this is called a *dirty float* or a *managed float*. Technically, it is a floating exchange rate, but only technically.

When it is necessary, central banks work in tandem. During and after the financial crisis of 2008, central banks around the world coordinated their efforts to drop rates at the same time. This was carefully done to negate any exchange rate maneuvers as each gave their respective country more money to provide the necessary liquidity to ease the pain.

UNINTENDED CONSEQUENCES

I think I am justified—though where so many hours have been spent in convincing myself that I am right, is there not some reason to fear I may be wrong?[54]
—Jane Austen (1775–1817), English writer

Sometimes the fiscal spending on social programs or infrastructure is so focused on domestic issues that it is hard to see how this could impact the exchange rate at all. It seems bizarre that government funding of a local addiction clinic or culverts in a small town can change the value of the currency, but it can. The domino effect (or *transmission mechanism*, as economists like to say) is through the interest rate. If the government has to borrow to spend, then it pays interest. The more governments borrow, the more pressure they put on the interest rate to rise. Once the interest rate increases, the exchange rate appreciates, and thus we have our connection.

OPTIMAL UNION

Unity in things Necessary, Liberty in things Unnecessary, and Charity in all.[55]
—Rupertus Meldenius, aka Peter Meiderlin and Peter Meuderlinus (1582–1651), German theologian and educator

Fixed or flexible, it sounds easy on paper to just exchange currency whenever you want, but this activity has transactions costs. Imagine what life would be like if every city had its own currency. Money trading would become a way of life if you travelled at all. On the other end of the spectrum, imagine if the world had only one currency (essentially a global fixed exchange rate) and one central bank with one world interest rate. As we saw with the Bretton Woods agreement, cracks would form in the system because regions are so different.

Nobel Prize winner Robert Mundell wrote a paper in 1961 on the theory of optimum currency areas, in which he says there are some regions or countries for which a single currency can work. You just need to know the costs and the benefits of a common currency. If the benefits exceed the costs, then it makes sense to go for it.

The major benefits of a common currency are the ability of that currency to act as a medium of exchange over a larger economy and the reduction in transactions costs of exchanging the currency between countries. This openness should increase the volume of

---

54. *Sense and Sensibility* (1811).
55. *Paraenesis votiva pro Pace Ecclesiae ad Theologos Augustanae Confessionis, Auctore Ruperto Meldenio Theologo* (1627).

trade[56] as well as integrate financial markets to a greater degree, making things like credit cards and bonds less costly to use.

The potential costs of a common currency are more complicated to explain but they have to do with the major criteria needed to make a region a good candidate for a common currency. They are as follows:

1. Labour mobility: It has to be easy for people to pick up and leave for employment. There can't be "frictions" due to work visas, licensing or accreditation requirements, workers' rights, language, portability of pensions, and unemployment benefits. The idea is that if work is scarce in one area, then workers should be able to easily move to another area if jobs exist. If it isn't easy to move for work, then different currencies could make the adjustment instead. For example, if unemployment exists in one country, then the level of imports should fall due to the loss of household income. The depreciating currency could encourage the export sector and create jobs. A common currency closes this adjustment mechanism.

2. Common business cycles or correlation of shocks: If countries have similar economic experiences, then the benefits of a separate currency diminish. The exchange rate isn't needed as a shock absorber between countries if everyone experiences the same shocks in the same way.

3. Similar inflation rates across the region: Because a common currency operates like a fixed exchange rate, inflation from one region can spread to another.

4. Automatic risk sharing through government fiscal spending and taxation programs: Because a common currency removes a country's ability to have independent monetary policy, it will need fiscal policy to remove any imbalances in economies across the region. Countries that prosper will have to share tax revenue with those that do not because the suffering region cannot just depreciate its currency or use monetary policy to solve the problem.

EURO TALKING TO ME

Reality is never a golden age.[57]

—*Joan Robinson (1903–1983), British economist*

The most recent example of a common currency is the euro. First, the good news. Trade within the euro zone and the size of the capital markets have increased, and the common currency can take the credit for that. Now, the bad news. It seems some of the qualities needed to make a good currency area weren't met, which explains some of the problems the area is experiencing.

1. Labour isn't particularly mobile,[58] as seen by the massively different unemployment rates throughout the EU. It could be because of language and cultural differences. It

---

56. "A model of an optimum currency area," 2008, by Luca Antonio Ricci, http://www.economics-ejournal.org/economics/journalarticles/2008-8.

57. *Economic Heresies* (1971).

58. "Labour mobility in the euro area," September 2011, Deutsche Bank Research, http://www.dbresearch.com/PROD/DBR_INTERNET_EN-PROD/PROD0000000000278645.PDF.

could also just be due to the structural unemployment, where the skills of the applicants in one region don't match the job openings[59] in another.

2. The external shock of a global financial crisis did not impact each of the euro-zone countries in the same way. Some were hit harder than others due to differences in national debt levels and the importance of commercial banking within each country.

3. European countries that have done well are reluctant to "bail out" countries that didn't do so well. In fact, this lack of helpfulness was enshrined in the Maastricht Treaty[60] in its "no bail-out clause." The European sovereign-debt crisis changed all that with the creation of the temporary European Financial Stability Facility (EFSF) in 2010, whose mandate was to preserve financial stability by giving aid to member countries in difficulty. The bail-outs began and haven't stopped, with the money coming from EU states and from the IMF. In 2012, the permanent European Stability Mechanism (ESM) was established to handle all new bail-outs from here on out. One thing is for sure, if the euro is going to survive, euro-zone countries have to become more fiscally integrated and practice more fiscal federalism.

TRUE NORTH STRONG AND FREE

[On leaving England at the age of seven.] "My parents migrated to Canada in 1876, and I decided to go with them."[61]
—*Stephen Butler Leacock (1869–1944), Canadian writer and economist*

The EU could take a few pointers from Canada on how to do this. Essentially, Canada is a federation of provinces and territories with the two official languages of English and French. The provincial governments control their own fiscal policy over most of the important things—provincial taxation, education, healthcare, social services, and natural resources—but have a common currency and monetary policy with the rest of the country. Canada, through federal taxation, also has automatic transfer payments from the richer provinces to the poorer to equalize the impact of economic disturbances. Labour is relatively mobile in theory, but people tend to work and then come "home" again. There are certainly cultural differences across the country that make coming home attractive. Many of the barriers to mobility because of licensing issues have been removed through the efforts of the Forum of Labour Market Ministers—Labour Mobility Coordinating Group (FLMM-LMCG). Wow! I wonder if anyone ever remembers this acronym. One occupation that is not mobile is the legal profession—probably because of the interplay between provincial and federal law, you need specialized provincial training be an effective lawyer. From the EU's perspective, Canada is a terrific model to emulate. It may be because Mundell, the "father of the euro," was a Canadian that he so clearly saw the possibilities and the requirements of a successful currency union.

---

59. "Euro area labour markets and the crisis," Structural Issues Report, October 2012, European Central Bank, http://www.ecb.int/pub/pdf/other/euroarealabourmarketsandthecrisis201210en.pdf.
60. This is the treaty that created the European Union, which ultimately led to the euro.
61. *Sunshine Sketches of a Little Town* (1912).

GOSSIP COLUMN: ROBERT MUNDELL

Robert Mundell (1932–) grew up in Kingston, Ontario, and attended a one-room schoolhouse, which seems old-fashioned but the first year of my schooling was also in one, so I won't make much of it. Somewhere along the way he went to high school in Maple Ridge, British Columbia. (When he won the Nobel Prize he used $2,000 from his winnings to host 37 of his classmates at their 50th anniversary at a nearby golf course.[62]) He earned his undergraduate degree from the University of British Columbia (UBC). For graduate studies he moved just south of the BC border to the University of Seattle in Washington State, where he got his MA. Then it was off to MIT to complete his PhD in 1956. He did part of his doctoral studies at the London School of Economics, working with his MIT thesis supervisor (a future Nobel Prize winner) James Meade on international capital movements. Then it was back to the USA for a post-doc at the University of Chicago. It looks like Mundell became a very mobile student.

He continued to move, teaching at universities all over the world, including the John Hopkins Bologna Center of Advanced International Studies in Italy, where he fell in love with the country. (Later, in 1969, he would buy a run-down, 65-room, twelfth-century castle in Siena and restore it as his home—his Nobel Prize winnings would come in handy here. He says the purchase was a hedge against inflation, but that argument only matters if he sells the place, and it doesn't sound like he wants to. But back to the main story.)

In 1961, he published the Nobel-Prize-winning paper "A Theory of Optimum Currency Areas" in the prestigious *American Economic Review*, called the AER by economists. Most would give their right arm to publish in this journal. Needless to say, he caught the eye of the IMF leadership and the organization actively recruited him. He stayed at the IMF from 1961 to 1963, working for Marcus Flemming. It was at the IMF that Mundell wrote about the impotence of monetary policy if exchange rates were fixed. He also showed that fiscal policy was a very powerful tool when rates were pegged because interest rates don't rise within the country. This model is called the Mundell-Flemming model after the two researchers who independently came to the same conclusions.[63]

After the stint at the IMF, Mundell went back to the University of Chicago, the home of Nobel Prize winners galore and the Chicago School of Economics, which isn't a place but a school of thought popularized by Milton Friedman. Near the end of the Bretton Woods agreement, a conflict broke out between Freidman and Mundell about whether the USA should float or fix its exchange rate against the currencies of the world. The exchange rate floated and Mundell lost.[64] Wounded, he came home to Canada to become the chair of the economics department at the University of Waterloo.[65]

It was at Waterloo that Mundell's life took another turn for the worse as he and his wife Barbara, with whom he had three children, divorced. Mundell's work suffered and his academic publications essentially ceased. He also took up painting, drinking martinis, and overeating.[66] He left Waterloo after just two years to become a professor at Columbia University in New York, and has been on the faculty there ever since. It was from here that he supported Republicans in favour of supply-side economics

62. http://business.highbeam.com/435424/article-1G1-63321506/nobel-laureate-uses-winnings-fund-class-reunion.
63. http://www.imf.org/external/pubs/ft/fandd/2006/09/people.htm.
64. http://www.economicprincipals.com/issues/2012.05.27/1371.html.
65. The University of Waterloo is near and dear to my heart. Coauthor Rick, my husband Martin, and many of our dear friends are graduates of Waterloo. I also live about 10 minutes from campus.
66. http://www.thecanadianencyclopedia.com/articles/macleans/mundell-wins-nobel-economics-prize

(the other major economic idea he put forth[67]) and European leaders in favour of the euro. Much of his economic influence shifted to the popular press and to politicians.

Sometimes events can take a turn for the better, for he met and married a much younger woman by the name of Valerie Natsios, a poet. By the end of 1997, their son Nicholas was born. He was just a toddler when Mundell's oldest son William told him that he had won the million-dollar Nobel Prize in 1999. The Nobel made him a superstar.

Mundell continues to travel extensively for both academic and consulting purposes. He favours China in recent years and has numerous honourary professorships and is the chairman of a number of Chinese research institutes. China has even named a university after him—the Mundell International University of Entrepreneurship in Beijing—and he has become a citizen of the Municipality of Beijing, which means he conveniently doesn't need a visa to travel there.

He thinks the Chinese strategy of keeping the yuan low is a good one. In fact, he is critical of the European Central Bank for not doing the same thing.[68] Mundell is still a big believer in the euro and hopes that the euro-zone countries heed the conditions necessary for success. You can see his many interviews about the euro on YouTube.

During his Nobel acceptance speech, he sang Frank Sinatra's "My Way," which seems to be a fairly accurate description of his career as an economist. In the 1999 ceremony he was 67, and he hasn't slowed down or stopped doing things his way since.

THE WORLD WIDE WEB

The fate of our times is characterized by rationalization and intellectualization and, above all, by the disenchantment of the world.[69]

—*Maximilian Weber (1864–1920), German sociologist and political economist*

There are good and bad ways to experience globalization. This chapter just laid out the terminology, but later in the book we will look at the debates—debates about foreign investment, international debt levels, and fixed versus flexible exchange rates. These debates matter because they can change the path a particular government follows. This can be potentially catastrophic when the governments involved are from poor countries. Ultimately we need to keep our eye on the goal of increasing human welfare around the world as we look at the issues. (There's one debate we won't discuss further: whether or not countries should have free trade. I think you can tell where I stand on the issue—and it really is microeconomics.)

Emma tweets:

@EvelineAdomait The balance of trade is X-M. The balance of payments includes capital. Central Banks can fix the exchange rate #commoncurrency

---

67. Supply-side economics, popular during Reagan's presidency, is the idea that tax cuts for businesses can create so much income that the tax revenue to the government can actually go up. This is also called trickle-down economics.
68. http://www.bloomberg.com/news/2013-03-25/mundell-says-ecb-tolerating-euro-strength-worsened-debt-crisis.html.
69. *Wissenschaft als Beruf* (*"Science as a Vocation"*) (1918).

Economic Policy

*Political necessities sometimes turn
out to be political mistakes.*

*—from
Saint Joan: A Chronicle Play in Six Scenes
and an Epilogue (1923),
by George Bernard Shaw (1856–1950), Irish playwright*

CHAPTER 11

Policy Matters

States are great engines moving slowly.[1]
—*Francis Bacon (1561–1626), English philosopher, scientist, and politician*

The stir-fry is ready. Emma takes the near-empty tray of appetizers to the counter and combines the remnants on a single platter. While moving the stir-fry off of the stove, Libby signals to Justin where to find the stack of plates in the cupboard, and he proceeds to set the table jutting into the living room. Salim looks around the room for the dining chairs and places them around the table in front of each plate. In the kitchen, David opens the top drawers until he finds the cutlery and proceeds to grab enough utensils for six people. To stop the incessant beeping, Brooke opens the microwave and, using tea towels to protect her hands, takes the organic brown rice to one of the hot pads Libby had put at one end of the table. Emma sets the now-much-smaller offering of appetizers at the other end of the table as Libby brings the large bowl of stir-fry and fills the centre spot reserved for her main dish. Everyone works silently with efficient coordination.

"Take a seat," Libby says. "Let's eat!"

Justin takes some rice and then passes it to Brooke on his right. "This looks great Libby! Definitely worth the wait. Just remember to leave room for cheesecake everyone."

"Don't worry, Justin," Brooke says. "We have the whole evening ahead of us and stir-fry is one of those meals that fill you up but an hour later you can eat again."

Salim passes the rice to Libby and receives the stir-fry from Brooke. "I guess we should start talking about macro. Have any of you started to study for the final yet?" he asks.

Emma, next to Salim, replies, "I have reread all the chapters but I still have to redo the online quizzes as practice."

David jumps into the purpose of the evening with, "You know, one of the things that confuses me is what 'government' means in this course. I always thought that the central bank was the government, but Professor Adomait never calls it that."

"Yeah," says Salim, "but in China the central bank is basically the government."

Brooke adds, "I think we just have to keep fiscal and monetary policy separate and she wants to make sure we get the right political body connected to the right policy."

"It is an interesting part of Canadian history," says Justin. "Currency used to be printed by individual commercial banks. In fact, in 1935 the Bank of Canada started out as a private institution that sold shares to the public. Then the government of Mackenzie King nationalized it in 1938 when it bought up the shares. The major banks still printed bank notes, but in 1944, all of the private banks were ordered to remove their bills from circulation, and only the Bank of Canada can print bank notes now."

"I think I read somewhere that the Bank of Canada owns a lot of Canada's debt. Anyone know why?" asks Libby.

Emma, bubbling with excitement, responds, "I know, I know: If the government runs a deficit and doesn't want the interest rate to rise, it sells the debt to the Bank of Canada."

"You sure about that?" asks Salim.

"Positive!" replies Emma. Everyone seems pretty impressed as they dig into the food once again.

---

1. *Advancement of Learning* (1605).

WHO'S IN CHARGE?

A task becomes a duty from the moment you suspect it to be an essential part of that integrity which alone entitles a man to assume responsibility.[2]

—*Dag Hammarskjöld (1905–1961), Swedish diplomat, Nobel-Peace-Prize-winning UN Secretary-General*

We have covered a lot of ground in the appetizer chapters—defining and measuring all of the major macroeconomic variables. This chapter takes the next step and asks, "What can a government do (if anything) to change its country's economic circumstances?" What are the tools of the trade, so to speak?

In our opening story, David is correct in his concern over what seems like semantics. There are two economic players with key, but distinct, policy roles. The term *government* normally refers to the legislative and executive functions or branches of government. In this book, the term *government* refers more specifically to the Department of Finance, which sets the national budget for all of the other ministries in the Canadian parliament. Budgetary matters are fiscal policy.

What a government prioritizes in its annual budget tells you a lot about that government. All the parts matter: Who is taxed? What is the level of progressivity of the income tax system? Are there expenditures for social programs, infrastructure, or war? And what of the bottom line? Is it a deficit, surplus, or balanced budget? The budget paints a political picture that we will explore in the last chapter of the book.

The central bank is in charge of monetary policy, managing things like the money supply, interest rates, and the issuing of new bank notes.[3] In Canada, the central bank[4] is a crown corporation whose shares are actually owned by the Minister of Finance on behalf of the reigning monarch. The central bank's governor is not elected but appointed for a seven-year term by a board of directors. The government's deputy finance minister sits on that board but doesn't have a vote. Technically, the Bank of Canada is a servant to the Canadian government but operates at arm's length. How arm's length that relationship is determines the level of policy independence.

This chapter looks at policy options—what *could* be done if the government or central bank were so inclined. The last chapter will look at what economists on the right and left of the political spectrum think *should* happen with respect to fiscal and monetary policy.

SO, WHAT'S YOUR PROBLEM?

No one can be a great thinker who does not recognise, that as a thinker it is his first duty to follow his intellect to whatever conclusions it may lead.[5]

—*John Stuart Mill (1806–1873), English political philosopher and economist*

Before we talk policy solutions, let's recall the problems. This brings us back to business cycles. Specifically, we want to look at when the cycle isn't on the trend line and the

---

2. *Markings* (1964).
3. Coins are issued by the Royal Canadian Mint.
4. Crown corporations are found in Common Wealth countries and are created precisely to shield their activities from constant government interference. The Federal Reserve in the USA, which began in 1913, has the same kind of relationship with its government. However, its structure, given the size and the political system of the USA, is different from that of the Bank of Canada.
5. *On Liberty* (1859).

economy is experiencing either a recessionary or inflationary gap problem. There are two approaches we can take when addressing the economic malady. The first is to do nothing and let the economy self-correct on its own. The second is to make changes to fix the problem with discretionary policy. If we decide to use the latter approach, we have to decide which policy will do the job—fiscal or monetary.

Let's begin by trying to solve these economic gap problems by doing nothing and letting the economy automatically self-correct without intervention.

WAIT AND SEE

In every part of the universe we observe means adjusted with the nicest artifice to the ends which they are intended to produce.[6]

—Adam Smith (1723–1790), Scottish economist and philosopher

Let's say an economy is experiencing an inflationary gap—and the workers work very hard, and put in lots of overtime. Perhaps some of them start noticing that their employers are making huge profits and ask for a raise. Help-wanted signs start to appear everywhere and companies actively recruit trained workers away from competitors with the promise of higher wages. Because of this situation, wages go up, which in turn raises the cost of production. Higher costs mean higher prices, which ends up decreasing the quantity demanded by buyers. Actual inflation due to higher wages and prices reduces the size of the GDP gap as the economy slows to the trend line. Wage and price hikes correct the economy on its own.

Now let's say that the economy happens to have the opposite problem and is in a recessionary gap. Workers are probably worried about layoffs because employer profits are down and no one is hiring. In order for things to get to potential without policy intervention, employees have to take a real pay cut—the sooner the better. Once the pay cuts occur, the costs of production go down and companies start to hire again. Eventually, this moves the economy up to the trend line. It is important to note that this approach of "doing nothing and letting the recession take care of itself" requires that workers take a pay cut in order for it to work. It was during the Great Depression that Keynes questioned how likely workers were to take pay cuts—even in bad times—which led him to propose an active role for the government to fix things. For Keynes, the "do nothing" approach wasn't a good option.

AT YOUR DISCRETION

Discretion is the best form of calculation.[7]

—Honoré de Balzac (1799–1850), French writer

If the economy can't self-correct without help, then governments and central banks can step in and try to fix the problem. They can take a more active role using fiscal and monetary policy. To see what can be done, let's look at a recessionary gap problem again.

---

6. *The Theory of Moral Sentiments* (1759).
7. *La Fille aux yeux d'or* ("*The Girl with the Golden Eyes*") (1835).

Essentially, in a recessionary gap, there isn't enough spending or demand at current prices to get us to the trend line. What we need to do is to get a category of spenders (whether they are consumers, firms, governments, or foreigners) to buy more goods and services within the country and hope things will start to turn around.

Once any of them spend more, we get an additional impetus in the economy known as the *multiplier effect*. It goes something like this. Suppose businesses wake up one morning and feel confident[8] about the future. They decide to build new buildings and purchase new equipment. This will increase spending by at least the price of the buildings and equipment. Not only that, this will induce other players to keep the spending going. Some of these players would be the workers at the construction companies that build the buildings and at the factories that produce the equipment. As they get paid, part of their paycheques will purchase such things as food, movies, furniture, electronics, clothes, or anything else they want to spend their income on. This is the second round of spending initiated by the first round of investment. This leads to the third round of spending by the people who work at the furniture shops, electronics stores, shopping malls, and theatres. The initial investment spending gets multiplied with additional consumption spending and hopefully fills the gap.

When looking at an economy with an inflationary gap, we see that a spending cut by one of the key economic actors in the system, along with the multiplier effect on various rounds of consumer spending, will take the pressure off the economy and reduce overall GDP to the trend line.

In either case, all the leadership has to do is prime the pump and get someone shopping—or not shopping, depending on the gap problem. Next, let's look at fiscal and monetary policy in turn to see how that pump can get primed.

ON A BUDGET

This is not a Budget, but a revolution; a social and political revolution of the first magnitude.[9]

—*Archibald Primrose (1847–1929), British prime minister*

Let's start with fiscal policy, shall we? Here the government, at the Ministry of Finance, makes budget changes. If the economy is in recession, it can introduce spending programs. For example, between 1931 and 1936, Franklin D. Roosevelt in the New Deal spent millions on roads, railway lines, reforestation, national parks, dams, courthouses, schools, and lunch programs in order to try to get the economy out of the Great Depression. Governments can also initiate tax cuts to get households and businesses to spend. During Roosevelt's tenure, the food stamp program he set up gave subsidies to poor urban dwellers so that they could buy food. Measures like spending initiatives and tax cuts lead to a decrease in budget surpluses or an increase in government deficits.

However, the size of the deficit depends on the speed of recovery because the spending increases get offset by any tax revenue generated by the resulting higher incomes. If the economy starts to improve, governments automatically take more tax revenue out of

---

8. Keynes said that the business community was often guided by "animal spirits," or a spontaneous urge to action, rather than rational cost-benefit analysis.
9. Letter to *The Times* attacking the "People's Budget" (June 22, 1909).

the system and automatically put less in through subsidies, which dampens the rise. When incomes fall, even with no discretionary policy changes, the government will automatically spend more on subsidy programs and receive less in income taxes, thus cushioning the fall. This is known as an *automatic stabilizer* because any initial shocks get dampened automatically.

ACTUALLY STRUCTURAL

Finally, I believe in an America with a government of men devoted solely to the public interests—men of ability and dedication, free from conflict or corruption or other commitment—a responsible government that is efficient and economical, with a balanced budget over the years of the cycle, reducing its debt in prosperous times.[10]
—John Fitzgerald Kennedy (1917–1963), president of the United States

Sometimes economists will distinguish between actual budgets and structural budgets. Actual budgets are just as they sound—the actual level of GDP as part of the business cycle. Structural budgets assume that the level of output is at potential or, in other words, on the trend line.

What policymakers are trying to get at with the idea of structural deficits is that over one complete business cycle, the deficits generated in the recessionary part of the cycle should get cancelled out by the surpluses in the inflationary part such that the budget of a cycle would balance. Let's see how this follows.

In terms of budget equations, we can see that the difference between an actual and structural budget is the income level used to calculate the budget balance. Everything else is the same.

The actual budget equals

$B = tY - G$, where Y is *actual* income, t is the tax rate, and G is the level of government spending.

The structural budget equals

$B = tY_p - G$, where Y_p is *potential* income, and all the other variables are the same as in the actual budget equation.

In a recession, it is therefore possible to run an actual budget deficit but be balanced in the structural budget because actual output is lower than potential output. In the times of boom, the actual budget could be a surplus but the structural deficit balanced. Noticed that I have carefully told stories where the structural budget is always balanced even if the actual budget is not. If the government has a goal of a balanced structural budget, this implies that the government *should* run actual deficits in recessions and surpluses in inflationary gaps.

If a country decides to balance the actual budget, no matter where it is in the business cycle, this has the perverse result of making the cycle have larger swings. To see what I mean, let's look at what happens in a recession if the government decides it must balance the budget. In a recession, actual income declines. This means that the budget automatically slips into a deficit. In order to rebalance the budget, the government must either

---

10. Speech by Senator John F. Kennedy, Convention Hall, Philadelphia, PA, October 31, 1960.

raise taxes or lower spending, but these actions only cut income further, deepening the recession.[11] In times of boom, spending budget surpluses makes the hot economy even hotter. Those who favour balanced actual budgets are not suggesting the government should never run a surplus. They would be supportive of budget surpluses and wouldn't suggest the government needs to spend the money to balance the budget. Instead, the policy rule of a balanced budget addresses the temptation for governments to run chronic deficits, in good times as well as bad.

TYING THEIR OWN HANDS

Our destiny exercises its influence over us even when, as yet, we have not learned its nature: it is our future that lays down the law of our today.[12]
—*Friedrich Wilhelm Nietzsche (1844–1900), German philologist, philosopher, and composer*

In the USA, the elected politicians were so concerned about the size of the deficit that they passed a series of laws that would increase taxes and decrease spending as of January 1, 2013. Effectively, they were forcing the issue of an actual balanced budget. The Federal Reserve chairman, Ben Bernanke, concerned that the sudden reduction in the deficit would take too much stimulus out of the economy, popularized the term *fiscal cliff* because he predicted the economy would plunge over the cliff into another recession as a result of these laws. Some think the terms *fiscal slope* or *fiscal hill* more accurately reflect the truth of the matter, but *fiscal cliff* definitely made the media sit up and take notice. A last-minute political reprieve made its way through the various levels of government to postpone the full effects of the proposed budgetary changes. The U.S. government stepped back from the edge—at least for a while.

GETTING THE JOB DONE

Now an' then an innocent man is sent t' th' legislature.[13]
—*Frank McKinney Hubbard (1868–1930), American cartoonist and writer*

As governments tweak their budgets, there are more concerns other than just the size of the deficit and resulting debt. These concerns have to do with the efficacy of fiscal policies to achieve the goals they were meant to accomplish. Some issues include:

1. *Lags:* Preparing a budget can take months. But even once everything is signed, sealed, and delivered, a government can't begin to spend immediately. For example, the Canadian government currently wants to build a bridge across the Detroit River into the United States at the Windsor–Detroit border crossing. However, it will take more than a decade from the beginning stages of the project to when the first car crosses the bridge to the USA. If the purpose of this bridge was to get Windsor out of a recession, the actual spending may come too late because by then the recession will probably (and hopefully) be long over, and the spending might arrive just in time to make a boom even bigger. The

11. Left-wing economists think the severity of the Great Depression was due to government attempts to balance their budgets.
12. *Menschliches, Allzumenschliches: Ein Buch für freie Geister* ("*Human, All Too Human: A Book for Free Spirits*") (1878).
13. *Back Country Folks* (1914).

purpose of the bridge can't be to solve a recessionary gap problem but rather for longer-term growth opportunities. "Spending your way out of a recession" means that the kinds of government spending must be designed to have immediate effects.

The contour should come last, only a very experienced eye can place it rightly.[14]
Eugène Delacroix (1798–1863), French painter

Because of these kinds of lags, governments look for "shovel-ready" projects to inter-ject quick stimulus spending into the economy during a recession. This means that only projects that are ready to go now get funded. The phrase "shovel ready" was the govern-ment of Canada's mantra during the recession after the 2008–2009 financial crisis. The implications of this kind of spending meant that it was virtually impossible to travel any-where through the Canadian province of Ontario during the summer of 2009 without hit-ting traffic slowdowns due to road and sewer repairs in small towns. It turns out that municipalities had maintenance projects on the back burner that they couldn't afford to complete, and the federal government tapped into these local projects to quickly let the spending hit the streets (literally). Furthermore, strict rules were placed on when the proj-ects had to be finished. I recall teaching at my university in a building that was re-roofed as part of a larger renovation funded with stimulus money. The noise overhead in my classroom was so distracting to the students that I had to ask the contractors to stop their work while I taught. They said they couldn't because they had only two months to finish the job or they wouldn't get paid. As a result, the university moved my class to a new makeshift location.

As part of the same government "action plan" to get the economy out of a slowdown, the Canadian federal government offered tax credits or subsidies to "ordinary Canadi-ans." This is the tax side rather than the spending side of the budget. Most of the tax rebates were for renovation projects a homeowner undertook up to a certain dollar limit before a certain deadline. The hope was that homeowners could be "shovel ready" more quickly than governments could. New windows and doors, anyone? How about a new furnace, deck, or driveway? Most of the projects were in the construction sector, with contractors working overtime to meet the deadlines. It wouldn't have done much good for recessionary stimulus spending to, say, give tax credits to new parents for a post-secondary education fund or 30-somethings for their retirement savings. For these people there isn't a shovel in sight. Education or retirement tax policy is all about long-term growth rather than relief from short-term cycles.

Striving to better, oft we mar what's well.[15]
—William Shakespeare (1564–1616), English writer

2. *Crowding-out effects:* Even if you get the timing right for an intervention (sounds like an addiction problem), it is possible for government spending on projects to "crowd out" or replace other forms of spending that normally would have happened in the economy. The crowding-out effect can happen on two fronts because it changes the interest rate as

---

14. *Journal* (1822–1824 and 1847–1863).
15. *King Lear* (1608).

well as the exchange rate. Let's take a look at each front separately and see how this situation can sometimes feel like three steps forward and two steps back.

The interest rate story of crowding out goes like this. Let's say a government increases spending on various projects and begins to run a deficit. It now has to borrow the funds by selling bonds, which works to decreases the price of bonds and increases the interest rate. This higher interest rate now decreases the level of borrowing by private-sector participants like businesses or consumers because the cost of borrowing is higher. The result is a slowdown in private-sector spending. This is why you will often hear people complain about "big government." Many businesses want a smaller government footprint so that they are not crowded out from growing their businesses.

Any change in the interest rate also changes the exchange rate, which leads to another kind of crowding out. If the government borrows and raises interest rates, this makes the domestic capital market more attractive to international investors (read "savers"). Capital flows into the country, which means these international investors must buy the domestic currency in order to earn these attractive interest rates. This puts upward pressure on the currency. However, a currency appreciation discourages net exports because exports are now more expensive and imports relatively cheaper. This leads to a decrease in the trade balance. The deficit spending by the government replaces some spending by foreigners through trade.[16] Economists sometimes call this the *twin deficit problem*—government budget deficits and international trade deficits tend to go together.

3. *Supply-side economics:*[17] Most economists see fiscal policy as a tool to increase or decrease the demand for goods and services in the economy. A few economists think that this is the wrong approach and advocate for tools to change the supply side of the economy mainly through tax cuts to businesses and to their employees. Supply siders, as they are called, think that tax cuts will cause businesses to invest more in productive capacity and induce labour to work more. They believe that not only can the economy get back to a trend line because of these incentives, but they will allow the trend line to move up the chart to reflect the increase in potential capacity.

Supply siders think it's possible that tax cuts are so effective at stimulating the economy, to the point that the government actually collects more total tax dollars than before, even with lower tax rates. A visual representation of this is called the Laffer curve after Arthur Laffer, who actually doesn't take credit for the concept. He harkens the idea back to Keynes. The main implication is that if you are on the right side of the curve, a drop in the tax rate can actually give the government more revenue. In reality, for most countries in the world, the tax rate is actually not past the top of the curve and supply-side economics supplied those countries that tried these policies with less revenue.

The degree of crowding out and the appropriateness of specific fiscal policy is a matter of debate between right- and left-wing economists. We will come back to these issues in the last chapter of the book.

---

16. In terms of GDP accounting, the impact of some crowding out due to government spending would look like this: Recall Y = C + I + G + NX, where NX = X − M Y (up a little) = C + I (down due to interest rates hikes) + G (up due to deficit spending) + NX (down due to a currency appreciation).
17. Reagonomics was essentially supply-side economics.

The Laffer Curve

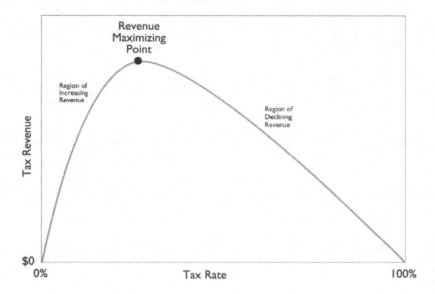

18. Biography by Mathew Forstater, Dictionary of American Economists, http://www.cfeps.org/pubs/wp-pdf/wp52-forstater.pdf.
19. Biography by David S. Landes, http://www.nap.edu/openbook.php?record_id=4547&page=209.
20. Biography by G. Debreu, B. Hansen, and C. J. Hitch. http://texts.cdlib.org/view?docId=hb967nb5k3&doc.view=frames&chunk.id=div00031&toc.depth=1&toc.id=.
21. http://www.britannica.com/EBchecked/topic/1085393/Abba-P-Lerner.
22. See the gossip column in chapter 1 of *Cocktail Party Economics* for more on Baron Robbins.

GOSSIP COLUMN *(CONTINUED)*

were too long and that there would be a market for such a journal. Given his past experience in printing, Lerner was certainly not afraid to venture into the world of publishing. All the founding group of LSE economists needed was money, and they were able to get visiting scholars to donate to the cause. *The Review of Economic Studies* exists today.

He earned his doctorate from the LSE but his studies allowed him to spend six months at Cambridge, where he mastered *The General Theory* by John Maynard Keynes. He was probably one of the few outsiders who actually did. Furthermore, he understood the logical implications of Keynes's ideas and was willing to push them further than Keynes did at the time. There is a story that Lerner pointed out the deficit and debt implications of Keynesian economics in one of Keynes's seminars and received a dressing down from the great man himself. Later, Keynes realized Lerner was correct and publically acknowledged his error because of the nature of the initial exchange. Lerner was asked to review[23] *The General Theory,* and he managed to explain many of the tricky, incomprehensible bits of the original work to his audience.

After finishing his doctoral studies, Lerner began a career in teaching and writing that is broad in terms of scope of topics—first in micro- and then macroeconomics, in theory and then policy. It was the important implications of Keynesian macroeconomics that led Lerner to write the book *Functional Finance and the Federal Debt* (1943), which is probably his most important and controversial work.[24] The basic idea is that governments shouldn't focus on principles of "sound finance" (such as restraints on deficit spending) as if a government were like a household. Governments aren't like households because they can print money. Government policies of taxation, spending, and deficits are just the means to accomplishing the end of full employment output and stable prices. The government's goal should never be about finance but about the economy. For Lerner, the ends justify the means. This was counterintuitive to most people, even the Keynesian converts of the time.

Once in the USA, his travels leave one breathless. He worked for nine different universities and colleges, with the longest tenure of 12 years (1947–1959) at Roosevelt University[25] in Chicago. Most places were for only a couple of years, and even during his time in Chicago, he consulted for the RAND[26] Corporation, the Israeli government, and the Economic Commission in Switzerland. The only word that comes to mind with that much travel and a set of twins is *stress.* At some point Abba and his wife Alice divorced. (Abba wouldn't remarry until he was 57, to Daliah Goldfarb, after his move to Michigan State University.[27])

Many of his biographers note that Lerner was not a typical professor of his era. He refused to wear a tie or shoes but opted for an open-collar shirt, baggy pants, and sandals. (As a young man, he looked like Woody Allen, and like Tevye from *Fiddler on the Roof* when he was older.) Furthermore, his personality was unconventional, and extremely logical; he said exactly what he thought (maybe because he came to the game so late that he didn't want to waste time). Furthermore, his politics weren't neat

---

23. Keynes, "General Theory of Employment, Interest and Money," *International Labour Review* (1936).
24. Lerner showed that price must equal marginal cost if resources are to be allocated efficiently. This proof is very significant but absolutely not controversial. See *Cocktail Party Economics* Chapter 9 for more on maximizing social welfare.
25. Named in honour of Franklin and Eleanor Roosevelt in 1945. The curriculum is based on the principles of social justice.
26. RAND (Research ANd Development) is now funded by the U.S. government and private donors and functions as a global, non-profit think tank. It was first started to offer research and analysis for the U.S. armed forces by Douglas Aircraft Company. Through a series of mergers, Douglas Aircraft is now part of Boeing.
27. For a simple chronology of his life, see http://socialarchive.iath.virginia.edu/xtf/view?docId=lerner-abba-ptachya-1903--cr.xml.

and tidy and so he offended folks on the left and the right. He espoused right-wing free-market principles as the means to left-wing socialist ends. His view was that the market was the servant of society and not the other way around. If the market wasn't up for the job (because of market imperfections), then decentralized government ownership was a good option. He essentially wrote the handbook[28] on how to run a command economy. The important distinction between ends and means seems to be a recurring theme.

He worked well past retirement into his 80s. At the end, the focus of his work was on stagflation (more on that later in this chapter) and market-based solutions to solving the problem. His prescriptions were clever but impractical and therefore never adopted.

Lerner was an economist more appreciated in hindsight than in the moment. He probably should have won a Nobel Prize, which would have given him a more credible platform to preach from. However, his life reads more like that of the Jewish prophet John the Baptist[29] than an economic messiah.

LIQUID MONEY

What is scarce is money. The lack of money to spend on goods is what keeps the unemployed resources from producing more goods.[30]

—*Abba Ptachya Lerner (1903–1982), Russian-British-American economist*

Whereas fiscal policy is under the purview of the Ministry of Finance (or the Treasury), monetary policy is under the control of the central bank. As we saw earlier in this book, central banks change the money supply with the purchase or sale of T-Bills. This throws the ball into the hands of the commercial banks, which can multiply the impact of the central bank's actions through commercial lending changes. The size of the money supply involves the coordinated efforts of the central bank, commercial banks, and borrowers. If commercial banks and the public don't want to play along with the central bank, it is hard to make them do so.

Central banks track all kinds of numbers as they try to read[31] the economy—the money supply (for example M1, M2++, M3), interest rates, inflation rates (as measured by different price indices), exchange rates, business inventories, investor confidence indicators, and real GDP. With this data, they set targets for things they can control in order to make the right monetary policy choice for the economy as a whole. Measuring economic data is one thing, but the ability to have control of an economic variable is quite another.

---

28. *The Economics of Control—Principles of Welfare Economics* (1944).
29. John the Baptist was an eccentric prophet who foretold of the Messiah. He was beheaded for speaking against the incestuous marriage of Herod.
30. *On the Causes of Unemployment* (1951).
31. Business Outlook Survey, http://www.bankofcanada.ca/publications-research/periodicals/bos/.

BANQUE DU CANADA

The Bank [of Canada] gave it a college try, it really did.[32]
—*John Crow (1937–), Bank of Canada governor*

For instance, throughout its history, the Bank of Canada has targeted or tried to control lots of different economic variables that were subsequently abandoned. For example, during the Bretton Woods agreement, it targeted the exchange rate but gave that up because the Canadian dollar kept needing to be devalued.

Later in the 1970s and 1980s, the Bank of Canada shifted focus to targeting the inflation rate in the economy but it had no direct way to do this. Because central bankers adhered to the quantity theory of money,[33] they believed that slowing the growth in the money supply should slow inflation as well. Central bankers could target the value of a specific definition of the money supply (for example, M2 or M2+), which should change how much prices change if the velocity of money happens to remain constant. Unfortunately, the velocity of money was not constant, and, furthermore, depositors became quite comfortable shifting money between different kinds of bank accounts (or definitions of money) because of financial innovations (for example, ATMs and a greater variety of bank accounts offered by the banks). Targeting a meaningful definition of the money supply that would actually control inflation was as difficult as herding cats. There were way too many definitions of money to control them all at the same time. As a result of targeting a particular definition of the money supply, interest rates (or the price of money) unexpectedly spiked, which led to a recession.

Enough was enough, and by the early 1980s, the Bank of Canada[34] switched to targeting interest rates instead of money aggregates (the M's) in order to control inflation. For many years, it targeted one specific interest rate—the bank rate, which is the interest rate the central bank charges the chartered banks on loans. It was up to the commercial banks to set all of the other interest rates in the economy (for example, the mortgage rates and prime rates), but these interest rates tended to move in tandem with the bank rate, so setting one is like setting them all.

ONLINE CENTRAL BANKING

As soon as an Analytical Engine exists, it will necessarily guide the future course of the science. Whenever any result is sought by its aid, the question will then arise—by what course of calculation can these results be arrived at by the machine in the shortest time?[35]
—*Charles Babbage (1791–1871), English mathematician, philosopher, and computer scientist*

At the end of the 1990s, Canada brought in a new electronic system for commercial banks to facilitate their interactions with each other on a daily basis, called the Large

---

32. Quoted in "In pictures," *The Globe and Mail* online (2006–11–18).
33. See Chapter 9, Taking Stock and Going with the Flows, to recall this idea. The quantity theory of money says that $MV = PY$, where M is the money supply, V is the velocity of money, P is the price level, and Y is real GDP.
34. See the discussion paper by economist David Laidler "The quantity of money and monetary policy," 1999, http://www.bankofcanada.ca/wp-content/uploads/2010/05/wp99-5.pdf.
35. *Passages from the life of a philosopher* (1864).

Value Transfer System (LVTS).[36] This system allows commercial banks to continuously update the net flows of large money transfers[37] between them.

At the end of the day, if one bank is short on what it owes another bank, instead of borrowing from the Bank of Canada, the bank borrows from a bank that is in a surplus position for an interest rate that is ¼% less than what it would have to pay the Bank of Canada. The lending bank will do this because it is making ¼% more than the Bank of Canada would pay. The interest rate at which banks borrow and lend to each other is called the *overnight rate.*

Even though the overnight rate is an agreement between commercial banks, its value is targeted by the Bank of Canada. The Canadian central bank is pretty good at keeping the overnight rate at the official level. Monetary policy for the Bank of Canada is very intentional, with statements about the exact percent for the overnight rate. These statements are made eight times a year on predetermined[38] days. Between those days, the overnight rate is targeted because, on a daily basis, the Bank of Canada will enter the government of Canada securities market[39] if the overnight rate drifts off course. If the overnight rate drifts up, the Bank of Canada will buy T-Bills in an overnight agreement[40] to lower the overnight rate to the official target. If the overnight rate drifts down, then the Bank of Canada will sell T-Bills in an overnight contract in order to raise it back to the specified target interest rate.

I wish to have no connection with any ship that does not sail fast.[41]
—John Paul Jones (1747–1792), Scottish-born naval officer[42]

During the course of a business day, the central bank also acts as the banker for the government of Canada. The Receiver General writes cheques and receives payments that end up in the government's accounts at the Bank of Canada. I hope you recall me telling you that any accounts held by the Bank of Canada are not part of the money supply—only commercial bank accounts are part of the money stock. It is very probable that in the daily operations of a federal government, the flows that go into the government accounts at the Bank of Canada don't match what leaves. This is unintentional monetary policy because it changes the money supply in the system but it wasn't part of any plan. If more funds flow in, then the money supply in the banking sector falls, and vice versa. The central bank actively neutralizes these flows by estimating the flows in the morning and making adjustments midmorning, but erring on the side of ensuring that more money comes into accounts than goes out. It continues to monitor the accounts throughout the day and in the afternoon, if the government's accounts are too large, it auctions funds from these bank accounts off to the commercial banks, which buy them as a source of funds for extending loans.

---

36. http://www.bankofcanada.ca/wp-content/uploads/2010/07/lvts_primer_2010.pdf.
37. The minimum amount in this system is $50,000, but this system handles more than 87% of the value of the transfers of money between institutions. Paper transfers or small electronic transfers (such as preauthorized debits or direct deposits) may be higher in volume but are much lower in value.
38. http://www.bankofcanada.ca/monetary-policy-introduction/key-interest-rate/schedule/.
39. http://www.bankofcanada.ca/markets/government-securities-auctions/?page_moved=1.
40. These are one-day contracts called Special Purchase and Resale Agreements (SPRAs). The Bank of Canada will buy T-Bills one day only to sell them back the next. If it sells T-Bills overnight only to buy them back the next, these are called Sale and Repurchase Agreements (SRAs).
41. Letter to Le Ray de Chaumont (November 16, 1778), as quoted in *The Naval History of the United States* (1890), by Willis John Abbot.
42. Served in the American Revolution and later in the Russian navy.

A COUNTER PARTY

Of course as business becomes more complicated it grows more difficult to tell so clearly whether both sides are equally prospered.[43]
—*Dr. Frank Crane (1861–1928), American minister and writer*

Commercial banks mainly deal with each other through the LVTS, which normally isn't a problem. However, during a financial crisis, counterparty risk raises its ugly head. This means that if a commercial bank lends to another commercial bank, at the end of the day the bank wants to know that the counterparty—in this situation another commercial bank—will pay it back. There is always a risk when lending funds. In financially tumultuous times, the risk of not getting paid back increases to the point where many banks stop lending to each other. The commercial banks that need funds to cover their shortfall must borrow from the central bank at higher rates, and the commercial banks with surpluses sit on their excess reserves, earning lower ones. Bank profits are down and commercial banks become more cautious about lending because they want to keep more cash on reserve. At times like these, central banks need to interject more liquidity or money supply into the banking system to keep the economy from grinding to a halt.

I am convinced that purely mathematical construction enables us to find those concepts and those lawlike connections between them that provide the key to the understanding of natural phenomena.[44]
—*Albert Einstein (1979–1955), German-American physicist*

So far in our discussion on policy, we still haven't connected monetary policy to the broader economy. For that, we need to talk about the interaction between commercial banks and the GDP-producing public.

Let's start in a recession and say the central bank wants to encourage spending. The central bank would respond by lowering the overnight rate. Holding its breath, the central bank waits to see if the commercial banks respond by lowering the interest rates they charge businesses and consumers. Once the commercial banks post lower rates, this should increase traffic with their loans officers because lower interest rates make borrowing more attractive. Depending on who comes into the retail bank, these customers use the borrowed funds to buy real things—new cars, homes, equipment, and so forth. Once the businesses that sold the cars, homes, or equipment get paid, they start their own round of spending and we have a multiplier effect.

In an inflationary period, the central bank will raise the overnight rate, which in turn raises all the other interest rates, putting the brakes on investment and consumer borrowing. To get from the central bank to real GDP requires a fairly long domino effect. The central bank changes the money supply and overnight rate. This causes banks to change their interest rates and their willingness to lend. The public responds by changing how much they are willing to borrow. At any point the monetary policy can fail. What if banks don't change how much they will lend or what if the public doesn't change how much they want to borrow?

---

43. *Four Minute Essays* (1919).
44. "On the Method of Theoretical Physics—The Herbert Spencer Lecture," delivered at Oxford June 10, 1933.

Once the borrowing occurs, and depending on what the customer buys with the borrowed funds, we have lag issues similar to those seen with fiscal policy. For example, if a homeowner or business borrows to build, it can take time to plan and execute the project. This means that the second round of spending can be a long way in the future and the dominoes hit each other in slow motion. The Bank of Canada estimates that an overnight rate change takes about a year and half to be felt by the real economy. This entire process is known as *conventional monetary policy*. If this is conventional, then it's time to talk about the unconventional.

UNCONVENTIONAL BECOMES CONVENTIONAL

Le mot impossible n'est pas français.
The word impossible is not French.[45]

—Napoleon Bonaparte (1769–1821), French ruler

When monetary policy is conventional, official statements by the central bank governor to the public about the future of interest rates sound very general and vague. Central bankers say things like "future interest rates are contingent on inflation expectations—blah, blah blah." In terms of their conventional bond market operations, when the central bank buys and sells securities, it only deals in "directly issued government of Canada bonds denominated in Canadian dollars" with a very select group of players[46] backed with high-quality collateral. This is a very exclusive bond market.

Unconventional monetary policy came about because of what is called the *zero-lower-bound* interest rate problem. This means that short-term interest rates are so low that they really can't go lower.[47] Unconventional monetary policy tries to get around this problem of ultra-low short-term rates by changing the rates on longer term, riskier debt.

Here are the basic ways a central bank can expand the money supply and increase liquidity in financial markets when it isn't possible to lower short-term rates any further:

1. Central banks make explicit statements about the short-term interest rate they will commit to as a matter of policy. This gives certainty about the short-term interest rates for an extended period of time. So how does this affect longer rates? Long-term rates are connected to and include expectations about short-term rates. After all, why would you commit to a five-year bond price if you can make more with a series of short-term bonds? Even if the central bank can't lower short-term rates any further, the certainty about how long those rates will last means that commercial banks know their cost of borrowing. This should take some of the risk out of committing to longer-term rates with their customers, and longer-term interest rates should fall. The Bank of Canada made such a commitment after the financial crisis of 2008–2009.

2. Central banks can buy longer-term government bonds directly. This raises the price of longer bonds and lowers their rates. By buying the bonds, the central bank can increase the amount of money in the system, which is known as quantitative easing. The Bank of Canada has never done this—ever.

---

45. Letter to General Jean Le Marois on July 9, 1813.
46. http://www.bankofcanada.ca/wp-content/uploads/2010/07/term_conditions_spra-sra.pdf.
47. Japan was the first country to get into this situation and paved the way for unconventional monetary policy to be used in the USA during the crisis.

3. The central bank can buy debt from the private sector, targeting those sectors where credit constraints are severe. In the economic crisis of 2008–2009, the Federal Reserve in the United States took bad assets off the books of commercial banks in exchange for "good" government securities. These bad assets were in mortgage-backed securities with the street name "toxic assets" because during the crisis there wasn't really a market for them. When a central bank changes the quality of the assets in the banking sector, this is called *qualitative easing*.

The situation was very much different in Canada but even here, during the same period, the Canadian Mortgage and Housing Corporation (CMHC) bought good-enough mortgages off of the books of commercial banks to give them the liquidity so that they could be lent out again and keep the mortgage market going.

The combination of qualitative and quantitative easing is often called *credit easing* because it should lower the spread between safe government debt and longer-term private-sector debt. Lots of easing goes on in the world, but not in Canada. Due to tighter bank regulations, we managed to avoid the problem of commercial banks with toxic assets on their books.

TOPSY-TURVY ECONOMICS

Topsy-turvy economics is just what is appropriate for an economy that is suffering from unemployment. An economy suffering from unemployment is an upside-down economy for which only a topsy-turvy economic theory is of any use.[48]
—Abba Ptachya Lerner (1903–1982), Russian-British-American economist

Governments and central banks can get too cozy with each other. So what is the problem? It is not an issue if central bankers go to dinner parties with government officials. A friendly, cooperative relationship is a good thing. The problem occurs when the central bank helps the government out financially. If the central bank helps too much, the economy can go into hyperinflation, and that's when things get really bad.

Let me explain how this can happen. It starts with the finance department deciding to spend more by borrowing. This means that it prints government bonds to sell. Instead of selling them to the public and dealing with the crowding-out effect that we mentioned earlier in the chapter, the finance department convinces the central bank to buy the bonds. The central bank buys the bonds and credits the account of the Treasury. So far nothing bad has happened. But that is about to change. The government promptly goes shopping, buying goods and services in exchange for cheques—cheques that hit the banking system as deposits and create money. Effectively fiscal policy is being financed with monetary policy. This is known as *monetizing the debt*, where the government owes the central bank, and if it is done carefully and cautiously it could be a good thing. However, if this happens too much (and like any addiction, too much can easily happen), then massive amounts of new money hit the economy, leading to inflation.

Whether monetizing the debt is a good or bad idea is of course a controversy. From Abba Lerner's perspective this is a perfectly reasonable approach if the government doesn't want interest rates to rise. Right-wing economists, like Milton Friedman, think this is the

---

48. *The Economics of Employment* (1951).

kiss of death for an economy. But I am getting ahead of myself. More in the last chapter on that subject.

STAGFLATION

In short, we must face problems which do not lend themselves to easy or quick or permanent solutions.[49]

—John F. Kennedy (1917–1963), American president

So far we have seen that if an economy is below the trend line in a recessionary gap, then expansionary fiscal or monetary policy can be used to try to get up to the potential GDP. However, if the economy is in an inflationary gap above the trend line, then contractionary policies are appropriate. Unemployment requires more spending and inflation requires less. Simple, right? Not so fast. What happens if we get high unemployment and high inflation together? (This is what we mean by *stagflation*—a stagnant economy and inflation.) This is a very difficult problem to solve and the standard monetary and fiscal prescriptions just won't work well.

The pitcher goes so often to the fountain (that it gets broken).[50]

—Miguel de Cervantes Saavedra (1547–1616), Spanish writer

The reason they won't work has to do with the underlying cause of the situation. Economies get the problems of high unemployment and high prices because of what we call "cost-push" inflation.[51] In other words, the reason prices are high has to do with the high cost of production from such things as oil shocks. When OPEC formed its cartel in the early 1970s, oil prices quadrupled. This shock pushed the world into stagflation. It is possible to use expansionary fiscal and monetary policy to get rid of the unemployment, but this would further increase prices. Therefore, policymakers must be very careful not to overdo their intervention tactics so as not to start inflation spiraling upward. This is especially true if they use monetary policy to fund government deficits.

In the past, the monetary causes for inflation weren't so clear, and double-digit inflation hit North America in the 1970s. Once inflation takes a foothold in an economy, people start to expect it and it becomes a self-fulfilling prophecy through wage demands. If workers expect inflation, then they also expect wage increases during negotiations. Higher wages force up the prices of goods and services and, voila, the expectation of inflation becomes real.

The idea that governments should just let the economy self-correct without any intervention isn't quite so easy a solution either. In order for the economy to self-correct, workers need to change their wage demands according to the economic climate. This isn't so difficult if the economy is in an inflationary gap. When workers get a pay raise—and who doesn't love a pay raise—then the economy slows down to potential. However, if the economy is in a recession, then workers need to take pay cuts to get to potential. Workers generally resist pay cuts. (Surprise, surprise.) Now let's add cost-push

---

49. Address at the University of Washington's 100th Anniversary program (November 16, 1961).
50. *Don Quixote* (1605).
51. The business-cycle type of inflationary gap is demand-pull. In other words, demand is too high and needs to be cooled down a bit.

inflation like an oil shock, which also generates unemployment. This means that every time oil prices increase (which has happened often since the oil crisis of the early 1970s), a corresponding wage decline is necessary to offset the higher costs of production, thereby restoring unemployment to the natural rate. This is painful all around.

You need a strong ideological and political stomach to let the economy correct itself out of stagflation, and the North American governments of Trudeau and Nixon in the 1970s couldn't do it. Instead, the U.S. and Canadian governments legislated wage and price controls to stop wages and prices[52] from rising while fueling the flames of inflation with monetary policy. There is some evidence that controls worked back in 1975 during Canada's anti-inflation board period by setting expectations. However, the 1970s were marked by labour unrest and frequent strikes as unions resisted taking any sort of real pay cuts. In the end, inflation was tamed by tough monetary policy but it required painful recessions to stamp out any imbedded expectations of inflation. Of all the economic problems to have, stagflation takes the most finesse to solve.

SPECIALIZED TOOLS

A bad workman blames his tools.[53]

—English proverb

Economists have learned a few things about effective economic policy. In fact, the very first co-winner[54] of the Nobel Prize in economics[55] was Dutch economist Jan Tinbergen, who found that governments need an instrument they can use for every economic target they want to change. Mundell[56] found that some target–instrument combinations are better than others. That is why in most countries, it is the job of the government to target full employment with the instruments of tax and spending programs and the job of the central bank to target inflation with the instrument of interest rates. Mundell[57] also showed that if you have two targets, such as a fixed exchange rate and inflation, then the central bank cannot target both at the same time. This is why we have a flexible exchange rate in Canada.

---

52. Along with coauthor David Colander, Lerner developed that Market Anti-inflation Plan (MAP), which essentially gave tradable credits to businesses to produce anything below their previous production. These credits could be sold to firms that wanted to produce above last year's production. New businesses would be given credits according to a fairly complicated formula. The administration of such a scheme is mind-numbing.
53. *Jacula Prudentum; or, Outlandish Proverbs, Sentences, Etc.* (1640), by George Herbert.
54. Jan Tingergen's (1903–1994) co-winner was Ragnar Anton Kittil Fisch (1895–1973), a Norwegian economist who founded the discipline and name of econometrics and coined the term *macroeconomics* in 1933.
55. The Nobel Memorial Prize in Economic Sciences, officially known as the Sveriges Riksbank Prize in Economic Sciences in Memory of Alfred Nobel, was first awarded in 1969 and isn't part of the Nobel Prizes awarded by the Nobel Foundation.
56. Read the gossip column from the last chapter.
57. http://faculty.haas.berkeley.edu/arose/Mundell.pdf.

POSITIVELY NORMATIVE

Therefore judge not before the time.[58]

—1 Corinthians 4:5a

So far, I have tried to focus on what economists call *positive economics*. I have described and explained how the economy works. I have given you mostly facts and stories of cause and effect.

In the remaining chapter, we will look at the controversies, the ideological differences, and the arguments about what different economists think governments ought to do. Some of this is still positive—either the model works a certain way in the real world or it doesn't—but once we add politics and values, this shifts over in what economists call normative economics. "Coulda" is going to become "shoulda."

Justin tweets:

> @EvelineAdomait When the govt or CB do things on purpose this is called policy. Stagflation is a nasty problem. #policymatters

---

58. Douay-Rheims 1899 American edition.

The Economic Debates

*I object to a quarrel because it
always interrupts an argument.*

*—from
Magic: A Fantastic Comedy (1913),
by Gilbert Keith Chesterton (1874–1936), British writer*

CHAPTER 12

Side Views

We cannot therefore settle on abstract grounds, but must handle on its merits in detail what Burke termed "one of the finest problems in legislation, namely, to determine what the State ought to take upon itself to direct by the public wisdom, and what it ought to leave, with as little interference as possible, to individual exertion."[1]

—John Maynard Keynes (1883–1946), British economist

"Well that was delish!" Emma says, as she wipes her mouth with a napkin.

Libby laughs, "Thanks, I'm glad I got the stove working again . . . that was a moment of panic."

"And now for my famous cheesecake," Justin announces as he jumps up to take it out of the fridge. The cake looks marbled with chocolate and caramel swirls. "I also brought some fruit salad for you, Brooke," Justin says as he goes back to the fridge to take out his fruit bowl.

"Thanks, this cheesecake looks really good. If I weren't a vegan, I would be tempted."

David looks long and hard at the cheesecake and says, "You know, this reminds me of economic theory. Everything is mixed together in one cake but you can still see the differences between the chocolate and caramel really clearly."

"All I know is that I wouldn't mind knowing who Professor Adomait thinks is right for the exam," comments Salim.

"I don't think that is going to happen," Brooke replies. "She is such a stickler for knowing everything. I am leaning toward a Keynesian approach to macro. I think governments need to help. Free-market systems just lead to crisis after crisis."

"No way!" exclaims David. "It is the governments that cause the problems. They should just provide the framework for the free-market system to operate and butt out."

Ever the peacemaker, Emma interjects, "Maybe both of you are a bit right. Maybe there has to be a lot of government intervention but of a certain type."

"But governments don't know when to stop and it can become the wrong type really easily," David shoots back.

Libby and Justin look at each other, and Libby says, "Let's talk about this over dessert before we come to any conclusions. And in the grand tradition of the Chicago School of Economics,[2] remember that no matter how heated this gets, we stay friends. OK?"

THE GREAT ECONOMIC DEBATES

Extremes meet.[3]

—Honoré Mercier (1840–1894), Canadian lawyer, journalist, and politician

At last we come to the economic debates, which tend to cluster politically into left-wing and right-wing agendas.[4] I want to make the observation that although politics looks clearly divided at the polls, people's

---

1. *The End of Laissez-Faire* (1926).
2. See the PBS series *The Commanding Heights,* where economists from the Chicago School talk about their seminars, at http://www .pbs.org/wgbh/commandingheights/lo/story/index.html.
3. *Tableaux de Paris.*
4. Right-wing policies tend to be free market, low debt, less government intervention, low taxes, and private property. Left-wing polices tend to be heavily regulated, higher debt, more government intervention, higher taxes, and public property of key sectors.

opinions on a variety of topics are much more nuanced and can sit anywhere on a left–right continuum. Sometimes people vote for the best package of policies even if they don't agree with every single plank in the party platform. This is certainly true for economists and their ideas. There isn't just one set of right-wing and one set left-wing views on economic issues. For instance, Abba Lerner, whom we talked about in the gossip column in the previous chapter, would be considered left-wing in terms of the goals he wanted the government to achieve, but fairly right-wing in methods he wanted the government to use. Depending on the issue in the election, it is possible he could vote either way (although I think people often vote with their values even if they don't appreciate their party's methods).

I will structure this section as a sort of catechism—a series of questions and answers in some semblance of logical order. For each question, I will give the theoretical basis from the left and from the right as well as the resultant policy prescriptions. Many of the theories are reactions to previous ideologies. Therefore, I will cover each topic with some sense of history, bouncing back and forth between the left and right. Please don't assume that where I end up is the last word. Normally, it is just the most recent incarnation of ideas on one side and the previous ideas from the opposite side of the political spectrum remain in play.

Now that we have that out of the way, let's begin our question-and-answer section with the question that gave birth to macroeconomics.

Q1: Do markets—particularly labour markets—reach equilibrium (or clear), and what does this mean for unemployment?

Words ought to be a little wild, for they are the assault of thoughts on the unthinking.[5]
—John Maynard Keynes (1883–1946), British economist

A1: Since the days of Adam Smith, economists saw markets as an equilibrating system of supply and demand relationships. When the system experiences a supply or demand shock, then prices (including wages) and quantities adjust according to the forces at play. In the classical system of the economists before Keynes, markets, given enough time, will always clear on their own, which means they reach a new equilibrium without excess supply or demand left in that particular market. Classical economists explain why people are not working in one of two main ways that find their home in right-wing politics. They thought that either markets are in disequilibrium with an excess supply of labour that will eventually sort itself out in the long run as wages fall to a new equilibrium, OR (and this is a pretty big OR) the unemployed are simply lazy and don't want to work. The first is a case of temporary short-run involuntary unemployment and the latter is voluntary "unemployment." Neither requires intervention to solve because the first just needs time to reach equilibrium and the second isn't primarily an economic problem but a social one.

The long run is a misleading guide to current affairs. In the long run we are all dead. Economists set themselves too easy, too useless a task if in tempestuous seasons they can only tell us that when the storm is past the ocean is flat again.[6]
—John Maynard Keynes (1883–1946), British economist

Keynes entered into the fray during the Great Depression, when people didn't buy into the idea that the misery around them should be bearable because it was a short-term

---

5. *New Statesman and Nation* (July 15, 1933).
6. *A Tract on Monetary Reform* (1923).

economic reality. Neither did they believe that it would eventually sort itself out on its own. They also didn't accept the idea that unemployed people simply didn't want to work. At the time, free-market capitalism was under attack by communism. Ironically, it would be the ideologically left-wing Keynes who would be capitalism's saviour.

He argued that what economists thought would be short term could actually end up being very long term because of resistance to downward wage and price movements. In order for markets to clear in the long run, prices and wages need to move freely both down as well as up. In a sense, the situation of involuntary unemployment was essentially at equilibrium because downside wage and price stickiness was changing the market in the short run. Aggregation of the many workers who are unwilling to take pay cuts (or employers reluctant[7] to give them) means that wages are sticky in the downward direction. This downward rigidity when compounded by the fact that generally the working population was not spending and in fact was saving because of a tenuous economic reality[8] meant that businesses couldn't make a profit and began to lay off even more of the workforce. There just wasn't enough spending stimulus in the economy for it to equilibrate at full employment, which meant that many of the workers were, in fact, involuntarily unemployed at the going "stuck" or "sticky" wage rate.

In Keynes's view, full employment was only possible as a state of equilibrium if the government provided the spending to hire unemployed workers. Keynes favoured public works programs as opposed to tax cuts or a decrease in interest rates because that way the government could guarantee the amount of stimulus spending, whereas people might hoard the money they get from tax cuts instead of spending it and business investment might be unresponsive to lower interest rates. Furthermore, when interest rates are already low, increasing the money supply might become a "liquidity trap" because having more money in the system might not be able to lower rates enough to make a difference in the real economy. In this case, monetary policy is viewed as pushing on a string—in other words, not very effective. For Keynesians, discretionary fiscal spending is the way to go.

GOSSIP COLUMN: JOHN MAYNARD KEYNES (1883-1946)[9]

Keynes was the first born of three children to an overly cautious, scholarly, economist father and an outgoing, political mother. He spent much of his childhood ill, in and out of school with long stretches of homeschooling. His family was upper-middle class but he passed Eton's entrance exam (with coaching from his father) and won a scholarship to attend the school, where he boarded with other intellectually elite non-paying boys, surrounded by the paying wealthy. A very quick and intuitive thinker, he excelled in mathematics, the classics (particularly in medieval Latin poetry), and history, winning lots of prizes. At school, he was also elected to the debating society and revived and ran the Eton literary society. Keynes was popular with his classmates and liked (as intelligent young men usually are) by his teachers. He did have a critical streak, as his letters home are filled with comments about the stupidity or dullness of those in charge.

---

7. This may be out of a feeling of fairness or because of "efficiency wages," an idea made popular by Henry Ford. If Ford paid his workers more than the going wage rate, these workers didn't want to lose their jobs and worked harder, making Ford more profits. Productivity losses due to shirking were down and morale was up.
8. Keynes called this the *precautionary motive* for saving.
9. See the *Oxford Dictionary of National Biography* (Oxford DNB) for a very complete and interesting biography of Keynes.

GOSSIP COLUMN (*CONTINUED*)

Keynes went on to win a full scholarship to Cambridge, where he studied mathematics but very much enjoyed the extracurricular activities of student life. He belonged to the famous semi-secret society called "the Apostles." During Keynes's era, they became fascinated with the work of Cambridge philosopher George Edward Moore (1873–1958), which led them on a journey of personal freedom and private morality. Love, creative expression, and the pursuit of knowledge were paramount. Many of the Cambridge Apostles during this period became part of the Bloomsbury[10] group, a left-wing group of philosophers, writers, musicians, and painters, all passionate about the arts, who met on a weekly basis. This group provided Keynes with more than just intellectual companionship. Many of the members[11] of the group were either gay or bisexual men with whom Keynes had a succession of romantic relationships. (It is reported that he kept a statistical diary of his sexual encounters.)

That would change after he met the Russian ballerina Lydia Lopokova—although not immediately. In the early years of their courtship, he also maintained a relationship with the much younger Sebastian Sprott but in the end Keynes gave up men for Lydia. She managed to get an annulment from her slimy first husband/business manager. Lydia and Keynes were besotted with each other and wrote to each other every day they were apart. Three things would make their marriage less than perfect, however. The other members of the Bloomsbury group didn't like her and were vocal about it. Over time she managed to win them over, so this wasn't permanent. Then Lydia became pregnant but she miscarried and they remained childless.[12] Finally, Keynes suffered a series of heart attacks over many years and died a premature death at 62 years of age. (Lydia was a widow for 35 years.)

His career had as many twists and turns as did his love life. Keynes's first employment was for the Civil Service in India because he came in second on the civil service exam. The work bored him and he revised his fellowship thesis on probability, hoping to win a fellowship back to England. When it appeared he wasn't going to win because the examiners thought that he could try again the next year, he was furious. A fortnight later, his father's friend and colleague Alfred Marshall offered him a lectureship at Cambridge. Even though his cautious father advised against the move, Keynes took it.

Back in Cambridge he lectured, took on private students, became editor of the *Economic Journal* (which would last for most of his life), and wrote his first book *Indian Currency and Finance*, which he published with Macmillan. (He and Dan Macmillan had a relationship during their school years.) An expert on Indian currency and acquainted with the civil service, he was asked to be on a royal commission on Indian Currency and Finance. It was perfect fit and one where he impressed the other commissioners. Then WWI broke out and the Treasury asked for his help in the war effort, especially in the area of money, currency, and finance. Most of the Bloomsbury group strongly opposed the war and became conscientious objectors. They wanted Keynes to resign, but Keynes was torn and in the end stayed at the Treasury. This did not make his friends very happy.

---

10. Virginia Woolf is the most famous female member of the group.
11. They include, Duncan Grant, Lytton Strachey, James Strachey, and Sebastian Sprott.
12. Niall Ferguson got himself into hot water when he speculated that Keynes didn't worry about the long run because he was gay and didn't have children. When this hit the news, Ferguson posted an apology immediately.

After the Great War, Keynes was part of the delegation to the Treaty of Versailles. He left three weeks before the signing of the treaty, appalled, and started to write *The Economic Consequences of the Peace* at a fast and furious pace. It was done in three months. Macmillan Publishing didn't think there would be a big market for the book and wanted to do a smaller print run. Keynes negotiated with the company to reverse the normal publishing approach by paying for the production costs and giving the publisher a royalty. The book was an international best seller and Keynes became a celebrity.

The government asked him to serve on a royal commission on Indian Tariffs and he agreed, but before he was to leave the country, he resigned for a couple of reasons. The first was that he met Lydia. Second, he was offered a job working for *The Manchester Guardian* as editor of a monthly supplement on the economic and financial problems of the reconstruction of Europe. Keynes wrote many of the articles but he also lined up an impressive list of contributors. Many of his books started by airing his views in the public sphere, and some of these articles became part of his book *Tract on Monetary Reform.*

When Britain was considering whether or not to go back to the gold standard, Keynes was consulted and advised against it. His advice was ignored and he wrote a series of articles in *The Evening Standard* called *The Economic Consequences of Mr. Churchill.* Given how badly the gold standard worked out for Britain, Churchill (when he was the Chancellor of the Exchequer) would wish that he had taken Keynes's advice.

Between the wars, Keynes wrote in various newspapers, served on corporate boards, became active in the Liberal Party, and worked with various government committees, all the while honing his ideas about "managing" the economy. Back at Cambridge, he became a Fellow because he resigned his economic lectureship. (He could limit his teaching to eight lectures in the fall term on the subject of his current work.) A group of young economists—who called themselves "Keynes's circus"—formed after Keynes's publication of a *Treatise on Money* in 1930 to discuss his work, and Richard Kahn reported their[13] comments to Keynes. All of this fed into Keynes's most famous work, *The General Theory of Employment, Interest and Money,* in 1936—a book that stood the economic world on its head both in academic and government circles.

A year later, he had a heart attack that curtailed his activities somewhat although not in the arts. He was an active patron and helped many arts organizations obtain stable funding to operate. He was also a collector of rare books and paintings, which were later donated. All of these activities needed money, and it seems Keynes was genius at making (and sometimes losing) large sums of money on the stock, bond, and commodities markets for himself and his alma mater. At the beginning of his investment career, he tried to play the turning points of the markets with borrowed funds (known as leveraging) but later he took a more conservative long-term approach to these investments. He died wealthy, equivalent to a modern day multimillionaire.

During WWII, Keynes was called upon to help the Treasury with the budget as well on exchange rate matters. He worked very hard despite his health. Lydia must have been going crazy trying to keep him well, but it appears he was a workaholic as well as active in the arts scene.

---

13. The Cambridge Circus included Richard Kahn, James Meade, Joan Robinson, Austin Robinson, and Piero Sraffa, all famous economists.

GOSSIP COLUMN (*CONTINUED*)

After the war, Keynes was the head British delegate to the Bretton Woods month-long conference, where he was a leader—especially in establishing the international finance arrangements that would become the IMF and World Bank. He described the pressure as unbelievable to the chancellor once it was over. This was due to the sheer volume of work, the negotiations on behalf of the system in general and for Britain in particular, and the language barriers between delegates. Keynes suffered a mild heart attack while running upstairs at the conference. At his concluding speech, the role that Keynes played was honoured with multiple standing ovations.

Back in England, Keynes continued to work for the Treasury on financing the post-war international system between Britain and the Americans, but that proved politically contentious. Keynes wasn't always at the table to outline his views and often felt impotent and angry when the positions of the cabinet ministers were reported back to him. This couldn't have been good for his heart.

His last public appearance was a trip to Savannah (USA) for the first meeting of the board for the international fund and bank in March of 1946. This would end with two disappointments and a physical setback. He was disappointed that the Americans would not budge on the location of these two new international organizations. The Brits wanted New York but the Americans decided it would be Washington. (It is very likely that Keynes was outmaneuvered by Harry Dexter White, a senior Treasury official and, as it turns out, a Soviet spy.[14]) The Americans also decided to hire the directors on the cheap, which wouldn't bode well for getting competent people to apply for the job. During his travels, Keynes became ill with a stomach bug because of a poorly cleaned cabin car. He arrived back in England exhausted. Keynes continued to work but slowed down before Easter by retiring to his Tilton farm in East Essex, to enjoy walks, take tea with his Bloomsbury friends, and read in the garden. On Easter Sunday, he died instantly of a heart attack.

If there is one word to describe John Maynard Keynes it would be the British term "brilliant."

Q2: How important is the fallacy of composition?

I do not know which makes a man more conservative—to know nothing but the present, or nothing but the past.[15]

—*John Maynard Keynes (1883–1946), British economist*

A2: As you recall from the introduction, the fallacy of composition states that you cannot assume what is true for an individual on a small scale will also be true for the larger group once we deal with a bigger system. Now the idea that one person doing something is a very different thing from everyone doing it isn't a strange idea even in microeconomics. For example, competition theory assumes this all the time when economists say that one firm experiencing an increase in costs does nothing to the market price but if every company has higher costs then the market price of that

---

14. *The Battle of Bretton Woods: John Maynard Keynes, Harry Dexter White, and the Making of a New World Order* (2013), by Benn Steil.
15. *The End of Laissez-Faire* (1926).

product will rise. What makes the fallacy of composition a particularly macro issue was how Keynes dealt with the interaction between savings and investment and the "paradox of thrift."

The story of the Keynesian paradox of thrift goes something like this. Businesses decide how much they want to invest and are ruled by investor confidence—or, as Keynes like to call it, "animal spirits"[16]—rather than by interest rates in making this decision. Once the level of investment (I) is set, these firms borrow from those who save. These savers provide the funds or savings (S) out of the part or fraction of their income they don't consume. ($S = sY_d$, where s is the savings rate and Y_d is disposable income.) In equilibrium, the level of investment equals the level of savings in the economy ($I = S$). If households suddenly decide to increase their savings rate (s) and save more out of every dollar of income (which they might if they are worried about the economy), they do so by consuming less of their income ($Y_d = C + sY_d$, where s is up, C is down, and Y_d is constant). This increase in the supply of savings is made available to business at lower interest rates (or price of borrowing), but those rates don't induce more investment spending—and this last part is the critical to the Keynesian story.

However, now businesses experience a drop in sales because households aren't shopping. They lay off some of their staff and those folks cut back spending, initiating the multiplier effect. As disposable income (Y_d) falls, the total value of savings will fall back to original levels even though everyone has a higher saving rate (s is up and Y_d is down to keep S constant). Frugality by households induces a recession, with disposable income (Y_d) down, consumption (C) down, and savings constant (S). This is a sad state of affairs that can only be solved by government intervention.

The more the state "plans" the more difficult planning becomes for the individual.[17]
—Friedrich August Hayek (1899–1992), Austrian-British economist

There are, of course, some right-wing criticisms of this scenario. First, if interest rates fall, this should induce some borrowing—unless people are saving by keeping cash under their mattresses or if commercial banks decide not to make the loans of the new savings they have on deposit. Those on the right think this kind of hoarding is unlikely because banks are motivated by profits and profits require banks to lend. Therefore any increase in savings should be matched with an increase in either consumer or business investment with no drop in aggregate sales. Second, in a global economy, even if domestic parties don't want to borrow, there are still foreign opportunities. Financial capital should flow out, which puts downward pressure on the currency. The lower value for the domestic currency should stimulate export sales. Thus the drop in domestic consumption is matched with a rise in foreign consumption and, more important, real GDP or national income (Y) stays constant. Third, even if people hoard the savings, the drop in demand should put enough downward pressure on prices that output will increase again.

---

16. I recommend the book *Animal Spirits: How Human Psychology Drives the Economy and Why It Matters for Global Capitalism,* by George Akerlof (Nobel Prize winner) and Robert Shiller. They have an interesting take on the concept of animal spirits that you won't find outlined in this particular way in standard macroeconomics texts. The five aspects of animal spirits they give are confidence, fairness, corrupt and antisocial behaviour, money illusion, and the role of stories.
17. *The Road to Serfdom* (1944).

Much of the debate between those who hold right-wing ideas and those who hold left-wing ideas has to do with how quickly market players can respond to a change in the savings rate in terms of investment decisions, money hoarding behaviour, and price rigidities.

Q3: Why do business cycles occur and what can we do about them?

A study of the history of opinion is a necessary preliminary to the emancipation of the mind.[18]

—John Maynard Keynes (1883–1946), British economist

A3: The question of why business cycles occur—the booms and busts—has been a topic of interest for a long time. There are many spots in history that we can use to launch into the theories that explain business cycles, but I will focus on the more modern explanations of the last century. Specifically, I will begin with Keynes.

In order to see how a Keynesian cycle occurs, let's start the economy on the trend line or at potential output. It's all good. So what suddenly changes? Keynes believed that business cycle booms and busts were due to changes in investor confidence or "animal spirits" such that members of the business community wakes up one morning with a "gut feeling" and make changes in their investment plans. This initial change in investment then leads to a multiplier effect because of the impact income has on consumption, and the economy is in recession.

Keynes believed that government should counteract the lack of spending by the business community and actively minimize the recessionary dip in the business cycle with government spending. If governments need the funds to spend and don't want to borrow from the public (in order to avoid the crowding-out effect), Abba Lerner showed that deficits could be funded with monetary policy in order to prevent any interest rate increases. The central bank would simply buy the government bonds and monetize the debt.

The right remedy for the trade cycle is not to be found in abolishing booms and thus keeping us permanently in a semi-slump; but in abolishing slumps and thus keeping us permanently in a quasi-boom.[19]

—John Maynard Keynes (1883–1946), British economist

CARRY ON AND THINK OF ENGLAND

The Keynesian revolution replaced the classical view of macroeconomics and would reign over government policies for quite a long time. Partially this was due to the following series of events. Keynes's book *The General Theory of Employment, Interest and Money* (1936), shortened to *The General Theory,* became a best seller and upon reading it American economist Alvin Hansen[20] became a Harvard Keynesian convert (although he

---

18. *The End of Laissez-Faire* (1926).
19. *The General Theory of Employment, Interest and Money* (1936).
20. Hansen (1887–1975) wrote *Fiscal Policy and Business Cycles* (1941), which cast the Great Depression in Keynesian terms and gave Keynesian solutions. He also co-developed the IS-LM model with British economist John Hicks, who is featured in Chapter 7 of *Cocktail Party Economics.* Hicks's wife Ursula Kathleen Webb Hicks (1896–1985) jointly started *The Review of Economic Studies* along with Abba Lerner and Paul Sweezy. It was a small world.

initially didn't agree with it). Hansen's most famous graduate student, Nobel-Prize-winning Paul Samuelson,[21] published an introductory economics textbook in 1948 that spread the Keynesian message throughout the world.[22] This was a very influential textbook and would embed Keynesian economics into the economics curriculum of post-secondary school campuses everywhere.

Reinforcing Keynesian economics, the post-WWII economies boomed and government economists around the world spoke about the inflation–unemployment trade-off[23]— each country either has an unemployment problem or an inflation problem but not both. Furthermore, a government could, depending on the politics of the time, change its spot on the "problem" continuum by manipulating fiscal and monetary policy. If the electorate was fed up with unemployment, the ruling party could expand the economy and generate some inflation. If the population was worried about inflation, politicians could agree to policies that would contract the economy, thereby removing inflation but generating some unemployment. Back then, governments saw themselves as steering the economy the way a driver steers a car, making corrections during the ride. However, by the stagflationary 1970s, the economy didn't seem so controllable anymore and Keynesian economics fell from grace.

Credit expansion can bring about a temporary boom. But such a fictitious prosperity must end in a general depression of trade, a slump.[24]
—Ludwig Heinrich Edler von Mises (1991–1973), Austrian-Hungarian philosopher, economist, and sociologist

All throughout the Keynesian revolution, Friedrich Hayek, along with other members of the libertarian Austrian School of Economics, warned of impending doom. They blamed business cycles on excessive increases in bank credit supported by the loose monetary policy of central bankers. Given that fiscal policies were monetized during the Keynesian heyday, there certainly was a lot of money growth going on during the post-WWII era. To the economists of the Austrian School, the inflation of the 1970s was inevitable. Their story said that excess credit eventually leads to excessive borrowing. Unfortunately, this borrowing is for unsound business projects ending in speculative bubbles. They believed that at some point, the credit expansion cannot be sustained, that bubbles burst and a recession is part of the correction process.

Even though Hayek received a Nobel Prize for some of this work, the ideas of the Austrian School were not popular with the mainstream, partly because their business cycle theory requires banks to consistently and purposely make bad loans. Economists didn't see this behaviour happening naturally—until the subprime mortgage market crisis of 2008, that is. It also needs very large swings in investment for self-correction, which also didn't seem to happen. Much of the discrediting of this theory was done by another right-wing economist, Milton Friedman.

---

21. Paul Samuelson (1915–2009) credits Hansen for the inspiration of his accelerator-multiplier business cycle model (1948).
22. *Economics: An Introductory Analysis* (1948), coauthored with William Nordhaus. By the 19th edition, the book had sold more than 4 million copies in 41 languages.
23. This was popularized by Bill Phillips (1914–-975) in what is known as the Phillips curve. The trade-off is due to aggregate demand shifts along a given aggregate supply curve. As demand increases, prices go up, as does output, which implies that unemployment is down.
24. *Planned Chaos* (1947).

Inflation is always and everywhere a monetary phenomenon in the sense that it is and can be produced only by a more rapid increase in the quantity of money than in output.[25]
—*Milton Friedman (1912–2006), American economist*

Friedman places the blame for swings in business cycles on excessive changes in the money supply and interest rates, not on bad bankers allowing businesses to borrow for subpar projects. In Freidman's theory, business and consumer borrowing behaviour is very sensitive to interest rates. This means that monetary policy is very powerful in controlling the economy. Monetary policy is the cornerstone of the Monetarist School of Economics based out of the University of Chicago (sometimes known as the Chicago School[26]—synonymous for a hotbed of right-wing economic ideas).

Essentially, Friedman revived the quantity theory of money, or MV = PY, which says that the stock of money (M) in the system must be used to buy the flow of expenditures (PY) in the economy assuming that the velocity (V) of money is stable. Furthermore, he said that because monetary policy was powerful but unpredictable due to long lags, the money supply (M) should only be increased just enough to match the real growth in the economy (Y). It should not be used to minimize swings in the business cycle because, odds are, when the policy finally kicks in, it would just make the swings worse.

Attempts to actively control the business cycle went somewhat by the wayside during the high-inflation years of the 1970s and 1980s. Rather, central banks and their governments shifted their focus to trying to control inflation. Central banks tried to control the money stock and governments implemented wage and price controls. Both strategies weren't as successful as everyone hoped they would be.

Just to put the nail in the Keynesian coffin, Friedman also reduced the importance of Keynesian fiscal policy as a tool to tame cycles by reducing the fiscal multiplier effect. He showed that people consume based on permanent or lifetime expected income and asserted that any income change in a single period doesn't necessarily change consumption. Without a propensity to consume out of income,[27] there is no Keynesian multiplier effect.

Last, in Friedman's theory, fiscal spending doesn't have a permanent effect on the economy. Although it is true that workers do have delayed responses to inflation, which explains some wage rigidity in the short run, once they respond any gains are lost. This means that governments can get a temporary increase in output when governments spend more, but it is only temporary. Once wages and prices rise, this isn't sustainable to the long run and the economy drifts back to the natural rate of unemployment. All the govern-

---

25. *The Counter-Revolution in Monetary Theory* (1970).
26. Milton Friedman and Arnold Harberger trained a group of young Chilean economists known as the Chicago Boys. These economists became prominent during the reign of Pinochet, and two years after the military coup Friedman visited the country at their request to give a series of lectures and seminars and to meet with government officials, including with Pinochet himself. Friedman never supported the government of Pinochet but this caused a quite the controversy such that when he was nominated for the Nobel Prize, his nomination was formally protested by four Nobel Prize winners in the sciences. Friedman maintained that going to help a country become free of the evils of inflation was no different from a doctor going to the country to help relieve a medical epidemic. The politics shouldn't change whether or not to help. He also believed that a free economy would lead to democracy. Needless to say there are many who disagreed with his actions, and controversy followed him even into death. When colleagues within his department wanted to name a research institute after him, a petition was circulated from outside the economics and business department to have a full-scale debate about whether or not this was appropriate given his ardent support of right-wing policies. Milton and Rose (his wife of 68 years and also an economist) co-wrote the book *Free to Choose*, which became a best seller and a 10-part PBS television series espousing free-market principles.
27. This is called the *marginal propensity to consume* (mpc). The consumption function is $C = C_0 + mpc\, Y_d$, where Y_d is the income to the consumer sometimes known as disposable income. ($Y_d = Y - T$, and T equals total taxes.)

ment would achieve is a change in who spends—the private sector spends less and government spends more. Friedman, a free-market economist, felt the private sector would do a better job of spending wisely and favoured government spending cuts as well as tax cuts and the privatization of government industries. After Friedman, monetary policy had the top spot on the policy agenda and Keynesian fiscal spending had slipped from its pedestal.

There is no means of avoiding the final collapse of a boom brought about by credit expansion. The alternative is only whether the crisis should come sooner as the result of voluntary abandonment of further credit expansion, or later as a final and total catastrophe of the currency system involved.[28]
—Ludwig Heinrich Edler von Mises (1991–1973), Austrian-Hungarian philosopher, economist, and sociologist

Many in the Austrian School point out that there isn't a great inconsistency between monetarism and their own view in terms of policy implications even if the stories about what causes business cycles are different. Both oppose discretionary fiscal and monetary policy. In the end, monetarism went mainstream and the Austrian school did not. The 2008 financial crisis provoked an Austrian School revival of sorts when the impact of financial deregulation and innovation led to the problem of moral hazard[29] in American banks. Banks made bad loans because they could get them off the books by selling them as asset-backed securities (ABSs)—a process known as securitization. The bad business decisions by banks, the inevitable housing bubble, and finally the credit crunch of 2008 are very much an Austrian School story.

It gives me great pleasure, indeed, to see the stubbornness of an incorrigible nonconformist warmly acclaimed.[30]
—Albert Einstein (1879–1955), German physicist

On the left, Hyman Minsky (1991–1996) expanded on the idea that business cycles had their origins in the financial system, but he included a wider array of financial products other than just the money supply. In fact, he felt that it was the new financial products that cause all of the action. His "financial instability hypothesis" is the following. After a sustained period of economic growth and financial calm, people become too confident and engage in riskier "get-rich-quick" borrowing. Leveraging[31] happens on a grand scale and asset prices rise. Eventually, this situation leads to a bubble in whatever market people madly invest (read "save") in—assets like housing, stocks, gold, and so on. Eventually asset prices burst in what is called a *Minsky moment*[32] and lending collapses. Moreover, much of the borrowing turns out to be very risky and borrowers sustain great losses and many default on their loans. This leads to a recession.

---

28. *Human Action: A Treatise on Economics* (1949).
29. Moral hazard occurs when people change their behaviour to take on more risk once a contract is signed—for example, a homeowner buys property insurance then decides not to lock his doors because his home is insured. This homeowner always locked the doors before.
30. Ideas and Opinions in the section "Address on Receiving Lord & Taylor Award" (May 4, 1953).
31. Leveraging is the act of borrowing at a low interest rate to invest (read "save") in something that promises a higher rate of return.
32. Coined by Paul McCulley of Pacific Investment Management Company to describe the Russian financial crisis in 1998.

Minsky's prescriptions are both short term and long term. In the short run, central banks have to save the system with monetary policy and governments need to spend to stimulate demand. This seems very Keynesian so far. It is Minsky's long-run emphasis that separates him. He was a big believer in strict regulations of the financial sector to prevent crazy behaviour in the first place. However, he thought that because of financial evolution and innovation, effective regulation would prove difficult to do in a democratic country. Minsky spoke in words rather than in mathematical models, so his ideas didn't become mainstream in academia or with central banks. He argued against the right-wing financial deregulation of the 1980s in the USA to no avail. The recent financial crisis of 2008–2009 brought his ideas back to the table.

He hath indeed better bettered expectation than you must expect of me to tell you how.[33]
—William Shakespeare (1564–1616), English writer

In the 1970s, Robert Lucas[34] brought new theoretical direction to both Keynesian and classical economics leading to New Keynesian and New Classical theories of business cycles. (Very innovative in the names, aren't they?) Lucas's concept had to do with *rational expectations* and is known as the "Lucas critique." It goes something like this. If people live in an inflationary world, then they don't just negotiate wages and prices based on past inflation but they make guesses about the future and ask for those increases instead. They are forward looking in their expectations rather than adapting to the past. Economic activity is based on the expectation of the future based on rational assumptions. If this is the case, then prices and wages all rise by the same amount and output doesn't change. Therefore, it isn't possible to use fiscal or monetary policy to change the level of real GDP because it will get undone by inflation expectations in contract negotiations. There no longer remains an unemployment–inflation trade-off. The only variable the government can control is inflation.

Now in saying a new, he hath made the former old. And that which decayeth and groweth old, is near its end.
—Hebrews 8:13[35]

The idea of "rational expectations" meshed perfectly with the neo-classical view that prices and wages adjust as we go. Milton Friedman's temporary impact of fiscal spending was now gone because prices and wages adjusted ahead of inflation, not in response to it. Neo-classical economists felt that changes to the business cycle can only occur because of surprises or unexpected shocks in demand because everything that is expected is already "rationally" incorporated into people's choices. In response, governments can sometimes surprise their constituents with unexpected interest rate declines or spending, but you can only fool people a few times before they catch on and the government loses all credibility. Surprises become expected. Neo-classical economists worry about the inflationary implications of any expansionary policy—even during a recession—and believe the spending isn't worth it.

---

33. *Much Ado about Nothing* (1598–1599).
34. Robert Lucas Jr. (1937–) won a Nobel Prize for this idea. His ex-wife had put into the divorce settlement that if he won the Nobel Prize within seven years of the divorce, she would receive half the winnings. He won within the time period and she got her money.
35. Dhouay-Rheims 1899 American Edition Bible.

Neo-Keynesians, on the other side of the fence, incorporated the theory of rational expectations into their approach as well. The key difference from the neo-classicals is that they told stories about why wages and prices get stuck, allowing fiscal spending to have an effect. (Recall that wage and price rigidities are necessary to have involuntary unemployment.) Wages and prices can become inflexible if people sign labour or business contracts that maintain wages or prices over a specified period. Before the contract is signed, individuals intend to guess what will happen to inflation but the duration of the contract is so long that it isn't easy to guess correctly. Even without a contract, in times of recession, employers may be reluctant to reduce paycheques in order to maintain the morale and labour effort of the workers still on the job. Therefore, even with rational expectations, some wage rigidity still exists in the system, allowing fiscal policy to change the value of real GDP and employment.

Once the rational expectations point was added to either the Keynesian or classical views, the effective role of discretionary policy by governments and central banks to remove business cycles diminished. Rational expectations reinstated the classical view of markets clearing, and therefore policy was again seen as unnecessary—even harmful. In terms of Keynesian economics, rational expectations decreased the impact of fiscal and monetary policy because it now depends on more subtle stories of wage stickiness in order to have involuntary unemployment. Economists were theoretically tying the hands of the bureaucrats.

The stories told by the neo-classical and neo-Keynesian economists didn't focus on supply-side reasons for business cycles, although they didn't rule them out. Things like oil prices and widespread unionization could lead to higher costs of production or stagflation, but the focus of the mainstream (whether neo-classical or neo-Keynesian) economists was on the demand side. There were a few, however, such as the right-wing supply siders, who focused on tax cuts to lower production costs[36] and increase output. Empirically, tax changes don't explain typical business cycles, however.

It is what we prevent, rather than what we do that counts most in Government.
—William Lyon Mackenzie King (1874–1950), Canadian prime minister

The story that truly connects supply to the business cycles is found in real business cycle (RBC) theory.[37] This theory says that cycles happen because of fluctuations in productivity changes due to technological change, natural disasters, or international frictions. Labour is rational in its expectations, in keeping with the Lucas critique. Workers make choices about how much they want to work given the prevalent interest rates and their current skill sets. If employee talents become obsolete due to technological change (for example, if coal mining jobs are out and computer programming jobs are in), then labour productivity falls and jobs are destroyed. According to this story of business cycles, this leads to a recession and wages should fall. As wages fall, people may choose not to work. This is very much a right-wing expected outcome because, according to this theory, markets always clear so there is no involuntary unemployment even though the economy

---

36. And potentially even increase tax revenues by the Laffer curve. In practice, it seems that none of the North American countries are on the wrong side of the Laffer curve, so any tax cuts do decrease revenue.
37. American Edward Christian Prescott (1940–) and Norwegian Finn E. Kydland (1943–) made important contributions to RBC theory, which, along with their work on time inconsistency (concerning the conduct of policy), was recognized for the Nobel Memorial Prize in Economics in 2004.

cycles for structural reasons. The cycle is real in that it involves output changes. From a policy perspective, RBC theorists believe only real things matter so governments should focus on long-run structural issues and not try to smooth the cycle with discretionary fiscal or monetary policy. They advocate stable rules that people can count on as they plan their lives instead.

Q4: Should exchange rates be fixed or flexible?

In truth, the gold standard is already a barbarous relic.[38]

—John Maynard Keynes (1883–1946), British economist

A4: As we saw in Chapter 10, International Cheques and Balances, the gold standard and the Bretton Woods agreement gave much of the world experience with fixed exchange rates. Although there isn't a consensus among economists based on a right–left divide about what is best, those of the far right-wing, as represented by the Austrian School, advocate going back to a gold standard, which implies a fixed exchange rate. This isn't because they believe that a fixed exchange rate is better but because it ties the hands of central bankers in terms of monetary policy. However, right-wing economist Milton Friedman was in favour of flexible exchange rates because he believed in the flexible movement of prices inherent in a free-market system. He believed that central banks should just control the growth in the money supply directly without needing to have their hands tied.

If one takes pleasure in calling the gold standard a "barbarous relic," one cannot object to the application of the same term to every historically determined institution. Then the fact that the British speak English—and not Danish, German, or French—is a barbarous relic too, and every Briton who opposes the substitution of Esperanto for English is no less dogmatic and orthodox than those who do not wax rapturous about the plans for a managed currency.[39]

—Ludwig Heinrich Edler von Mises (1991–1973), Austrian-Hungarian philosopher, economist, and sociologist

Left-wing economist Abba Lerner favoured a flexible exchange rate because he wanted the central bank to have the ability to support fiscal policy with monetary policy. Keynes, however, never favoured a flexible exchange rate even though he spoke against the gold standard after WWI. His main concern with the gold standard, as a particular fixed exchange rate, was the plan to peg the exchange rate to prewar values for gold, which he felt were too high. Keynes thought that this particular price of gold would result in an unnecessary restriction on the gold available to grow the economy because the country was committed to maintaining the exchange rate. The British economy painfully contracted and Keynes was proven right (not to his great pleasure, by the way). Britain subsequently abandoned the gold standard as a fixed exchange rate. After WWII, Keynes was sent to Bretton Woods as the British delegate and fully supported a fixed exchange system for international trade purposes.

---

38. *Monetary Reform* (1924).
39. *Human Action: A Treatise on Economics* (1949).

Q5: How damaging are government deficits and debt?

Economics is a very dangerous science.[40]

—John Maynard Keynes (1883–1946), British economist

A5: It took Abba Lerner to push the implications of Keynesian economics to its logical conclusions. In this line of thinking, deficits and debt are tools to serve the economy. Because the state can print money, he felt that these tools are not as worrisome as they are at a personal level. According to left-wing economists, the debt isn't as important as the economy because of the high cost of unemployment.

The right pushes back with the assertion that debt puts a drag on an economy, making it hard to grow. This is supported with a now very controversial study[41] published in 2010 by Carmen Reinhart and Kenneth Rogoff, who claimed that once gross external debt is 60% of GDP, the country's growth rate drops by 2%. If the level rises to 90%, the growth rate is cut in half. This research was used by right-wing politicians and policy wonks[42] as justification for the austerity measures proposed in Europe around the same time the paper was published. Unfortunately for the researchers, a group of grad students took their data and found coding errors in their Excel spreadsheet and omissions of some data points. This created quite a scandal in the academic world of economists. The data was then reviewed by three economists from the University of Massachusetts (Amherst)—a hotbed of left-wing economists—who did not overturn the basic findings of Rogoff and Reinhart[43] for the very high debt levels. They too found that when external debt levels are above 90%, the loss in growth is still about 1%. Although a percentage doesn't seem like much, the average growth for countries with lower debt was on average 3.5% and for the indebted countries it dropped to 2.3%.

In their work, Reinhart and Rogoff did not quickly jump to tough austerity measures as the antidote to the debt problem, but the right-wing political machine certainly did. Left-wing Paul Krugman[44] reacted to the fiasco (both the paper and the resulting policy measures in Greece) by pointing out that policymakers chose to listen to the voices that supported their ideological position not because the evidence was so compelling that they had to but because they wanted to. Economists do not speak with one voice, and politicians should listen to all sides of the argument before they make life really tough for ordinary people.

This kafuffle does not take the negative impact of debt levels off the table, however. Research[45] done by the European Central Bank showed that a relationship exists between growth in per capita GDP and debt levels for 12 euro countries from 1970 to 2010. The relationship isn't a simple linear one, but there is a relationship. Once debt levels reached between 90% and 100% of per capita GDP, growth slowed. In fact, the slowing may have occurred at lower debt levels (70–80%), but this is statistically more uncertain. Debt is a

---

40. *Essays in Biography* (1933).
41. "Growth in a Time of Debt," *American Economic Review* (2010).
42. A person who studies or develops political strategies and policies.
43. http://www.nytimes.com/2013/04/26/opinion/debt-growth-and-the-austerity-debate.html?_r=0.
44. http://www.nytimes.com/2013/04/19/opinion/krugman-the-excel-depression.html?_r=0.
45. "The impact of high government debt on economic growth and its channels: An empirical investigation for the euro area," http://www.sciencedirect.com/science/article/pii/S0014292112000876.

very important issue in the euro zone because each country cannot print money to fund its spending due to the common currency.

Q6: What should governments do?

I work for a Government I despise for ends I think criminal.[46]

—*John Maynard Keynes (1883–1946), British economist*

A6: The question of what governments should do is very much a political one. Let me give you a basic summary of the policy solutions for the different political camps.

For the left, a recession can be fixed primarily with fiscal policy. The government should quickly implement fiscal policy because of the tremendous cost of unemployment to society. Leftists believe the monetary authorities should serve the government in this endeavour by monetizing the debt, especially when interest rates are so low that monetary policy alone is like pushing a string. Leftists are not overly concerned about inflationary pressures at low levels of inflation. At high levels of inflation, policies like wage and price controls and other wage-containment strategies along with a slowing of the money supply make the most sense. (To be honest, the left hasn't had much success with fighting inflation, but they have mitigated the cost of unemployment during times of low inflation.)

For the right, there really isn't any discretionary policy that can solve either the problem of inflation or unemployment. In fact, there is a great risk that governments and central banks can make things worse. Instead governments should support the free-market system so that it can solve the macroeconomic problems on its own. Furthermore, central banks should be very controlled in their actions and withstand any governmental pressure to expand the money supply beyond the real growth in GDP. For those on the right, national debt is a very bad thing and should be avoided at all costs. If austerity measures are needed, then so be it. It is short-term pain for long-term gain.

In countries where inflation is very high, right-wing economists propose very tough measures. It is sometimes called "shock therapy"[47] because it combines substantial cuts in government spending and in the growth of the money supply in hopes of quickly removing the "rational expectation" of inflation. Some economists think the sudden shock will result in less pain[48] in the long run than if governments try to remove inflation slowly but surely.

New objectives and new money cannot solve these problems.[49]

—*John F. Kennedy (1917–1963), American president*

Given the Lucas critique or "rational expectations," economist Thomas Sargent found that a credible (or believable) central bank with anti-inflationary policies is critical. People have to believe that governments will do everything in their power to reduce inflation for people to change their expectations at the negotiating table. The cost of this disinflationary process is greater if central banks try to trick the public by saying one thing and

---

46. Letter to Duncan Grant (December 15, 1917).
47. Milton Friedman called this *shock policy*, whereas Jeffery Sachs called it *shock therapy* to connote the therapeutic nature of the policy to get healthy again that does not glorify the process.
48. Sometimes the pain is measured by the *sacrifice ratio*, which is the percent of GDP loss required to take inflation down by 1%. There is a trade-off between the small losses of years of chronic unemployment or one really bad year. Often one bad year has less aggregate loss than cumulating years of losses. However, richer countries can take the shock of one bad year easier than the poor because one bad year in a poor country usually results in many deaths.
49. Delivered to a Joint Session of Congress on May 25, 1961.

doing another[50] in hopes of easing unemployment. Once a central bank is known to fool the public, people who negotiate the wages and prices essentially ignore the government's (unbelievable) policy statements.

Fortunately for Canada, once the Bank of Canada announced it was fighting inflation in the 1990s, the public believed it partly because of the resulting spike in unemployment. Inflation fell from 5% in 1990 to less than 2% in 1992. The most important thing for any central bank is its credibility. When the governor of the Bank of Canada announces the target rate it is willing to live with, because the central bank delivered on its promises in the past, the Canadian public believes it, even if citizens don't like the direction the governor is taking.

WHERE DO WE GO FROM HERE?

It is better to debate a question without settling it than to settle a question without debating it.[51]
—*Joseph Joubert (1754–1824), French writer*

I am reluctant to tell you my particular position on these important questions partly because there are very smart people (with supporting data) on both sides of the fence. But I will give it a go anyway.

Let's start with the easy one. Gold is good for jewelry but I don't think it is good for currency anymore. I don't think we should go back to the gold standard because there just isn't enough gold in the world to act as "grease" for a growing world economy. Furthermore, gold discoveries, erratic as they are, would affect economies in unpredictable ways. I also don't think we should tie the hands of central bankers because of the threat of inflation. They should act with credibility and great transparency instead. Exchange rates are too good of a price mechanism in addressing unemployment issues between countries, and we shouldn't give that up in the name of inflation. The problems in the euro zone are partly due to the constraints a common currency places on countries to deal with their unemployment problems.

In times of low inflation, low interest rates, and high unemployment, the social cost of unemployment is so high, and the odds of prices rising are so low, that we need a good dose of Keynesian spending to get things going. Letting the economy self-correct in this case causes untold misery. But this spending needs careful analysis, because if the underlying reasons for the unemployment are structural rather than cyclical, then throwing money at the problem won't necessarily solve it. Spending can easily lead to inflation, which makes the misery worse. Now the unemployed face higher prices.

I think some government debt is fine. In fact, if the government had no debt, it would transform how central banks would have to administer monetary policy. Our entire monetary system is based on debt (loans that become deposits). The way the central bank changes the money supply is through the sale and purchase of government T-Bills (part of the government's debt). Without government debt, our current monetary system would not exist. However, once the debt-to-GDP ratio gets beyond a certain amount (more

---

50. Many central banks in developing countries tried to trick their citizens into thinking they would slow the growth of the money supply but didn't actually do so in practice.
51. *The Notebooks of Joseph Joubert* (1983), translated and edited by Paul Auster.

research is needed to find the upper limit—but 90% is certainly too much), then the accumulated debt and the resultant interest payments make it very difficult for governments to solve unemployment problems or fund needed programs.

If the economy has stable inflation and interest rates along with low unemployment, a government should run a surplus to pay down the debt and build up capacity for bad times, which are inevitably around the corner. Governments need to be wary of what Milton Friedman called the "permanency of a temporary program." Left-wing economists often argue for spending in bad times, but they should be more vocal for cuts in good times to be consistent with a cyclically balanced budget[52] of the type suggested by Abba Lerner. More often than not, the left never speaks of cuts but relies on the tax revenue increases in good times to reduce but not eliminate the size of the deficit.

During times of high inflation, high interest rates, and high unemployment, we have to do the hard thing and get rid of inflation first because unemployment becomes almost impossible to solve in a world of rational expectations, escalating prices, and market uncertainty. This means cutting money growth and raising interest rates, which will make unemployment worse—hopefully for a very short time because the government acts credibly, with integrity, and the public believes the government. It may also be worth it for the government to put wage controls into place to modify expectations about inflation. This is easiest to do among public-sector employees but the government has to be prepared for labour disruptions, which can make the recession worse.

Countries with high inflation and unemployment usually end up in civil unrest. Proposing painful austerity measures to fix the situation becomes a really "tough sell" to the public. Even if you convince people initially, these measures become difficult to sustain in democratic countries where different interest groups have loud voices. The recent crisis in Greece is a good example of this. In places where governments rule with an iron fist, it might be easier to implement austerity measures but the people who live there soon find that their leaders expand their control beyond the economy to their very liberty. It seems to me that you need a very economically literate electorate to make this work in a free country. Hopefully, this book contributes to that literacy.

A popular Government without popular information, or the means of acquiring it, is but a Prologue to a Farce or a Tragedy, or perhaps both. Knowledge will forever govern ignorance: And a people who mean to be their own Governors, must arm themselves with the power which knowledge gives.[53]
—James Madison (1751–1836), American president

The economic world in between these extremes is trickier, and I don't have a clear answer for you. It depends on so many factors that it is truly debatable.

Libby tweets:

@EvelineAdomait Both the left and the right have good points. We need more research by economists from both sides. Economic debate in the public arena is critical and sometime we have to let history play the theory out so we can learn. #informedvoter

---

52. The story of Joseph's interpretation of the pharaoh's dream in the Old Testament is particularly applicable. The seven thin cows that consumed the seven fat cows were interpreted as seven years of plenty followed by seven years of want. Joseph suggested that the Egyptians save grain in the seven years of plenty to use in the seven years of want. Pharaoh put Joseph in charge of the government program to do so. This was a 14-year balanced budget.
53. In a letter to W. T. Barry dated August 4, 1822.

Concluding Remarks

Out of respect for what is handed down to me as sacred,
I refrain from drawing any conclusions
from my nonunderstanding.

—from
Stages on Life's Way (1845),
by Søren Aabye Kierkegaard (1813–1855),
Danish philosopher and theologian

CHAPTER 13

A Friendly Ending

"I could tell you my adventures—beginning from this morning," said Alice a little timidly: "but it's no use going back to yesterday, because I was a different person then."[1]

—*Lewis Carroll, pen name for Charles Lutwidge Dodgson (1832–1898), British author, mathematician, and clergyman*

The cheesecake and vegan fruit tray lay decimated in the centre of the table. All six students lean back on their chairs, holding their various drinks and talking.

"I don't know about you," says Brooke "but that was a fantastic meal. Good job everyone!"

They all nod in agreement. Justin points out that there is one slice of cheesecake left and says, "I can cut it in half if anybody wants to share."

Salim and David respond at the same time with, "Sure." This causes a burst of laughter among the group as Salim and David split the remaining piece.

Emma turns to Libby and says, "Thanks for letting us come here tonight. This was really helpful and I feel that a lot of the ideas I was fuzzy about are now clear. I still don't know what I think about what governments should actually do, but I at least understand the issues better."

Justin agrees, "Yeah, and I should be able to hold my own in a discussion on the economy when I debate my dad. That should make for some interesting conversations."

Libby laughs at Justin, "I wouldn't mind seeing that."

Justin smiles in a hopeful way, "We have a family dinner tomorrow night, if you want to join us."

Libby blushes and says, "Sure, I would love to."

All the other students look at Justin and Libby with new eyes but say nothing.

Emma, ever the diplomat, diverts the attention away from Justin and Libby, stands, and raises her glass. "I propose a toast—'To great friends!'"

They all stand in response and clink their glasses.

SUBSTANCE OF THINGS HOPED FOR[2]

The day is not far off when the economic problem will take the back seat where it belongs, and the arena of the heart and the head will be occupied or reoccupied, by our real problems—the problems of life and of human relations, of creation and behaviour and religion.[3]

—*John Maynard Keynes (1883–1946), British economist*

I am sorry to say that this dinner party is now over. Not much left to do but to clean up, gather our things, and go home. What about you? I hope your experience through this material was life changing—that you know more than you did before you started reading. I also hope that for some of you, this will begin a love affair with economics—as happened for me when I took my first introductory economics course.

---

1. *Alice's Adventures in Wonderland* (1865).
2. Hebrews 11:1.
3. *First Annual Report of the Arts Council* (1945–1946).

The overarching idea behind this book is that I believe that economics—whether macro or micro—is a social science and deals with people, people as they relate to each other in economic systems and, in the case of *Dinner Party Economics*, the economy as a whole.

Some might think, as they look through economics textbooks and academic journal articles, that economists are applied mathematicians who measure and model economic outcomes—that we are in a cold, detached discipline, which makes us appear as either heartless theoreticians or nerdy bean counters. In reality, economists are passionate about what they think is economically right and wrong—especially about macroeconomic topics. We worry about the state of the world and how to make it a better place. Normative statements (or non-testable opinions) given by economists are usually the norm, like the following one by Keynes.

Too large a proportion of recent "mathematical" economics are mere concoctions, as imprecise as the initial assumptions they rest on, which allow the author to lose sight of the complexities and interdependencies of the real world in a maze of pretentious and unhelpful symbols.[4]
—John Maynard Keynes (1883–1946), British economist

I have carefully tried to cover all of the big ideas in macroeconomics, giving a fair representation of all of the various opinions out there. You will have to make up your own mind about what you think about them. Hopefully, you feel better prepared to craft an intelligent opinion on the role that governments should play and the implications for a global economy. Now that you know the basics, you should also be able to follow any of the major newspapers or popular economics blogs[5] as they discuss macroeconomic issues. Some writers are more technical than others, but once they tell you the ideas they are writing about, you should be able to follow the gist of the discussion.

THE BEGINNING OF THE END

Every limit is a beginning as well as an ending.[6]
—Mary Anne Evans, pen name Georg Eliot (1819–1880), English writer

This book is supposed to be about ideas expressed in words rather than mathematics. I have done my best to stay within that restriction I set for myself. There are only two relatively simple graphs in the entire book and very few equations. All in all, I told fairly complicated stories in a way that hopefully makes sense without high-powered mathematics. (In truth, I imagine some of you might think that math would have made more sense of the material, but that wasn't the objective.) Now that the book is done, I have to say that I am quite proud of it. It does what I wanted it to do.

---

4. *The General Theory of Employment, Interest and Money* (1935).
5. The biggest Canadian blog is Worthwhile Canadian Initiative, http://worthwhile.typepad.com/worthwhile_canadian_initi/.
6. Taken from *Middlemarch* (1871).

FAST AND FURIOUS TOO

Many books require no thought from those who read them, and for a very simple reason;
they made no such demand upon those who wrote them.[7]
—*Charles Caleb Colton (1780–1832), British author, clergyman, and art collector*

Keynes wrote his book *The Economic Consequences of the Peace* in three months. I have
to confess that the first draft of this book was also written in three months in order to
make a publishing deadline. I took too long to start writing, partly because, for a very
long time, I thought that there wasn't much I could add at the introductory level that
would be value-added information. Now that this book is done, I think I was wrong.

A man finds he has been wrong at every preceding stage of his career, only to deduce the
astonishing conclusion that he is at last entirely right.[8]
—*Robert Louis Stevenson (1850–1894), Scottish writer*

   Dinner Party Economics is so different from any other book out there. It isn't a textbook and it isn't a macroeconomic opinion piece. I have endeavored to be comprehensive
yet not technical (I know, I know, some of you are thinking . . . really?). This book is a
great way to acquaint you with all of the macro issues without needing to go into the nitty
gritty of macro models found in typical introductory macroeconomics textbooks (textbooks that, I might add, are very well written and visually interesting to read). This book
is the perfect companion to any macroeconomics textbook because it covers why macroeconomic ideas are so important in a conversational way. It will also help you understand
the other books in the popular press that are written with a definite opinion about the
economy. Often these books tell a very specific story, and it is good to know that there is
actually some disagreement out there about how that real story plays out. I like to think
that this book is the bridge between a textbook and an opinion piece. Now that you have
read *Dinner Party Economics*, I hope you agree with me.

THANKS ALL AROUND

A grateful mind
By owing owes not, but still pays, at once
Indebted and discharg'd.[9]
—*John Milton (1608–1674), English poet and politician*

Haste can make waste—along with significant errors—but I didn't really have a choice in
writing in haste. (I will, of course, have to repent in leisure.) That is why I am so grateful
to my colleagues who agreed to read a chapter on short notice, scrutinizing for errors.
The biggest help came when they commented on the subtleties of ideas that they felt
needed further clarification.

---

7. *Lacon,* vol. I (1825).
8. *Crabbed Age and Youth* (1878).
9. *Paradise Lost* (1667; 1674).

One of the things that makes this book unique is the first appetizer (or chapter, if you will) called Measure for Measure. Most introductory texts begin the macro section by listing all of the important economic variables that the text will cover with a brief overview of each. I decided to start *Dinner Party Economics* with a justification for why the study of economics, in general, and macroeconomics, in particular, is fundamentally about human well-being. Professor Michael Hoy gave me wonderful feedback on this chapter, making sure I didn't overstate what constitutes positive economics, the role of happiness in well-being, as well as to clarify the work of Amartya Sen. He also was very encouraging that this chapter is really the best place to start a meaningful discourse on macroeconomics because it gets to the heart of the matter.

I would also like to thank Professor Bram Cadsby, an expert in international economics, who corrected my understanding of the Doha round, the impact of the most-favoured nation (MFN) status on the GATT, as well as the difference between a free trade zone and a customs union. His feedback was swift and detailed. *Dinner Party Economics* is better for his input.

Professor Atsu Amegashie read the chapter on stocks and flows and corrected my thinking about proportional taxes and flat taxes. I thought they were essentially the same thing, but they aren't among the public finance crowd. My thanks for his careful reading of this chapter and the lively ensuing discussion with respect to some subtle points I was making about stocks and flows in the quantity theory of money.

Some of my colleagues were so kind as to actually ask to review a chapter. Professor Laurent Cellarier read both my introduction and the chapter on growth and helped me be more precise about what is possible in the long run. He also reminded me that macro-economists care very much about how various markets interact with each other in general equilibrium.

Professor Louis Christofides read many chapters, but his input on the final chapter led to a few great conversations about the idea of unemployment. He was particularly helpful in clarifying my understanding of real business cycle (RBC) theory and how traditional RBC theorists think about the role of unemployment: Basically, there isn't any, and it seems the word *unemployment* is removed from their lexicon. He helped me find alternative ways to say what I wanted say without mentioning the "u" word. I really appreciate his attention to this chapter during a very busy time in his life. (Congratulations on the birth of your grandson, by the way!)

Last, but certainly not least, I owe Professor Brian Ferguson a huge (I mean really huge) debt of gratitude because he is an expert on the history of economic thought and knows the lives of important economists as if they were his relatives. He helped me pick every gossip column economist, sent me sources about them, read each gossip column, and made fairly significant editorial changes when he felt it was necessary. He also read the last chapter to make sure I really did give a fair shake to all sides of macroeconomic debates. Brian was my "go-to" economist when I wanted a second opinion—thank you, thank you, and thank you. Oh, and did I say thanks?

LOOK, VIRGINIA, I HAVE A ROOM OF MY OWN

A woman must have money and a room of her own if she is to write fiction.[10]
—Adeline Virginia Woolf (1882–1941), English writer and Bloomsbury member

I spent most of the summer in the guest bedroom. Since *Cocktail Party Economics*, my older son has moved out and I now have a room of my own to write in uninterrupted. Over the summer, both my husband and younger son left me in relative peace as I pushed myself to produce a chapter a week. Neither of them seemed to mind that I was inattentive. I think my younger son was actually glad that I wasn't "bugging" him as he prepared to leave home for university. My husband kept me supplied with great food, even if I didn't keep up my part of the household chores. All I can say is that the laundry did get done, but I won't comment on the state of the bathrooms. One of the only benefits of writing quickly is that the pain is over faster.

MUTUAL ADMIRATION SOCIETY

Le sort fait les parents, la choix fait les amis.
Fate chooses our relatives, we choose our friends.[11]
—Jacques Delille (June 22, 1738–May 1, 1813), French poet and translator

I would also like to thank my writing partner, Richard Maranta. This is our second book together and we are still friends. We both kept plugging away at the book during the summer of 2013 despite the feelings of panic that we wouldn't make the deadline. This book is a testament to the adage "Keep calm and think of England." It was also fortuitous that the weather wasn't particularly summery and we could stay focused on working incredibly hard. *Dinner Party Economics* has been in my voice, so I think it is only fair to let him have the last word.

RICHARD SPEAKS

Discretion of speech, is more than eloquence; and to speak agreeably to him, with whom we deal, is more than to speak in good words, or in good order.[12]
—Francis Bacon (1561–1626), English philosopher, statesman, and writer

Well I hope you have enjoyed our second book as much as I enjoyed helping write it. Actually, I lied. I should say, "as much as I enjoyed completing it." I think Evie would

---

10. *A Room of One's Own* (1929).
11. *Malheur at Pitié* (1803).
12. *Essays* (1625).

agree. Like many things, it's the final product that gives the most satisfaction, and for me, this book is pretty satisfying for a number of reasons.

First, as I mentioned in the conclusion of our last book, it gives me great satisfaction to help people say what needs saying, especially people with passion. Evie is one of those people, and genuinely believes in educating students so that they can be equipped not only to find jobs, but also to understand the issues so that they can speak intelligently and work to improve the well-being of themselves and others. I don't pretend to be an economist, but I love helping people get important messages out to a wider audience. This book, I think, helps make economic concepts more accessible and provides a good basis for people to dive in further if they so desire.

Second, I think macroeconomics is one of the most important topics there is. If you care at all about the well-being of other human beings, you really should care about this topic and know something about it. Many of the solutions to painful world problems, such as global warming, poverty, sickness, and warfare, have economic causes and thus will have economic solutions. As Evie has pointed out, it's a complicated business and there are many views concerning how we should best go about improving the well-being of all people. But that is the goal. I hope you have been given at least some basis to begin understanding the issues and help decrease the gap of global ignorance when it comes to the larger economic ideas.

When I started writing this section, I was tempted to thank the economic crisis of 2008 and the problems in Europe for making this book something people would find relevant. But to be honest, I wish those things never happened. I hope you feel the same. Yes, life would be dull without that kind of drama to fill the newspapers, but hopefully, like you, I want what's best for people, and it's better if we can avoid these problems altogether. Maybe we can learn to talk about more positive things. If economics can help governments do a better job of fixing problems globally and avoid the tragedies that we see daily, all the better.

The End